Colección Támesis

SERIE A: MONOGRAFÍAS, 230

TELEVISION IN SPAIN

FROM FRANCO TO ALMODÓVAR

Spaniards are amongst the most avid consumers of television in Europe, watching some four hours daily. And in the past decade Spanish viewers have enjoyed an explosion of local production, especially in quality drama and comedy. Spanish TV has not just held its own against Hollywood but has banished US shows to the margins of the schedule. Any follower of Spanish cinema who turns to television finds that the programmes most appreciated by both audiences and critics are as creative and original as any feature film.

This book offers close readings of TV programmes broadcast from the 1970s to the present day. They embrace drama, comedy, and talk/reality shows and are currently available on DVD. It also treats the obsessive theme of television in Almodóvar, Spain's most celebrated film director, arguing for a re-reading of his work in the light of TV studies. In addition to analysing particular programmes, the author examines TV channels, production companies, governments, and the role of the press, academy, and audience.

Television in Spain provides readers with a new guide to Spain's most popular and dynamic medium, which celebrates its fiftieth anniversary in 2006.

PAUL JULIAN SMITH is Professor of Spanish at the University of Cambridge.

PAUL JULIAN SMITH

TELEVISION IN SPAIN

FROM FRANCO TO ALMODÓVAR

TAMESIS

First published 2006
by Tamesis, Woodbridge

ISBN 1 85566 136 5

Tamesis is an imprint of Boydell & Brewer Ltd
PO Box 9, Woodbridge, Suffolk IP12 3DF, UK
and of Boydell & Brewer Inc.
668 Mt Hope Avenue, Rochester, NY 14620, USA
website: www.boydellandbrewer.com

A CIP catalogue record for this book is available
from the British Library

This publication is printed on acid-free paper

Transferred to digital printing

CONTENTS

ILLUSTRATIONS

Illustrations 16, 17 and 18 are reproduced by kind permission of El Deseo.

ACKNOWLEDGEMENTS

My thanks to the faculty and students of the Universities of Cambridge and Stanford, California, where I taught while writing this book. I would also like to thank the Spanish friends who sent copies of TV shows they had taped for me. Earlier versions of material from chapter one and six are published in *Bulletin of Hispanic Studies*, *Hispanic Research Journal*, and Brad Epps and Despina Kakoudaki (eds), *Sexual Politics and the Cinema of Almodóvar* (Minneapolis: Univ. of Minnesota). Material from the book was read at conferences and invited lectures in the US at Harvard and the City University of New York Graduate Center, in the UK at the universities of Aberdeen, Birmingham, Cambridge, and University College and Queen Mary, London, and in Spain at the Jornadas sobre televisión en España, organized by Manuel Palacio. I am most grateful for all these invitations to share my work. Professor Palacio also originally suggested I write on *Aquí no hay quien viva*. The University of Cambridge has kindly contributed to the production costs of the volume. While every effort has been made to contact copyright holders the author welcomes corrections and additions.

London, April 2006

For Jonathan, David, James, and Alfred

Introduction: From Franco to Almodóvar

Texts, producers, institutions

It is fair to say that Spaniards are not proud of their television. After they took stock of fifty years of broadcasting in 2006, the consensus of the press, political parties, and viewers' associations was that Spanish television is trash (*telebasura*). Educated citizens dismiss the medium as the *caja tonta* or "stupid box". Yet Spaniards are amongst the most avid consumers of television in Europe, watching some four hours daily. And in the past decade there has been an explosion of local production, especially in quality drama. In a supposed era of globalization, Spanish TV, unlike Spanish cinema, has not just held its own against Hollywood but shunted US shows to the margins of the schedule. A top-rated drama or comedy such as TVE's *Cuéntame cómo pasó* (*Tell Me How It Happened*) or Antena 3's *Aquí no hay quien viva* (*No-one Can Live Here*), reaches a bigger audience in a single night than all Spanish feature film production in a year; and a day's broadcasting of the five channels of national reach (public Televisión Española or TVE 1 and 2, private Antena 3 and Tele5, and the regional consortium known as FORTA) offers more hours of content than a year's feature film production. Clearly those who are concerned with Spanish culture and society cannot afford to neglect Spain's most popular and dynamic medium. Indeed in the debate leading up to the recent historic vote that legalized same-sex marriage (June 30, 2005) the gay characters in the sitcom *Aquí no hay quien viva* proved a flash point for controversy.

The sheer volume (or "flow") of television content must thus be borne in mind by those who brand the medium "trash." After all, we do not dismiss the novel as a genre because much commercial publishing is considered unworthy of critical attention or acclaim. Moreover, changes in distribution and exhibition mean that television no longer seems as ephemeral as it once did. A feature film now takes most of its profits and audience in the first weekend of release. A TV series may engross millions for years or even decades, forming a vital part of the affective and everyday life of a nation. Re-released on DVD, seasons of such shows become as durable as the classics of cinema. One of the names given to "boxed sets" of such DVDs in Spain is revealing of the value ascribed to this lovingly memorialized television: it is "cofre," a word also used for a jewel box or chest. Any scholar of Spanish cinema who turns to television may well find that the programmes most appreciated by both audiences and critics (those that top the ratings and win national prizes) are as creatively original as any feature film. Certainly they provide ample opportunity for an analysis that is aesthetic as well as industrial.

As Manuel Palacio (my main local source for Spanish television history) has noted (13), academic Spanish TV studies remains in its infancy and all that we have so far is a political history of the medium which is "partial" in both senses of the word. The only book in English, now somewhat dated and out of print, is devoted wholly to institutional questions of the transition period (Maxwell). As in other countries, popular studies of television tend to be anecdotal or nostalgic. It is surprising how little attention has been paid to content, that is to individual programmes. What is new, however, is that a small number of Spanish scholars such as Palacio, his collaborator José Miguel Contreras, and to some extent Lorenzo Díaz, less viscerally hostile to the medium than their earlier colleagues, have now undertaken invaluable empirical work that has cleared the way for a more sympathetic approach to Spanish television content. Meanwhile British scholars such as John Ellis, John Caughie, and John Corner (all of whom I cite in this book) have offered a more positive approach to television in general than the ideological critique derived from the Frankfurt School or British cultural studies that was once dominant. They suggest we view television as a privileged form of witnessing and working through, as a repository for "serious drama" which deserves proper consideration and evaluation, and as a focus for comedy as a "televisually-guided" form of social innovation. The practical and theoretical conditions are thus in place for a radically new study of Spanish television.

The main aim of this book is to offer for the first time close readings of televisual texts. The texts have been chosen for their inherent interest and creativity, for their objective importance within the medium (length of run, ratings, and prizes), and their subjective value to audiences (shown by ratings once more, but also backed up in many cases by consumer websites). With one exception, my chosen programmes are all currently accessible on DVD. Two subsidiary aims of this book are to establish connections between TV texts and other media (as in the case of serials based on classic novels) and between Spain and other countries (as in the adaptation of British or American formats to a Spanish TV ecology). The focus, however, is on the specificity of television in Spain, aesthetically, industrially, and nationally.

My first text is *Cuéntame cómo pasó* (chapter 1), a period drama aired by TVE1, which has been the most critically and popularly successful of the 2000s. *Cuéntame* (2001–) is clearly a "quality" product with high production values, frequent exterior shots, and a luxury cast headed by movie star Imanol Arias as the troubled patriarch of the Alcántara family. Dismissed by some critics as facile nostalgia, *Cuéntame* can be read rather as a sophisticated attempt to witness and work through recent Spanish history for a broad audience that encompasses all ages and classes. Chapter 2 treats two classic-serial adaptations made by TVE in very different conditions. *Fortunata y Jacinta* (1980) was produced during the transition to democracy while the public broadcaster still held the monopoly; *La Regenta* (1995) was made and shown at a time of bitter competition between TVE and the still new private stations, who stood accused of lowering the quality of scheduling. Rather than focusing on the process of adapting two compendious and prestigious nineteenth-century novels for the small screen, I investigate rather how industrial change may interact with aesthetic form, asking how the radically different broadcasting climate affected the relatively stable genre of the classic serial, already familiar in Spain from British imports. As in the case of *Cuéntame*, I do not dismiss period drama as nostalgic or regressive "heritage," but rather attempt a sympathetic assessment of its unique televisual pleasures.

The third and fourth chapters address ruralism and urbanism on TV. First I examine a popular and long-running rural comedy (or perhaps "dramedy") of the late Francoist period *Crónicas de un pueblo* (*Chronicles of a Village*, 1971–4). This is a test case for the relative autonomy of aesthetic form. Commissioned directly by the regime as a propaganda vehicle, *Crónicas de un pueblo* engages critically with this founding concept at the formal level of mise-en-scène and performance. Shot entirely on location in a rather run-down village set in the bleak Castilian meseta, *Crónicas* is populated with care-worn character actors and extras who could have come straight from Víctor Erice's *El espíritu de la colmena* (*The Spirit of the Beehive*, 1973), a feature film made at the same time as the TV show but set some thirty years before. I argue that the show implicitly calls attention to rural tensions in Spain at a crucial time of depopulation and migration to the city. Certainly the avowed didactic lessons of *Crónicas* (such as the "dignity of labour") are undercut by the unavoidable evidence of poverty and underdevelopment displayed before our eyes. I contrast *Crónicas de un pueblo* with rural representations in Francoist newsreel and feature films, especially as rerun on current television. The next chapter looks at the urban sitcom in the 2000s, a genre arguably imported from the US but transformed beyond recognition in a Spanish context. *Aquí no hay quien viva*, at the time of writing (July 2005) the most popular programme in Spain, is, like *Crónicas de un pueblo*, an ensemble comedy based around a small community, in this case a shared apartment building in a big city clearly based on Madrid. Addressing televisual form closely here, I argue for the specificity of narrative structure and of shooting and cutting style both within single episodes (which play for a lengthy 90 minutes) and across the "arc" of the second season of 14 shows that aired over Spring 2004. Nostalgia for community is here crosscut with indulgent delight in consumerism. The breakdown in traditional family structures leads, amongst other things, to newly visible same-sex partnerships and households.

Chapter 5 attempts to engage with the most fragile and ephemeral of television genres: reality and talk shows. Here once more a US genre (Letterman/Leno's late-night formula) is radically transformed in a Spanish, or more properly, Catalan context. *Crónicas marcianas*, which plans to take an extended hiatus at the end of July 2005, has played for two hours from around 12.30 am four times a week since September 1997. Well over one thousand shows have been broadcast. Based in Barcelona and hosted by unrepentant Catalan Javier (or Xavier: he uses both spellings) Sardà, *Crónicas marcianas* is both one of the most popular and profitable shows on Spanish television, attracting a substantial "quality" audience of educated young people, and the most cited in the bitter controversy over trash TV. Like the comedies we have examined earlier, this talk show (whose live antics cross-fertilize with the reality genre) is highly collective, featuring a large number of guests who interact unpredictably with each other and the presenter every night. I argue that in spite of the ghoulish delight (Spanish: *morbo*) with which the show chronicles celebrity culture, *Crónicas* stages a certain model of sociability and festivity which is distinctive in Spain and which deserves sympathetic attention. Shifting to cinema, the final chapter examines television as the "dark continent" of Almodóvar's cinema, the crime scene to which the filmmaker obsessively returns, and suggests a strategic reversal: that we read Spain's best known cineaste in the light of TV theory.

If these texts have their own inherent interest then they cannot be separated from the individuals who produced them. Given the collective nature of TV authorship, the range of producers I deal with in the book is wide and some of them fulfil more than one function. Eduardo Ladrón de Guevara, a one-time anti-Francoist militant who spent long periods in hiding, is the creator and scriptwriter of *Cuéntame*. As script coordinator, he also bears responsibility for the development of the show across a number of seasons. Because of thematic and ideological consistencies across media and within his TV creations, Ladrón is a clear case of an individual television author within the constraints of collective production. The classic serial is another interesting case of the movement between cinema and television. Before they undertook the huge task of adapting a literary monument for TVE, both Mario Camus and Fernando Méndez Leite were known above all as directors of feature films, with varying success. Certainly the sensibility of the two series seems to owe more to their directors and screenwriters, albeit filtered through different production processes, than to the established profiles of the literary authors, Galdós and Alas.

Antonio Mercero, creator and frequent director and scriptwriter of *Crónicas de un pueblo*, is perhaps the most outstanding example of a TV auteur in Spain. The only professional to have worked with great success in the Francoist period, the transition, and (in private television) the full democracy, Mercero is celebrated both for his skill in casting character actors in major roles and as the only Spaniard ever to win an Emmy. The contemporary urban sitcom *Aquí no hay quien viva*, on the other hand, is credited to two young and inexperienced "creators," one of whom went on to be script "runner" or coordinator of the team-written teleplays and to direct many episodes. There is an interesting conflict here with the show's veteran executive producer, José Luis Moreno, who is known for variety shows that appeal to an audience directly opposed to that of his sitcom. Finally, *Crónicas marcianas* is the product of an independent production company, Gestmusic-Endemol (part of a "Catalan cluster," rivalling Madrid's media dominance), whose two executive producers, the brothers Mainat, have long collaborated with presenter Sardà, in radio as well as television. Arguably the nightly regulars on the show (especially the flamboyant Venezuelan Boris Izaguirre) are also indispensable to its production process. As we shall see, the disagreement in sources as to how much of the show's talk is scripted and how much improvised raises an interesting question about creativity in live television.

Producers, broadly defined, are thus inseparable from institutions, the subject of most of the previous scholarship on Spanish television. Given continuing controversies over government meddling in the media, successive Spanish governments are the main institutional actors. Throughout the book I discuss government regulation (such as the 2005 report on the future of broadcasting by the "Committee of Wise Men") and in chapter 2 I deal at length with the question of "public service" broadcasting, arguing that it does indeed have relevance for Spain. Since private television began at the late date of 1990, commercial broadcasting has also wielded considerable institutional influence. In chapter 4, I offer a general account of private television and its relation to competition and consumerism, and a corporate study of the chequered history of the most successful private broadcaster, Antena 3. The rapid rise of independent producers feeding the new schedules of private channels is traced in chapters 4 and 5, which examine Miramón Mendi and Gestmusic-Endemol, respectively. What clearly emerges is that the content of programming cannot be reduced to the political positions of those who control and own it: if Francoist technocrats had bothered to watch *Crónicas de un pueblo* they would surely have been surprised by its revelation of rural underdevelopment; if Silvio Berlusconi, majority owner of Tele5, made time in his busy schedule to watch *Crónicas marcianas* (which has even inspired an Italian clone) he would be shocked by the Leftist politics of its presenter, who did not stint from attacking the Partido Popular ("People's Party") during the 2004 electoral campaign.

Hugh O'Donnell's pioneering studies of Catalan and Basque *telenovelas* (a genre not common in Madrid-produced programming) reveal the importance of the governments of the self-governing historic nationalities of the Spanish state in both the promotion of minority languages and innovation in televisual genres. The first *telenovela* produced in Spain was in Catalan: *Poble Nou* aired with great success on TV3 from January to December 1994, and has since been followed by many successors. In the same year Basque-language ETB1 began broadcasting the long-running soap opera *Goenkale*. Such shows have not just played a vital role in the reconstruction of national identities and linguistic "normalization." They have also consistently engaged with social issues vital to local audiences. My central concern in this book, however, is with the more culturally valued genre of series drama (generally called simply *serie* in Spain), which is not to be confused aesthetically or industrially with soap opera. *Telenovelas* imported from Latin America (known because of their inordinate length as *culebrones* or "big snakes") were popular successes in Spain some twenty years ago, but are now no longer shown in Spanish prime time.

Beyond networks, production companies, and governments, other institutions have considerable influence on the televisual field in Spain. The bitter hostility of the print media to television gave birth to what has been called the "black legend" of Spanish television (Palacio, 84–5). This has remained dominant since the 1970s and only rarely intersects with the changing historical reality of the medium. Print, both press and book publishing, is also compromised by its affiliation with multimedia parent companies such as Prisa. I try to supplement reference to *El País*, the Leftist daily most quoted by foreign academics, with citation from *El Mundo*, the centrist daily that is less clearly affiliated to a single political party and less damning of the TV medium. Beyond journalism, university departments of media studies with a vocational bent (generally known as "Comunicación audiovisual y publicidad") have produced such valuable empirical studies as Javier Bardají and Santiago Gómez Amigo's corporate account of one important independent producer. The first academic collection in Spain on television came from the Barcelona-based company Gedisa. Between 1999 and 2004, it published some twenty titles, including excellent studies by Palacio and Enrique Bustamante.

The awards given by the Television Academy or the TV listing magazines, such as *TP*, are valuable guides to industry and audience preferences, as are the websites www.formulatv.com and www.muchatv.com. The latter combine consumer reviews with production materials and lists of series' episodes, complete with data for screening, ratings, and share. I have also drawn extensively on the trade press, especially *Television Business International* (London) and *Cineinforme* (Madrid). The hybrid nature of television, its unique reach from public to private and national to domestic, thus requires that an equally diverse range of research resources be addressed by its students.

Two histories, two approaches

In *Seeing Things: Television in the Age of Uncertainty*, John Ellis offers a discontinuous and provisional history of television modes and practices, focusing on the UK and US. As his subtitle suggests, Ellis starts from the understanding that "the television industry enters the new millennium in a state of profound uncertainty" (1), most particularly in relation to new production and distribution technologies. But (like Manuel Palacio in Spain) Ellis remains convinced that TV "will continue to play an important part in society, commensurate with the amount of time people spend in its company." Ellis's chronology is based on the introduction of a new modality of perception through broadcasting, which he calls "witness." This is defined as "a particular form of representation that brings with it a sense of powerless knowledge and complicity with what we see." The liveness and intimacy of television has intensified this sense and brought it into the home.

For Ellis there have been two distinct eras of television in consumer society. The first is that of "scarcity," coinciding with the standardized mass-market and public service broadcasting (2). The second is that of "availability," corresponding to a "diverse consumer market which accentuates and commodifies

. . . difference between citizens in the name of choice." Where once TV presented definitive programming to a mass audience, it now offers "a diffuse and extensive process of working through . . . a constant worrying over issues and emotions . . . without ever coming to any final conclusions." This practice is helped by new electronic image processing of TV graphics (which work over pre-existing images) and is subject only to the little studied but vital process of scheduling, which Ellis claims is "central in determining the nature of any tele-vision service and any national televisual universe." While Ellis takes care to insist that not all television is socially useful or effective (3), he does claim that the "everyday ordinariness" of the medium, so often criticized, is in fact its "founding strength" and one that can only intensify (4). Defending television from "blanket condemnation," Ellis thus proposes a historical perspective that is also theoretically novel.

For Ellis electronic witnessing is not simply seeing; rather it involves "a degree of direction of understanding" or "level of narration" (13). Thus tele-vised sport has always required commentary. Live TV drama also relied on a form of witnessing unknown to film or theatre: "[bringing] viewers into extreme proximity with outpourings of emotion" (32). If in the era of "scarcity" television promoted modernization, it was through "an intimate relationship with the everyday lives of its audiences" (43). This new kind of public–private temporal sequence was both annual (sporting and political calendars) and daily ("the assumed regular rhythms of the household"). TV's force for social integra-tion is seen in famous examples of complicit witnessing: *Cathy Come Home* (1966), a pseudo-documentary drama on housing problems, provoked national debate and the setting up of a powerful pressure group (46). As Caughie has also noted, this "national private life" produced, like that of families, "fierce and slightly embarrassed loyalties" (47).

Throughout Europe the public service television which could produce such drama, whose "primary ethos was national unity" and whose primary aim was "education" (56), was under increasing pressure from a commercial model, often dismissed as "Americanized" but in fact based on a coalition of regional, populist, and entertainment interests. With the now universal arrival of private broadcasting, TV still offers "an important social forum": "reconciling the divi-sions that come with differences" (72). This is the new role of "working through," which television shares with other institutions such as the school, police, and hospital. It is a role characterized by the "uncertainty and openness" seen in the narrative organization of series drama (82).

National unity thus gives way to the concerted "display of national disunity" (87), an attempt to negotiate multiple antagonisms. Television graphics (treated, layered, framed) can be read as an attempt at interpretation: "under-standing and speculation" (97). Even in television drama, where "empathy replaces speculative understanding" (122), social themes are "worked through" much more explicitly than in film, while TV narratives are "contingent and co-present," far from the ruthlessly predestined plots of Hollywood (124). Meanwhile scheduling has become far more complex in the shift from offer- to demand-led television (from public service "scarcity" to consumerist "avail-ability"). With sophisticated audience research feeding back into production, the schedule has become "the mechanism whereby demographic speculations are turned into a viewing experience [and] the distillation of the past history of a channel, of national broadcasting as a whole, and of the particular habits of national life" (134).

Given the huge differences between national life in post-War Spain and in the UK, it is striking and surprising how closely Ellis's account of the transition from a public service regime of "scarcity" to a consumerist regime of "avail-ability" coincides with Manuel Palacio's deceptively and modestly titled *Historia de la televisión en España* (*History of Television in Spain*). Palacio also coincides with Ellis in his initial belief in the social importance of television, stressing that it offers access to a communal history from the inside, as in "el ritual individual-colectivo que supone la retransmisión de los grandes acontecimientos que congregan a decenas de millones de espectadores" ("the individual–collective ritual of the broadcasting of great events which bring together tens of millions of viewers," 11). Moreover TV consumption is a key foundation of socialization, providing communal memories that reinforce national and generational identities: those who fondly remember *Los chiripitifláuticos* (a children's show with a nonsense name, from the 1970s) will always constitute a distinct group. Citing (like Ellis) the parallel of still photog-raphy, Palacio notes how much Spanish writing on television is nostalgic and anecdotal, based on oral testimony (12).

Yet Spanish TV studies has its own distinct problems. Unlike in the case of film (well served by the Filmotecas), there is no easy access to RTVE's archives, which remain mainly uncatalogued. Moreover television is universally despised by Spanish journalists and the educated classes who read them. The almost exclusive field of study has been government influence on broadcasting; but even this has failed to produce a reliable "political history" of television in Spain (13). Given the circumstances, Palacio does not attempt a "linear history" of a medium whose development was contingent and singular. He notes two vital circumstances: if television had been born in Spain before the late date of 1956 it might not have been saddled with a unique funding mechanism (govern-ment subsidy and advertising revenue); and if commercial television had arrived before the equally late date of 1990 then its impact on the public sector would not have been so devastating.

Palacio sheds valuable light on the "pre-history" of television in Spain, which is said to have begun in 1938 with a "Fonovisión" experiment in which, using equipment lent by the Nazis, General Franco transmitted an audiovisual message to an underling (22–3). When broadcasting proper finally began in 1956, almost twenty years later, the regime's loyal daily *ABC* praised televi-sion's potential for "propaganda and education" (37) and the opening night coincided with the celebration of Christ the King and the eve of the anniversary of the founding of the Falange (39). Echoing the first film made in Spain, the first broadcast to exploit a national network beyond Madrid was of the Mass celebrated in El Pilar, Zaragoza (49). Yet unlike in other government monopoly systems, the Spanish system was from the outset commercial: attempts to introduce a BBC-style licence fee failed when the first viewers proved unwilling to provide the necessary collective commitment (44). By 1958, Televisión Española was courting advertisers with the slogan "Un escaparate en cada hogar" ("A shop window in every home," 45). In 1959 entertainer Tony Leblanc complained he was unable to appear on television, as he could find no advertising agency to sponsor him (48). Television in Spain was thus an early and unstable example of public-private partnership.

There had been some scepticism as to the future popularity of television in Spain. An early director of programming described the "ethnological" reasons against it: climate, life style, and the supposed "imaginative qualities" of the Spanish masses (54). But successive surveys made by RTVE showed an immediate take up, if only through the collective mode of consumption known as "teleclubs." By 1966 urban Spaniards were more likely to have a television set at home than hot water (51% against 40%) (64). But it was at this time of unprecedented economic expansion that the negative image of television took hold, based in part on the perceived illegitimacy of the Francoist regime. The "Golden Age" of drama saw the publication of scripts in 1962 (76) and in 1963 a special issue of *Triunfo* (a vital journal for anti-Francoist resistance), which emphasized the role of television in unifying urban and rural Spain and in promoting "noble vulgarización" (78). But a decade later writers display an implacable hostility to a medium held to be politically and economically subservient: *Cuadernos para el Diálogo* and Manuel Vázquez Montalban (in 1972 and 1973, respectively) coincide in their blanket attack (84–5). Curiously this is a period when the cultural distinction of television is at its highest: with the shift from live to recorded drama the most prestigious film directors of the era came to work in television (Palacio lists some thirty of them) (87).

Likewise, during the transition to democracy, attacks on TVE increased in intensity, most especially from *El País* (which offered more measured commentary on other fields). Yet monopoly broadcasting produced some of its most radical and respected work: the director of one 1977 episode of *Curro Jiménez* (the bandit reminiscent of a Spanish Robin Hood) proclaimed that he had made a "didactic" work on class struggle and anti-imperialism (88); the years immediately preceding the Socialist victory in 1982 saw many programmes firmly anchored in collective memory, from political discussion on *La clave* to uncompromising historical drama in *La barraca* (1979) (96). Palacio calls attention to some elements of the adaptation absent in Blasco Ibáñez's original novel: both the opening song and invented dialogues comment quite explicitly on the importance of peaceful cohabitation and the dangers of civil war (157). After the Socialists came to power, TVE produced no fewer than nine big-budget, prestigious drama series set in the period 1900–39 (160). Similar series focused either on a single figure (*Cervantes*) or on a narrative of historical process (*Fortunata y Jacinta*), both exemplary in their different ways. Such public service programming, successful in a regime of scarcity, was to prove incompatible with the competitive rigour of "availability" (167). However, even the pioneering dramas of the 1990s (*Farmacia de guardia* [*All Night Chemist*], *Médico de familia* [*Family Doctor*]) are informed by a progressive or "politically correct" ideology, seasoned only by conservative supporting characters (183).

What is striking in Palacio's broad historical narrative (which is interrupted by stand-alone analyses of genres such as drama) is the persistence of the term "pedagogy." Where Ellis's "working through" is located ambivalently in both producers and consumers, Palacio's pedagogy is clearly top down. From Francoist autarchy to Socialist democracy, television is understood as a tool of education, schooling the populace in changing modes of socialization. What is important is that even those who attack the medium in Spain do so from this same standpoint, arguing that television has not succeeded in educating the Spanish public as it should. Such an approach not only fails to acknowledge the new objective reality of television following the ending of state monopoly; it also neglects the subjective value of the medium as a depository of individual memory. This unstable combination of the objective and subjective (national history and personal experience) is what characterizes the most popular television drama of the 2000s, *Cuéntame cómo pasó*.

Works cited

Bardají, Javier and Santiago Gómez Amigo. *La gestión de la   creatividad en televisión: El caso de Globo Media*. Pamplona: EUNSA, 2004.

Caughie, John. *Television Drama*. Oxford: Oxford University Press, 2000.

Ellis, John. *Seeing Things: Television in the Age of Uncertainty*. London: I. B. Tauris, 2002.

Maxwell, Richard. *The Spectacle of Democracy: Spanish Television, Nationalism, and Political Transition*. Minnesota: University of Minnesota Press, 1994.

O'Donnell, Hugh. *Good Times, Bad Times: Soap Operas and Society in Western Europe*. London: Leicester University Press, 1999.

———. "Media Pleasures: Reading the Telenovela." In Barry Jordan and Rikki Morgan-Tamosunas (eds). *Contemporary Spanish Cultural Studies*. London: Routledge, 2000, pp. 295–303.

Palacio, Manuel. *Historia de la televisión en España*. Barcelona: Gedisa, 2001.

Electronic source

O'Donnell, Hugh. "Peripheral Fissions? Soap Operas and Identity in Scotland, Ireland and the Basque Country." July 12, 2005 <http://people.brunel.ac.uk/~acsrrrm/entertext/2_1_pdfs/odonnell.pdf>.

1

The Approach to Spanish Television Drama of the New Golden Age: Remembering, Repeating, Working Through (*Cuéntame cómo pasó* [*Tell Me How It Happened*, 2001–])

Two problematics: art and industry

In its coverage of the newly elected Socialist government's plans for the future (published on March 21, 2004), *El País* called attention to the "reforma y saneamiento" ("reform and cleaning up") of television as a priority. Under the heading "¿El fin de la televisión de partido?" ("The End of Party Political Television?"), Rosario G. Gómez reported that President José Luis Rodríguez Zapatero had announced that not one more euro would be given from public funds for "la manipulación y la programación basura" ("manipulation and trash programming"). *El País* offers an apocalyptic sketch of the current state of public broadcasting in Spain:

> Zapatero hereda una televisión estatal endeudada como nunca en su historia, una audiencia en constante descenso, una programación infestada de programas basura, con una credibilidad informativa bajo mínimos y una condena por manipulación sobre la mesa. (Gómez, 12)

> Zapatero inherits a state television service in deeper debt than ever in its history, an audience in constant decline, a schedule infested with trashy programmes, and a news service whose credibility is below zero and which has charges of manipulation pending.

The Socialists proposed a new Statute for RTVE (aiming to bring back truth, plurality, and objectivity in the media) and the creation of a Consejo de Medios Audiovisuales ("Council of Audiovisual Media"). The founding membership was given as: Academician Emilio Lledó; the philosophers Victoria Camps (a vitriolic critic of *telebasura* in the pages of *El País*) and Fernando Savater; Media Studies professor Enrique Bustamante; and the veteran linguist and Academician Fernando Lázaro Carreter, who was to die before the Council met.

The contradictions in the Socialists' policy are clear. How can the new government's threat to withhold funding from specific content fit with its commitment to plurality and independence? And how can the literary and philosophic skills of the new "Committee of Wise Men" (as it was soon dubbed) address economic and technical problems such as TVE's burden of debt and declining audience? The composition of the Council could hardly have been further from that of the Spanish TV audience and it contained only one specialist in the field.

Leaving aside the specific context of Gómez's article (the controversy over the TV coverage of the March 11 terrorist atrocities at Madrid's Atocha Station), we can see that it repeats a long-standing and surprisingly consistent discourse of hostility to television in the Spanish print media. What I argue in this first chapter is that a new, more sympathetic approach is required to this vital medium. Contrary to the stereotype of the "abominable decade" (Díaz), the offering of Spanish television has been transformed for the better over the past ten years. Since 1995 domestic drama has consistently beaten all other programming in prime time. While the 1960s is sometimes described as the "Golden Age" of Spanish television (boasting as it did the live drama broadcast from TVE's studios at Prado del Rey [e.g. Palacio, 126]), I would propose that, on the basis of this unprecedented explosion of quality fiction, the current period merits the title of "new Golden Age". As has been argued elsewhere (Smith, "Quality TV?"), this huge wealth of material, often superior in quality to the feature films that are more widely studied both at home and abroad, deserves proper and sympathetic attention. As I mentioned in the Introduction, the Spanish television demographic corresponds much more closely to the composition of Spanish society as a whole than does the cinema-going public; and the nightly audience for a single episode of a top-rating, innovative TV drama (such as *Farmacia de guardia* [*All Night Chemist*, TV3 1991–5], *Médico de familia* [*Family Doctor*, Tele5 1995–9], or *Cuéntame cómo pasó* [*Tell Me How It Happened*, TVE1 2001–]) surpasses the annual audience for all Spanish feature films.

Although Spanish scholars sometimes insist that their television journalism is a unique case in which specialist reporters are paid to exhibit ignorance and prejudice about their chosen field, similarly dismissive attitudes have long held sway in other countries. Significantly, however, recent academic studies in both Spain and the UK have coincided in making closely argued defences of television as a medium. These new studies (by José Miguel Contreras and Manuel Palacio [*La programación*], John Ellis [*Seeing Things*], and John Caughie [*Television Drama*]) allow us for the first time to sketch a new approach to Spanish television that is both artistic and industrial.

The gap between theory and practice appears to persist, however, in two accounts of the state of the field. Caughie begins his study of "serious" British drama (the scare quotes are his) by examining six continuing "problems" in TV studies. We may take each of them in turn. Although Caughie proposes that TV must be dragged out of the interpretative "isolation ward" (Caughie, 2) to which it has been confined, he still argues for the "specificity" of the medium and its criticism. Much writing about television, he claims, is "haunted by the desire for film", even though the "diversity of the television text . . . turned out to be less like a film than we had thought" (9). The "possibilities of meaning and subjectivity in television", menaced as the medium is by banality and famil-iarity, will thus be quite different from those to be found in cinema. The second problem is history. While cinema scholars have a continuous, albeit incomplete, corpus of primary material to study from the 1890s to the present day, televi-sion's past is either inaccessible (early live transmission went unrecorded; later taped programming was routinely wiped) or critically dismissed. "Classic cinema" is revered, but "old television" is scorned. Comparing television to the family photo album, Caughie claims that TV, tinged as it is by embarrassment and pride, "establishes commonalities of shared experience and communities of memory" (13).

Historical amnesia is related to Caughie's third question: the national. Scholars such as Jameson, arguing for the lack of "monumental" figures in TV, forget that they speak mainly of the US, which remains dominant in cinema but not in a television medium that is local in content and national in regulation (16). The up side of the local is that TV challenges universal theories; the down side is that national specificity can slide into parochialism (17). Moreover, the nature of the TV text is itself a problem for the development of appropriate theory. While cinema first evolved as image without sound, broadcasting began as sound without image. "Television drama", writes Caughie, "uses the word to tell us about the world". "Film", he says, "allows us to dream; television drama invites us to be responsible" (18).

Far from the phantasmatic seductions of film, TV is (in a fifth problem) notoriously everyday, "continually subject to . . . distraction" (20). Arguing against theories of undifferentiated "flow", however, Caughie writes: "There is no single form of attention appropriate to television. . . . Flow . . . moves in currents of distraction and eddies of engagement" (20). This leads us to the final problem, that of value. Since criticism, whether romantic or Marxist, has tended to assign value to difference, it cannot account for television "where a signifi-cant part of the pleasure seems to lie in repetition, recognition, and familiarity" (23). Yet serious drama has historically attracted large and committed audiences in the UK, as elsewhere in Europe. Caughie argues that this genre "gives us a certain purchase on certain questions of theory and criticism, meaning and value . . . important for an understanding of the recent history of British culture" (23–4).

There is little doubt that Spanish television in general, and serious Spanish drama in particular, offers a similar critical purchase. Indeed, as we shall see, scholars such as Manuel Palacio have argued as much. However, it is instructive to contrast Caughie's six theoretical problems with the six practical problems that industry professional José Miguel Contreras claims are currently trans-forming the Spanish "model" of television (Contreras and Palacio, 89). The first is technological change (the rise of digital), which renders previous plan-ning obsolete. The second is business: the transformation of long-standing corporate structures through the convergence of telephony, computing, and entertainment companies with television. The third is legislation. After passing through the phase of deregulating the state monopoly, the Spanish government is now confronted by a newly competitive medium. Content comes fourth. New media and new channels have changed the very idea of what constitutes a "programme". Modern formats and methods of production have reactivated creativity as the generative source of the medium. The fifth element is the audience or rather "audiences" ("públicos") (90). Audiences are now more selective, experimental, fragmented, and interactive, in response to an ever expanding offer. Finally there is the problem of markets. The internationalization of the television market, writes Contreras, is now a reality and the medium now crosses frontiers at both individual and collective levels.

The specificity of television, championed by Caughie, thus returns in the new light of Contreras's technological and commercial changes. These further problematize the already incomplete history of the medium. Caughie's national differences are intensified by Contreras's stress on continuing and unpredictable government legislation, while the former's stress on the complexity of the TV text is echoed by the latter's emphasis on creative transformations in content. Finally, Caughie's vision of the everyday and the persistence of value is set against Contreras's somewhat paradoxical account of the emergence of new, more diversified audiences in a time of increasingly international markets. In order further to explore this complex conjunction of theory and practice we may now appeal to the two diverse but complementary theoretical models mentioned in the Introduction to this book: "working through", which is for Ellis the main characteristic of television in our current "age of uncertainty"; and "pedagogy", which is for Palacio a recurrent aim of Spanish television since its inauguration.

Witnessing and working through: *Cuéntame cómo pasó*

Palacio and Contreras stress the uniqueness of the Spanish broadcasting environment. Unlike countries like the UK in which one public and one private channel battle for the general audience, while the remainder settle for minorities, in Spain there is a four-way competition between broadly equal rivals: the public broadcasters TVE1 and FORTA (the consortium of subsidized regional stations) and the private Antena 3 and Tele5 (91). Often these four channels are separated by just one rating point. Given TVE's historically unstable funding formula this is a recipe for financial chaos: in the early 1990s costs exploded and revenue plummeted. It is a conundrum the PSOE's panel of non-specialists is unlikely to solve.

What is extraordinary under these uncertain circumstances (outlined in Contreras's "six changes") is that in 2001 TVE was able to originate *Cuéntame cómo pasó*, a period series that remained in 2005 the most popular and prestigious drama in the country (Illustrations 1, 2, 3). A family narrative, *Cuéntame* magically resolves Caughie's six problems. The series exploits the specificity of television (its potential banality and everydayness) to offer, week by week, a national history of the late Francoist period, which remains relevant to modern viewers (see Estrada). Unapologetically domestic, still it avoids parochialism by addressing broadly political concerns (solidarity, repression), accumulating unimpeachable "value" through the expertise of its production values (from quality casting to seamless special effects). A consummate TV text, it (in Caughie's terms once more) uses the word to tell us about the world and establishes commonalities of experience and communities of memory (see Smith, "The Emotional Imperative"). In an era of availability (relentless consumerist competition) *Cuéntame* seems to hark back to a now distant televisual time of scarcity, when public service broadcasting had the last, definitive word, promoting national unity and social integration by exploiting the regular rhythms of the household, both on and off screen.

The recent publication by a university press of a *Cuéntame* script (Ladrón de Guevara) and the release of the first two seasons in lavish DVD boxed sets not only establish new forms of consuming a once ephemeral TV text; they also suggest that current Spanish television can attain the cultural distinction it had lost since the Golden Age of drama in the 1960s, when scripts were also published in book form. Emeterio Diez, the academic editor of the volume, binds together two scripts by Eduardo Ladrón de Guevara, one from *Cuéntame*'s first season and one from the earlier and now cancelled contemporary drama *Querido maestro*. Diez thus seeks to establish Ladrón as an auteur in the strongest sense of the term, proclaiming him a "critical" and "disenchanted" voice in the culture of leisure (7). Ladrón's auteurist authority is demonstrated in three ways. First his distinctive "voice" is held to be constant across multiple media (theatre, print, and television) and genres (sitcom and series drama). Secondly his oeuvre is said to be intimately connected to his own biography: when the varied characters of *Cuéntame* visit swinging London, steal a copying machine, or play with *chapas* (home-made table soccer players) they are simply repeating the writer's avowed experiences of the same period. Finally Ladrón's writing as a whole is held to be underwritten by consistent themes that structure and unify it: the disappointment (*desencanto*) of idealists in both the political and the personal arenas (23).

As scriptwriter for the first of the wave of top-rated domestic drama, *Farmacia de guardia*, Ladrón has been a key player in the changes that have swept Spanish television content. But as a former anti-Francoist militant who spent much of the late Franco period in exile or hiding, Ladrón also echoes the "pedagogy" so prominent in Palacio's history of Spanish television and the overt Leftism of the prestige dramas of the 1970s and 1980s. He is proud of his "class consciousness" (9) and still resolute in his verdict on the Dictatorship. It was a "terrible" time when only a few, brave Spaniards fought for freedom, while the rest were "shitting themselves" with fear (105). Ladrón claims to have avoided "reactionary, Francoist discourses" in the series at all times. As we shall see, this defiant didacticism (which seeks to educate forgetful viewers on their heritage) is somewhat mitigated in the shift from script to screen. But the production process was beset by rumours (recounted by Diez, unconfirmed by Ladrón [102]) that the much delayed project was finally approved only after an intimate meal between two married couples: the executive producer and female

1. Father, Antonio (Imanol Arias)

2. Mother, Mercedes (Ana Duato)

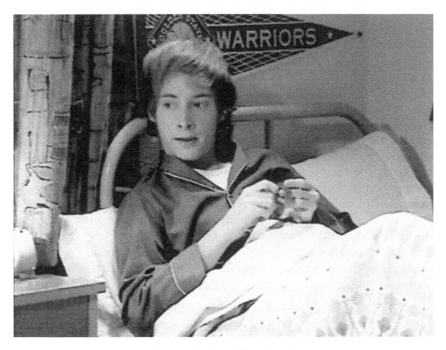

3. Son, Toni (Pablo Rivero)

star (Miguel Ángel Bernardeau and Ana Duato) and the then Spanish President and his wife (José María Aznar and Ana Botella). However, the constant press complaints that TVE is subject to political manipulation by its paymasters here seem difficult to confirm. While Diez speculates that the series might reflect the Partido Popular's vision of the transition to democracy (102), there is no doubt that much of Ladrón's radical and individual "voice" made it through the unavoidably collective process of television production. Moreover, as script coordinator, he was responsible for setting the guidelines for even those scripts he did not write himself.

The ideological ambiguity of *Cuéntame* derives to a large extent from the fact that the bitter pill of Ladrón's disenchanted didacticism is sugared by the nostalgic reaction of older viewers, irresistibly attracted by the meticulous production design (period costumes, furniture, and toys) and the incorporation of fragments of "old TV" glimpsed on the new black-and-white set that has pride of place in the family's living room. Such programming (from children's shows to news) not only provokes an ambivalent mix of loyalty and embarrassment, analogous to the snapshots in the family album; it also allows TVE to exploit a unique resource: the national broadcasting archive, to which outside researchers have only limited access.

But if *Cuéntame* has direct access to the intimate televisual autobiography of viewers, it also benefits from sophisticated scheduling. Playing on a Thursday (the strongest-rating night before the weekend dip), *Cuéntame*, a unique period drama in a clutch of contemporary series, even triumphed over the new fashion for reality shows. A "tent pole" with a vengeance for TVE1, reaching at its peak an exceptional 40% share on a channel that averages just over 20%, *Cuéntame* runs for an extended 70 minutes and combines comic and dramatic subplots. It thus coincides with distinctively Spanish tastes and schedules: the "golden moments" of highest viewing are at a late 10.45 pm (Ladrón de Guevara, 111) and repeated episodes are played back-to-back until past midnight. *Cuéntame* has proved Ellis's suggestion that the schedule grid can be a distillation of both the past history of the channel and the particular habits of national life (Ellis, 134).

What, then, is the secret of *Cuéntame*'s success? Widely watched by both children and the old, *Cuéntame* seems to be a throwback to the "scarcity" era when a monopoly public service addressed the whole nation. What I will suggest, however, is that *Cuéntame* combines that traditional authority (to which only TVE, however denigrated, can aspire) with the open-endedness of consumerist availability. Worrying over the events and emotions they so voraciously and impotently witness, *Cuéntame*'s characters and viewers are led to "work through" national differences that can have no definitive conclusion. It is a hypothesis that we can now test against a single episode.

"Las Mejores Huelgas de Nuestra Vida"

Noviembre 1968

Desde que el doctor Barnard realizó el primer trasplante de corazón, la donación de órganos se extiende por el país. El marqués de Villaverde se dispone a hacer el primer trasplante español, con lo que Herminia comienza a inquietarse. Cuando le preguntan si estaría dispuesta a donar algún órgano, no solo se niega a hacerlo sino que, sin que se entere nadie, saca sus pequeños ahorros y se compra un nicho perpetuo en el cementerio.

Los profesores del colegio donde estudia Carlos y sus amigos recibe la orden del Ministerio de Educación de aceptar la coeducación, es decir, tener en clase a alumnos de ambos sexos, lo que provocará la reacción de los chicos y también del profesorado cuando dos niñas españolas, que llegan de la recientemente independizada Guinea, aparecen en el colegio. Carlos y sus compañeros protagonizarán un auténtico motín.

Cuando Gregorio Fuente, un compañero de Antonio, es detenido por asociación ilegal, Antonio y Mercedes temen que también detendrán a Antonio por ser amigo de Gregorio. El matrimonio pensará incluso que Antonio perderá el trabajo en la imprenta y en el ministerio. Finalmente, Antonio y Mercedes afrontarán el problema con valentía.

Inés, que ha roto sus relaciones con Jesús, tiene un encuentro con él para intercambiar los regalos que se hicieron cuando eran novios. Pero no se llevará a efecto cuando Jesús, por primera vez, se comporte civilizadamente con Inés.

Toni y sus compañeros de Facultad están obsesionados con el sexo en una época en que las relaciones sexuales apenas existían como hoy se entienden. Por eso, cuando Toni se plantea organizar un guateque en su casa, una joven radicalizada le criticará su actitud. Dicha compañera será la que le muestre un mundo universitario que desconocía, como era el de las asambleas y el de la represión policial.   (http://www.cuentamecomopaso.net/)

"The Best Strikes of Our Lives"

November 1968
Since Dr Barnard carried out the first heart transplant, organ donation is spreading throughout the country. The Marques of Villaverde gets ready to perform the first Spanish transplant and so [grandmother] Herminia begins to get worried. When she is asked if she'd be willing to donate an organ, she doesn't just refuse to do so but, without anyone finding out, withdraws her small savings and buys herself a permanent niche in the cemetery.

The teachers in the school which [younger son] Carlos and his friends go to gets an order from the Ministry of Education to go coeducational, i.e. to have kids of both sexes in the classroom. This provokes a reaction in both boys and teachers when two Spanish girls who hail from Guinea (which has just been granted its independence) turn up in school. Carlos and his friends will lead a real rebellion.

When Gregorio Fuente, a friend of Antonio, is arrested for belonging to an illegal organization, [father] Antonio and [mother] Mercedes fear Antonio will also be arrested because he is Gregorio's friend. The couple even think that Antonio will lose his jobs in the printing press and the ministry. In the end Antonio and Mercedes face up to the problem courageously.

[Daughter] Inés, who has broken up with her boyfriend Jesús, meets up with him to exchange gifts they gave each other during their relationship. But they don't go ahead with the plan as Jesús, for the first time, behaves in a civilized manner with Inés.

[Older son] Toni and his university friends are obsessed with sex in a time when sexual relations hardly existed as they do today. So when Toni suggests holding a party in his house, a radical young woman criticizes his attitude. This female friend will be the one to show him a university world that he didn't know: one of political meetings and police repression.

The eighth episode of the first season of *Cuéntame*, directed by Agustín Crespi and scripted by Eduardo Ladrón de Guevara, was broadcast by TVE1 on November 8, 2001 to an audience of 5.2 million and an audience share of 33.2% (the first episode, airing just two days after the tragedy of September 11, had won 4.3 million and 29.4%) (Ladrón de Guevara, 112). As the plot synopsis taken from the series' extensive website shows, the episode attempts, in generalist scheduling style, to engage a broad range of demographics in both age and sex: Antonio and Mercedes (Imanol Arias and Ana Duato) are the middle-aged protagonists and Toni and Inés (Pablo Rivero and Irene Visedo) their teenage children. Little Carlos (Ricardo Gómez) (whose adult alter ego gives a voice-over narration) attracts the child audience, while grandmother Herminia (María Galiana), the voice of the country in the city, pulls in the elderly. If TVE can no longer rely on the standardized mass-market offer of public service broadcasting, still it attempts to address diverse segments of the population in a

single show and bring together the two televisual Spains identified by
programmers.

The plotting of each episode is subject to strict formal requirements. For
example, the stars Imanol Arias and Ana Duato must appear in 30% of the
scenes; and each of the six principal characters in the Alcántara family must
have his or her own plotline. In a continuing series (the first season ran for 33
episodes; by the end of the third, 86 had been made) there must be a delicate
balance between narrative threads that are completed in a single show and those
that run over months or years (Inés's fumbling attempts to learn English here
will lead eventually to a trip to London and an English boyfriend). What is
notable, however, in this episode is the prominence of education as a theme and
setting. In a style reminiscent of the Golden Age comedia, the main action (here
Toni's initiation into university revolt) is comically echoed by the main subplot
(Carlos's staging of a strike motivated by the introduction of girls into his
same-sex classroom). A moral and political pedagogy is also implicit in the
other plotlines: the two parents learn to face political peril with fortitude; Inés
settles the argument with her boyfriend in a civilized fashion; even the grandmother's mysterious absences are shown to be motivated by a misplaced but
moving family loyalty: the purchase of a communal burial plot. This is a TV
drama that (unlike most recent Spanish feature films) invites its audience to be
responsible and to understand recent history.

Pedagogy sometimes comes close to propaganda, betraying too clearly the
authorial voice of the anti-Francoist militant screenwriter. It is not clear if the
references to, say, the independence of Guinea (one of Spain's last colonies) are
addressed to the innocent children within the show or the ignorant audience
outside. The most explicit moment retained from the script in the final show is
when teenage Toni lectures his fearful parents:

> ANTONIO: En España no pasa nada. Tenemos paz y trabajo. ¿Te parece poco?
> TONI: Papá, tenemos un televisor, tenemos una lavadora, vivimos más o
> menos bien, y pensamos que fuera del barrio no pasa nada . . . y claro que pasa
> . . .
> ANTONIO: ¡Pero qué va a pasar!
> TONI: ¿Por qué crees que detienen a la gente? . . . es por pensar de manera
> distinta.

> ANTONIO: Nothing's going on in Spain. We've got peace and work. Don't you
> think that's enough?
> TONI: Dad, we've got a TV set and a washing machine, we live pretty well, and
> we think that outside our neighbourhood nothing's going on . . . but something
> *is* going on . . .
> ANTONIO: What could possibly be going on?
> TONI: Why do you think they're arresting people? . . . It's just because they
> think in a different way.

Consumerism is thus no consolation for the lack of freedom of thought and
expression. Yet, as is conventional in TV drama, intellectual understanding is

replaced by emotional empathy. Toni's mother weeps because her son now "speaks like a lawyer": family bonds have been undermined by institutional discourses. The enigmatic and misunderstood phrase "correlation of forces" (picked up by Toni from his new radical girlfriend) is repeated mockingly, ominously, throughout the episode.

The characters thus witness historical change not only impotently, but also uncomprehendingly. In the very first sequence in the script (the second in the show itself) Carlos hears his father call a colleague a "Red", which he takes to mean a "Red Indian". Likewise the grandmother's misunderstanding of organ transplants is clearly presented to our more knowing view. Dramatic irony thus serves a pedagogical function traditional in TVE, which schooled Spaniards in the rights and responsibilities of democracy during the transition. Radical milestones in TV drama of that period, such as *Curro Jiménez* and *La barraca* (see Palacio, 153–4), were hardly more explicit.

From script to screen, however, the director of this episode both softens didacticism and undercuts sentiment. After the boys have protested at the presence of girls in their class, a female teacher in the script (but not the broadcast) reads them a dictation on the rights of women according to the United Nations charter. In the script Ladrón has the husband comfort his weeping wife; on screen Crespi simply cuts briskly to the next sequence. Elsewhere the necessary visual rhetoric of television qualifies the published script and problematizes pedagogy. The long-time familiarity of movie star Imanol Arias as the father, Antonio, directs sympathy and intimacy towards him in a way not evident on the page. Likewise the casting of veteran film player Fernando Fernán Gómez as a curmudgeonly priest in an opening sequence lacking in the script not only signals "quality" to a discerning audience; it also flags up "cultural continuity" to an older demographic. Toni Leblanc (whose professional collaboration with TVE dates back to the 1950s) also has a recurrent role in *Cuéntame* as the kindly kiosk owner. The casting thus confirms the intimate relation of television with national history and identity.

New possibilities of meaning and subjectivity are also expressed through performance and shooting style. Ana Duato as the mother is in this early episode introduced somewhat dismissively. Our first sight of her is of a bottom wiggling in time to Los Panchos' *La cucaracha* on the radio as she scrubs the floor. Fearful and emotional, she clearly fails to grasp what is at stake in the social changes of which we, the audience, are so aware. Yet, as the series develops over the seasons, Mercedes, with her expanding clothing business, will become the mainstay of the family, both emotionally and financially. The character will thus evolve with the audience in an intimate, psychological process that takes place in both real and fictional time.

Yet the camerawork suggests that such individual or private media narratives must be placed in a collective or public context. In both workplace and domestic sequences (Antonio's boss berates his workers, Mercedes and the kids fearfully await the missing father), the camera holds back, typically framing the actors in medium-long, group shots and letting the action play uninterrupted. Even in the shot/reverse shot conventionally used for conversation between two characters, the camera is more distant than is usual on television, avoiding tight close ups and keeping both participants in frame. It is a technique familiar from, say, Hollywood film melodrama of the 1950s, and one which pointedly distances itself from the overbearing close ups and exaggerated musical prompts of the Latin American *telenovelas*, which fell so swiftly from favour in Spain when domestic drama was upgraded.

Music, then, is another non-verbal resource that helps us to frame and interpret dialogue. *Cuéntame* typically uses period source music rather than a freshly composed score. Indeed the contemporary songs used in each episode are carefully listed on the show's website and cannily marketed on CD in an extension of *Cuéntame*'s hugely profitable brand. In the post-public-service era of availability, then, *Cuéntame* is not averse to exploiting the same consumerism whose arrival its scripts deplore. *Cuéntame*'s use of special effects is also fully up to date and slightly disconcerting. With the use of seamless blue-screen technique, the fictional characters are inserted into (and even interact with) documentary footage. In this episode the grandmother enters a period post office to withdraw her precious savings and the radical student beloved by Toni lectures authentic campus comrades on the "correlation of forces".

Most effectively, however, period footage is combined with location shooting. Thus the father, Antonio, emerges (in colour) from his job at the Ministry of Agriculture opposite Atocha Station to be engulfed by a (scratchy black-and-white) student demonstration met by merciless repression from the police. The camera falls to the ground and dark blood flows onto the pavement. The incident is reprised at the end of the episode, when Antonio has bravely stood up to his Francoist boss. The camera advances ominously towards the family at dinner and cuts to a flashback of the terrified father (in black-and-white once more) sheltering off the street, his eyes shut tight to the horrible spectacle just out of shot. As the credits roll we hear a strangely tinny orchestration of the anthem "We Shall Overcome" mixed with the wail of sirens. The published script ends, more reassuringly, with the family dinner scene.

Such non-verbal, ambiguous techniques seem to represent not so much pedagogic witnessing of national history as an emotional working through of traumas which can have no clear conclusion. While the final scene of the episode as broadcast confirms Ladrón's claim that Francoism was a "terrible" time when Spaniards were "shitting themselves", it also clearly displays a national disunity that is just as typical of the contemporary period. The series concept of *Cuéntame* emphasized topics which were of relevance to modern viewers. Some spectators might find uncomfortable reminders in this episode that the rule of the Partido Popular had also coincided with increasing wealth at the expense of political commitment. Moreover it is noticeable (and this is for Ellis a characteristic of TV's "working through" [97]) that *Cuéntame*'s expert special effects are sometimes used not for cinematic illusionism but rather to call attention to the elaboration of pre-existing graphic materials: there is no attempt to blend the scratchy monochrome of documentary film with the glossy colour of studio-shot video tape. If, as Ellis claims once more (82), the new role of television is, like that of schools, to reconcile difference in a diverse nation, the lesson taught by *Cuéntame* remains unclear and its process of working through the past, defiantly unfinished. Hence the irony of the episode's title: from the rueful perspective of a less politically engaged era, late Francoism was perhaps indeed the time of "the best strikes of our lives".

Remembering, repeating, working through

It is striking how often the characters of *Cuéntame* watch television. In the episode discussed above, Mercedes distracts herself from her dressmaking chores with an unidentified classic costume drama (retrieved from TVE's precious archives); the family stare at Francoist newsreel of student revolt in far flung countries; and grandmother Herminia is only reassured about her purchase when she sees the burial plot she has bought on a TV report. While it is one of the great strengths of the series that it makes explicit (and thus open to analysis) the role of television in reflecting and refracting everyday life, this ordinariness is the source of both theoretical difficulty and journalistic hostility towards the medium.

The least we can ask for is that accuracy replaces the prejudice of the black legend of Spanish television. *El País* itself had reported (November 30, 2003) on the success of locally produced drama, which occupied four of the top ten slots of the previous week in a list composed entirely of Spanish shows. *Cuéntame*, forced that week into second place by Antena 3's contemporary urban sitcom *Aquí no hay quien viva*, still held the record for the highest audience share of the year: 51% (Anon., 53). Surviving the shift from a protected regime of scarcity to a mercilessly competitive regime of availability, TVE showed it could still produce generalist programming for a national audience.

In its sheer abundance and implicit challenge to romantic conceptions of the uniqueness of the work of art, television drama is reminiscent of the Spanish drama of the Golden Age. And, as A. A. Parker famously argued of the comedia, it "speaks a language of its own which we must first learn" (27). Parker's five principles remain well known to specialists:

> (1) The primacy of action over character drawing; (2) the primacy of theme over action . . . (3) dramatic unity in the theme and not in the action; (4) the subordination of the theme to a moral purpose through the principle of poetic justice . . . (5) the elucidation of the moral purpose by means of dramatic causality. (Parker, 27)

At a time of radical uncertainty in the field of broadcasting, characterized by changes in technology, industry, and content, it may seem over ambitious to ascribe similar priorities to an approach to Spanish television drama of this new Golden Age. But some of Parker's principles still hold for the new medium.

Although the extended character arc of series drama is vital to its appeal, televisual dramatic unity is, as in the comedia, found more easily in the theme rather than in the multiple and varied action. For example, in the episode of *Cuéntame* we examined above, the theme of solidarity unites the six subplots allotted to each of the family members. And, as in the comedia once more, there is some evidence for poetic justice in this form of TV drama: the father who claims all is well in Spain is forced to eat his own words. But the organizing principle seems rather to be pedagogy, understood in the extended sense of an education in social responsibility. Indeed, in Autumn 2003, TVE ran a series of programmes explicitly designed to teach viewers about the Constitution, as it had done twenty-five years earlier. Such pedagogy is not incompatible with commercial competition. Contreras stresses that programmers are sensitive to social profitability: loss-making news and prestige drama enhance the channel's overall brand. *Cuéntame* is thus more typical of Spanish television as a whole than the *telebasura* attacked by Right and Left alike: the most scandalous shows have been commercial disasters, failing to find an audience (Contreras and Palacio, 104–5).

Turning from Parker's five principles to Caughie's six problems, we can now re-read TV studies in a new Spanish context.

(1) *Specificity*. Television is not film. While its visual pleasures are smaller, they are diverse and still require close analysis. But more typically broadcasting is verbal, using the word to tell us about the world. *Cuéntame*'s voice-over is emblematic of this framing and interpretation of the image through text.

(2) *History*. We must attempt to retrieve the history not just of television but also of discourse on television. The "black legend" of Spanish TV emerged at a specific moment for specific reasons. The blanket condemnation of the medium so frequent in Spain not only consigns to oblivion important programmes of the past; it also renders invisible current creative innovations.

(3) *Text*. The televisual text is based on repetition and familiarity, underscored by the regular rhythms of scheduling and domestic life. However, certain genres (such as "serious" drama) stand out from the herd, both formally and ideologically. Current Spanish fiction shows clear signs of textual "authorship" in work created by scriptwriters and coordinators such as Eduardo Ladrón de Guevara (and, I would add, independent executive producers such as Antonio Mercero).

(4) *The national*. Spanish television is increasingly national, not only in its public service heritage (which still underwrites much of TVE's programming) but also in the recent rise of domestic drama. As one media commentator writes, "US cultural hegemony lives on movies, not TV" (Gabler). If we are concerned with the specificity of Spanish culture, then television shows are a more significant field than feature films.

(5) *The everyday*. TV's flow is continuous, but it is not undifferentiated. The "eddies" and "currents" of attention cited by Caughie are clearly visible in the Spanish context, both through the ever shifting patterns tracked by audience research and through the varied responses of viewers, posted in chat rooms (fans of *Cuéntame* both lament the absence of a familiar friend during

the summer hiatus and solemnly recount the series' informational value for the study of Spanish history).

(6) *Value.* Most of the scholars I have cited engage with the Frankfurt School's critique of the culture industries. However, Caughie argues that pessimism is not as all-pervasive in Adorno as is commonly thought (228–9). A theoretical space thus opens for the discrimination of value within mass media. Empirical study has established clear criteria for "quality" from a production and consumption standpoint. There seems little doubt on both sides that what Spanish television offers has markedly improved in recent years.

In his essay "Remembering, repeating, and working through" (1914) Freud focuses on a particularly difficult, even tedious, part of the process of analysis. According to Laplanche and Pontalis, "working through" applies to resistances: "[it is] a sort of psychical work which allows the subject to accept certain repressed elements and to free himself from the grip of mechanisms of repetition" (Laplanche and Pontalis 488). Or again: "Working through permits the subject to pass from rejection or merely intellectual acceptance to a conviction based on lived experience". While TV viewing might seem to be a primary example of repetition compulsion (Palacio notes how Spaniards' daily consumption has continued to grow year on year [Contreras and Palacio, 69]), I have argued with Ellis that television is a forum for addressing national issues which, in an age of diversity, have no simple solution. Through the empathy of drama in particular, events that are resisted or known only intellectually (such as the terror of dictatorship) can achieve in viewers a conviction based on lived experience, or a convincing simulacrum thereof. This positive effect is, in the words of Salvador Cardús (another unexpected defender of television), a "virtuous reality" to set against the "catastrophe mentality" so often attributed to TV in Spain. The resistance, then, is in this case not only that of the viewer, but also that of the professional commentator, mesmerized by the black legend. A new approach to this new Golden Age of television drama would thus involve an acknowledgement, as in Freud, that while analysis may be interminable, it is no less necessary and valuable.

Cuéntame cómo pasó (*Tell Me How It Happened*, TVE1, 2001–)

Creator: Eduardo Ladrón de Guevara
Executive producer: Miguel Ángel Bernardeau
Co-producer: Mario Pedraza
Directors: Tito Fernández, Agustín Crespi, Antonio Cano
Script editors: Eduardo Ladrón de Guevara, Patrick Buckley
Scriptwriters: Eduardo Ladrón de Guevara, Patrick Buckley, Alberto Macías, Verónica Fernández, Javier Amezúa
Photography: Tote Trenas
Art direction: Gonzalo Gonzalo

Regular cast
Antonio: Imanol Arias
Mercedes: Ana Duato
Carlos: Ricardo Gómez
Herminia: María Galiana
Inés: Irene Visedo
Toni: Pablo Rivero

Works cited

Anon. "Los programas más vistos de la semana". *El País*, 30 Nov. 2003: 53.
Cardús i Ros, Salvador. "En defensa de la televisió: la realitat virtuosa". *Trípodos* 6 (1998): 31–44.
Caughie, John. *Television Drama*. Oxford: Oxford University Press, 2000.
Contreras, José Miguel and Manuel Palacio. *La programación de televisión*. Madrid: Síntesis, 2001.
Díaz, Lorenzo. *Informe sobre la televisión en España 1989–98: la década abominable*. Barcelona: Ediciones B, 1999.
Ellis, John. *Seeing Things: Television in the Age of Uncertainty*. London: I. B. Tauris, 2002.
Estrada, Isabel. "*Cuéntame cómo pasó* o la revisión de la historia española reciente". *Hispanic Review* 72 (2004): 547–64.
Gabler, Neal. "U.S. Cultural Hegemony Lives on Movies, not TV". *International Herald Tribune* Jan. 10, 2003: 7.
Gómez, Rosario G. "¿El fin de la televisión de partido?". *El País*, Mar. 21, 2004: 7.
Ladrón de Guevara, Eduardo. *Cuéntame cómo pasó. Querido maestro*. Ed. Emeterio Diez. Madrid: Fundamentos-Universidad Camilo José Cela, 2003.
Laplanche, J. and J. B. Pontalis. *The Language of Psychoanalysis*. London: Karnak, 1973.
Palacio, Manuel. *Historia de la televisión en España*. Barcelona: Gedisa, 2001.
Parker, A. A. *The Approach to the Spanish Drama of the Golden Age*. London: Grant and Cutler, 1957.
Smith, Paul Julian. "Quality TV? The *Periodistas* Notebook". In *Contemporary Spanish Culture: TV, Fashion, Art, and Film*. Oxford and Cambridge: Polity, 2003, pp. 9–33.
———. "The Emotional Imperative: Almodóvar's *Hable con ella* and TVE's *Cuéntame cómo pasó*". *MLN*, 119 (2004): 363–75.

Electronic source
Cuéntame cómo pasó. 21 Dec. 2004 <http://www.cuentamecomopaso.net/>.

2

The Classic Serial: Public Service, Literarity, and the Middle-brow (*Fortunata y Jacinta* [1980] and *La Regenta* [1995])

Two televisual eras: scarcity and availability

El año 1979 ha sido un año clave en la historia de la Radio y la Televisión públicas en España. Durante ese año, las Cortes Generales elaboraron el Estatuto de la Radio y la Televisión, que entraría en vigor el 2 de febrero de 1980. Ese Estatuto, hecho desde el diálogo entre las fuerzas políticas representadas en el Parlamento, es el instrumento para conseguir unos medios audiovisuales de comunicación al servicio de la comunidad y con plenas garantías democráticas.

En el aspecto del funcionamiento interno de RTVE, 1979 ha sido también un año muy importante. Tal como ya ha quedado reflejado en la Memoria de Contabilidad del Organismo, en ese período se consolidó la contabilidad administrativa o de presupuesto, y se creó la financiera o de gestión. Han sido, sin duda, grandes pasos para llegar a la transparencia económica de un organismo del Estado, financiado con recursos públicos.

Transparencia en las cuentas, eficacia en el gasto, equilibrio en la programación, imparcialidad ante los grandes acontecimientos vividos (elecciones generales y locales y referendos de autonomía) han sido las grandes líneas maestras que hemos querido que presidieran la actuación diaria de RTVE.

1979 has been a key year in the history of public radio and television in Spain. During this year Parliament drafted the Statute of Radio and Television which was to take effect on February 2, 1980. This Statute, created out of a dialogue between the political forces represented in Parliament, will serve to put audio-visual media at the service of the community and with fully democratic guarantees.

With reference to the internal management of RTVE, 1979 has also been a very important year. As has now been made clear in the Report on Corporation Accounting, during this time the administrative or budgeting accounts were consolidated and the financial or managements accounts were created. There is no doubt that this has meant a great step forward towards economic transparency in a state corporation that is financed by public funds.

Transparent accounts, efficient expenditure, balanced programming, and an impartial approach to the great events we have lived through (the general and local elections and the referendums on the self-governing regions), these are the general principles which we have attempted to follow in the daily business of RTVE.

(Director-General Fernando Arias-Salgado, in RTVE, 5)

Una nueva temporada televisiva ha dado comienzo. Una vez más, las cadenas, las empresas de producción, las compañías relacionadas con el mundo de la publicidad y varios miles de profesionales se han puesto en marcha para afrontar la batalla por la conquista de la audiencia.

Dentro de un año podremos ver los resultados y analizar lo ocurrido. De momento veremos desde qué punto partimos, cuál es la situación real de la televisión en España a finales de este año 95. A lo largo de los últimos meses se ha librado una feroz competencia entre las diferentes cadenas para situarse en la mejor de las posiciones posibles a fin de afrontar el futuro inmediato. La temporada 94-95 ha resultado apasionante en términos profesionales y muy atractivo desde la perspectiva del telespectador, que cada vez parece más satisfecho de la oferta televisiva española.

Another TV season has started. Once more the stations, the production companies, the advertising firms, and several thousand professionals have gone into battle to win over the audience.

In a year's time we'll be able to see the results and analyse what happened. For the time being we can see our starting position and the real situation of television in Spain at the end of the current year 1995. During the last few months there has been fierce competition between the different channels to get into the best possible position in order to face up to the immediate future. The 1994–5 season has been exciting in professional terms and very attractive from the point of view of the viewers, who seem increasingly satisfied with the offering of Spanish TV.

(José Miguel Contreras and Javier del Pino in GECA 9)

If we compare the Spanish TV annuals for 1979 and 1995, we might be forgiven for thinking they refer to entirely different countries, so completely did the televisual landscape change during the period. Even the format of the covers gives notice of distinct audiovisual regimes. The state-monopoly broadcaster's "chronicle of a year" shows a single picture of a cameraman at work. Shot from below, he looms as large as a Soviet hero-worker. Commercial consultancy GECA's "book of the telly" gives us multiple snapshots of the comely or eccentric stars of the period: celebrity newsreaders and game-show hosts, the presenter of a talk show on sex, and the happy couple at a royal wedding. Yet both annuals mark key moments in the history of television in Spain: the coming of the Radio and Television Statute, which regulated the state media for the new democracy, and the height of the battle between the public broadcaster and the new commercial stations.

While, as we shall see, the political impartiality and financial transparency of RTVE proclaimed by its Director-General were hotly contested, the objective conditions of broadcasting in 1980 are clearly set out in the "chronicle."

Televisión Española comprised two channels, one of "general interest," the other for "specialized programming" (9). The average daily audience for the first channel was over 17 million: 75.5% of the adult population on Tuesdays and 81.3% on Thursdays (11). The peak viewing time is (as today) a late 10.30 to 11 pm. The minority second channel, at that time still unavailable to many in the Peninsula, oscillated between a 2.5% share on Thursdays and 11.9% on Sundays. Scheduling was thus clearly complementary, with each channel peaking at a different time in the week.

The somewhat primitive audience research of the period (which had begun only in 1972) revealed that public approval of this monopoly programming had increased slightly year on year (11), although feature films were the most popular genre. Of individual shows, the most popular were documentaries, such as *Mundo submarino* (*Underwater World*) and *El hombre y la tierra* (*Man and Earth*, a globe-trotting nature show), with fourth place going to the "Grandes Relatos" ("Great Stories") strand, a slot often occupied by UK classic serials. The three photos chosen to illustrate the statistics are of a picturesque anemone, a bedraggled presenter (the respected pioneer of ecology, Félix Rodríguez de la Fuente) cradling a dolphin in his arms, and Welsh actress Sian Phillips as the bloody matriarch Livia in the BBC's costume drama *I, Claudius* (12–13). But this cultural programming is not universally welcomed. We are told that the least popular programmes are also those with *pretensión de culturalidad* ("cultural pretensions," 13). The moral, according to RTVE, is not that culture turns off audiences, but that the way in which the cultural element is presented is of primary importance. The sheer volume of cultural programming remains surprising, however. The first channel broadcast 56 hours of "classical music" in 1979 (although this included such middle-brow strands as a six-hour series of *zarzuela* selections) (58). The second channel scheduled no fewer than 201 hours of classical music, including twelve shows of ninety minutes called, simply, *Opera*. Special one-off concerts included popular classics such as Handel's *Messiah*, a gala performance at Vienna Opera, and the Festival Folklórico at Jaca (59).

Fifteen years later programming had changed beyond recognition. The top stories of the season were the rise of the home-made sitcom and "sex on screen" (9); and the prime attraction was "stars": new stars, "polivalent" stars, and the stars of "family viewing" (25). The newly arrived and hugely popular *Médico de familia* (*Family Doctor*, Tele5) will herald the explosion of local fiction in the decade to follow. Where the public broadcaster stressed culture, the private regime promotes pleasure. According to GECA, by 1995 customer satisfaction (now measured by the more sophisticated audience research of SOFRES) has surely increased year on year in line with average daily consumption: from 193 minutes in 1992 to 210 minutes in 1994 (9). "Housewives" are the most dedicated viewers, clocking up a total of 255 minutes a day. If GECA attributes this change to the increased competition that followed the arrival of commercial TV in 1990, they also acknowledge that TVE has now halted its "tremendous" decline in audience, with its first, generalist channel retaining its overall leadership. Average share for the year gives TVE1 27.6%; the private channels Antena 3 and Tele5 26.0% and 18.1%, respectively; the consortium of autonomous and regional channels known as FORTA 15.8%; and, finally, the minority state channel TVE2 9.3% (10). These figures disguise large differences, however, within the Spanish state: Catalan viewers give their national public channel TV3 a hefty 22.8%. Moreover this "battle" for ratings is about to get fiercer still: the subscription service Canal + has just achieved a million viewers and cable TV is about to arrive in Spain (11).

There could be no clearer illustration of what John Ellis has called the two eras of television: that of "scarcity" in standardized public service broadcasting and that of "availability" in a diverse consumer market (2–3). The question then arises of whether we can identify changes in content that correspond to these radical changes in audiovisual and, indeed, political regimes. Manuel Palacio has traced the history of the genre of "prime-time fiction" in Spain over some forty years. Unlike many academics and even practitioners, Palacio takes it for granted that TV fiction possesses its own "logic," different from that of other media and founded not only in the form (shot size, serial narrative) but in the mode of consumption (private as opposed to public) (*Historia*, 142). Aesthetics, often derived from cinema, also intersect with what Palacio calls "pedagogy": the reworking of the public culture of the present on the basis of the historic "sedimentation" of the past (144). While such educational prisms will necessarily vary from one moment to another, they are always in operation: Palacio notes the widespread appeal to historical or literary "consultants" in such series, who serve not only to guarantee the programmes' fidelity to the past but also to ensure their acceptability in the present (144).

While live drama of the earliest period is lost, by the mid-1960s TVE had entered what Palacio calls its "Golden Age" (146). A dramatic strand called *Estudio 1*, broadcast for fifteen years, aimed unashamedly to awaken the viewer's interest in theatre with productions of such classics as Arthur Miller's *The Crucible* (1965), Shakespeare's *Richard III* (1967), and Calderón's *El gran teatro del mundo* (*The Great Theatre of the World*, 1969) (147). The literary strand known as "Novela" ran for almost twenty years, adapting at great speed and in reduced financial circumstances novels such as *The Count of Montecristo* (1969) and *Little Dorrit* (1970) (148). The quest for international prestige soon led to higher budgets and prestige projects such as *La cabina* (*The Telephone Booth*, 1972), the only Spanish programme to have won a US Emmy (152).

By the 1970s TVE changed course, rejecting theatrical studio-bound production for cinematic-style literary adaptations often shot in authentic exteriors (153). Spain sought to emulate the BBC's family chronicle *The Forsyte Saga* (1967) and RAI's great-man biopic *Leonardo da Vinci* (1971), both of which were dubbed for Spanish transmission. The best known early example is veteran actor-director Fernando Fernán Gómez's *El pícaro* (1974), based on classic narratives of the Golden Age. For Palacio the years of the transition to democracy (1975–82) are those which are most unapologetically pedagogic, when TVE attempted to link past and present through exemplary life stories (e.g.

Cervantes [1981]) and adaptations (*Fortunata y Jacinta* [1980]) (153). *Curro Jiménez*, the Western-style bandit serial which boasted the participation of film directors such as Pilar Miró and Mario Camus (1976–8), made use of its War of Independence setting to construct a national democratic imaginary in opposition to an illegitimate "other" (154). The bandit's final heroic death scene provoked commentary from politicians and *folklóricas* alike (155). *La barraca* also contained explicit political commentary that was absent from its popular source novel: nineteenth-century characters are made to warn twentieth-century audiences about the dangers of renewed civil war (157). The still hierarchical and authoritarian TVE, directed by the reactionary Fernando Arias Salgado, saw such narratives as allegories of the tense Spain of the transition. The biopic of Cervantes also supplemented its source with a voice-over warning that any historical inaccuracies were intended to support the cause of freedom in contemporary Spain (158).

The 1980s, the last decade before commercial television, saw no fewer than twenty home-grown prime-time fiction serials, of which the great majority were period pieces. In this new Socialist era, the focus was on the period before and during the Civil War (160). Unsurprisingly, audience sympathies are directed exclusively towards the Republicans, with Nationalists virtually absent until the end of the decade (162). The 1990s see a further change in televisual regime. The cinematic series of a previous decade no longer fit new patterns of programming and consumption. *El Quijote* (1992), directed by noted cineaste Manuel Gutiérrez Aragón, flops when it is scheduled in a weekly slot. *La Regenta* (1995) is stripped like a mini-series over three consecutive nights in order to sustain audience interest (163). But the biggest industrial change is the emergence of contemporary drama, which now monopolizes prime time in a fashion that is, for local Spanish production, unprecedented in the history of the medium (162).

What is striking is the sheer prominence and persistence of the genre of the classic serial through huge historical and institutional changes. From Francoism, through the transition, to the consolidation of Socialist dominance, period drama held a major place on Spanish television. But if, as Palacio argues, in-house "fiction" remains the key element in lending legitimacy to a single channel or an entire TV system (143), then it is striking that he fails to differentiate within that broad category, even as he argues that TV fiction's main role is not to represent contemporary society to itself but rather to reconcile past and present. Another academic commentator attempting in 1989 to construct a "typology" of TV series also fails to divide the genre by categories such as period and source text, concentrating on such criteria as "temporal relations between episodes" (González Requena, 39), plot length (44), and plot structure (46). Significant also here is the corpus of series studied, which, as is typical of the period, is heavily skewed towards foreign production: the UK has as many titles as Spain (fifteen), and this figure is surpassed by the US (twenty-five) and "other countries" (twenty) (Jiménez Losantos and Sánchez-Biosca, 283).

The study of the classic serial genre (like its production) is thus less developed in Spain than in other countries, especially the UK, where the BBC has long broadcast literary adaptations and academics have, with equal tenacity, provided detailed readings of them. As we shall see, those readings will prove invaluable in our study of two vital Spanish series corresponding respectively to the two televisual regimes of public scarcity and private abundance: *Fortunata y Jacinta* (1980) and *La Regenta* (1995). But first I would like to propose a methodology for reading Spanish classic serials which integrates the political, social, and aesthetic fields by addressing three interconnected topics: public service, literarity, and the middle-brow. Such an approach is intended to bridge the gap between the few existing commentaries on these programmes, which tend to be by either purist literary scholars or pragmatic practitioners.

Politics, society, aesthetics

We have already seen that Arias Salgado proposed in 1979 that the state media would be at the "service" of a democratic community and cultivate the public's sensibilities through careful use of cultural elements (RTVE, 5). Conversely, Contreras stated in 1995 that audience "satisfaction" had been achieved through commercial competition and could be measured numerically through the daily ratings (GECA, 9). The uncanny persistence of the classic novel into the commercial era suggests that something of the public service ethos still survived. But on closer inspection, the concept is surprisingly slippery. British scholars discussing the pioneer of public service (the BBC changed from "company" to "corporation" in 1926) note that the public "was conceived as a national body of people, only differentiated by region" (Casey, Casey, Calvert, French, and Lewis, 185). Broadcasting was understood to be cultural, introducing the mass audience to serious music and drama that did not follow but rather led public taste in the arts (186). Even when commercial television was established in the UK in the 1950s it was intended not as an alternative to public service but as an "extension" to it, with a brief to "inform, educate, and entertain" (187). Indeed, Channel 4, a commercial channel set up in the early 1980s, was dedicated to "minority groups" within the national audience. Unlike in Spain, the British public broadcaster is funded not by advertising and direct government grants but by a licence fee paid by viewers. The BBC's relationship with the state is thus "complex" and, unlike in Spain once more, rarely directly controlled by the government. However, given the increasing "fragmentation" of national audiences, the debate has shifted from public service to "the changing relationship between providers of media and their consumers" (188).

It is interesting to contrast this British account with a Spanish argument for "rethinking public service in television" (Giordano and Zeller). Here the authors argue that the criterion for distinguishing between public and private is not so much the ownership of a channel as the nature of its programming (171). Current public channels defend poor programming with two arguments. The first is that of articulating national identity, employed by the notoriously poor-quality Valencian Canal 9 (172). The second is that popular programming generates revenue that can be used for higher-quality shows. Rejecting these arguments, the authors note that in Spain both public and private channels are vulnerable to political interference (173) and that TVE still requires organizational reform, analogous to that of the universities, to make it independent (174). Noting (like the British) the increasing complexity and diversity of society, the Spanish scholars argue that the "associative fabric" which television must reflect cannot be reduced to party politics (175). TV programming is thus to be understood as a "social good" that is as heterogeneous and plural as the new audience. Public broadcasting should be freed from the tyranny of the ratings; but it should not turn its back on society (178); and generalist entertainment programming should be combined with minority schedules dedicated to important segments of the public, especially those with "reduced cultural capital" (179). "Quality programming" (given in quotes) should embrace both the elite culture of music and theatre and those forms of popular entertainment that are not incompatible with quality (180).

Hence while some British academics seem resigned to the decline of public service, claiming that audiences will be increasingly differentiated by their ability to pay for special programming, Spanish scholars still hold out for the potential of public service, albeit redefined as a social good that embraces diversity and plurality (they call for access for such marginalized groups as gypsies). Ironically, then, the Britons, who still enjoy the service of a powerful public broadcaster, substantially independent of government manipulation and commercial pressure, are less sympathetic to elite and quality programming than their Spanish counterparts. I would suggest that this corresponds to a continuing sense of media hierarchy in Spain and a relative reverence for traditionally defined high culture. A report on the habits of cultural consumption in Spain in the mid-1990s (just after the broadcast of *La Regenta*) explores these contradictions and enables us to sketch a connection between media policy and social class.

According to the SGAE only a tiny minority of Spaniards take the time to attend classical concerts or the theatre, although many claim they would do so if what was on offer was more accessible or they knew more about it (40). Conversely 99.5% habitually watch television (93). There is a strict inverse correlation between objective hours of TV watching and both social class and education level. While those richest in cultural capital see only 178 minutes a day, the poorest (those to whom Spanish scholars say public service television should be directed) watch 229 minutes a day, and consume no other cultural products (95). All Spaniards claim subjectively to watch less television than the objective research indicates. But what is striking is that social class and education are positively related to increasing miscalculation of that time: the cultural "aristocracy" are more likely to underestimate their addiction to television than their lumpen neighbours. There is thus clearly a class stigma clinging to the medium. Satisfaction with different genres of programming is also class specific. Book and theatre programmes attract the lowest level of both interest and satisfaction (103). In other words, the elite cultural audience is the least satisfied with the scheduling dedicated to it. Contradicting the Spanish daily press's relentless hostility to television news, the latter is judged both the most interesting and the most satisfactory. Fiction series (divided into "dramatic" and "romantic") fall in the middle for both audience size and satisfaction.

We can crosslink this TV audience profile with that of another, less popular medium: reading. Only half of Spaniards read books regularly and, unsurprisingly, social class and education level are once more rigidly determining factors (120). Of those who do read, fiction dominates over non-fiction, and within that subset contemporary fiction is preferred by a large majority (122). Only 16.5% claim to read "classic" literature. But the cumulative audience for historical novels, romances, and non-fiction history books is not insubstantial. Given informants' general tendency to give opinions they think will please the researchers, the SGAE thinks it likely that lower-class respondents overestimate their modest hours spent reading, just as the upper class underestimate their relatively lengthy TV viewing time. In Bourdieu's terms, subjective dispositions thus interact continuously with objective positions in the cultural field.

We will see later that the "literarity" of classic TV serials is a mixed blessing, alternately emphasized and disavowed by producers and press. But it is clear from these data on cultural consumption that the classic serial stands at a crossroads between social classes and cultural tastes: educated, upper-class TV viewers are generally ashamed of the medium and dissatisfied with the meagre cultural programming it dedicates to them; uneducated viewers express mild interest in the elite pursuits of reading, concerts, and the theatre, if only in an attempt to satisfy researchers. There remains a surprisingly large group in the middle, who appear modestly satisfied with their dramatic or romantic TV series and with their historical novels. It is to this unstable and overlooked segment that the middle-brow genre of the classic serial is directed.

While the SGAE often talks of "elite" and "popular" choices it does not mention the middle-brow. Yet the term is attracting increasing attention in UK Spanish cultural studies. For example, in a recent paper ("Middle-brow"), Sally Faulkner has suggested that while Spanish popular comedies of the 1960s are about the middle-brow (the attempt by the upwardly mobile working class to adapt or adopt elite forms), social realist dramas of the 1990s are middle-brow in themselves (negotiating that same cultural conundrum for contemporary audiences). The *locus classicus* of the middle-brow remains Pierre Bourdieu's *Distinction*, first published in French in 1979. Bourdieu's subtitle (*A Social Critique of the Judgement of Taste*) suggests how we might make a link from the social to the aesthetic. For Bourdieu there are three class-specific cultures. The "legitimate" taste of aesthetic "aristocrats" (represented in music by Bach); the middle-brow culture of Gershwin and Jacques Brel; and the "popular" taste of Strauss waltzes and Petula Clark (16). Characteristically contradictory, the middle-brow thus embraces both "the minor works of the major arts" (such as orchestral music) and "the major works of the minor arts" (such as semi-popular *chanson*). It is typical of secretaries, technicians, and primary school teachers. Bourdieu writes later:

> In photography this taste prefers objects that are close to those of the popular aesthetic [i.e. mountain landscapes, sunsets, and woods] but semi-neutralized by a visible stylistic intention combining the human picturesque (weaver at his loom, tramps quarrelling, folk dance) with gratuitous form (pebbles, rope, tree bark). (58)

Such a taste entails a corresponding life style, favouring in food and furniture "a taste for tradition . . . and a sort of temperate hedonism . . . moderate even in its audacities" (267). Striving towards distinction, however, middle-brow taste exposes its exponents to anxiety in their newly aestheticized personal choices (such as clothing). Bourdieu's case studies of middle-brow life styles now have a pathos that is due only in part to their distance in time. One magazine article of 1970 proclaims that "For Today's Career Woman, Entertaining Means Planning" (321). An "up to the minute welcome" is expressed in "a simple green lacquer coffee table with steel trimmings" (322), while another hostess uses "a wicker basket to stack the dirty plates and cutlery." Or again, "a very modest nurse" is shocked when she hears a grammatical mistake, but "hates pretentious people" (324). She wears "classic clothes" ("a navy blue skirt") and only watches television "to pass the time" or "relax" (325). She listens to "meaningful" songs on the radio and rents a small flat on the Atlantic coast for her summer holiday. The lives of the bourgeois heroine of a Spanish classic novel or the modern housewife addicted to television talk shows could hardly be more circumscribed.

But what of the producers of this discreet and reverent culture? These new intermediaries are placed "half-way between legitimate culture and mass production" (326). Lacking the charisma of the genuine author, they "live in the unease of the inherently contradictory role of a 'presenter'" devoid of intrinsic value. Providing an insecure audience with "guarantees of quality" and "institutional signs of cultural authority," such producers represent a middle-brow culture that is "resolutely against vulgarity" (326). One of Bourdieu's examples here, tellingly, is "Sorbonne professors debating on TV" (326). It is a perilous position also occupied by those who adapt classic novels for television.

The literary adaptation: academy and press

> Fortunata, a glorious woman of the people, struggles all her life against the angelic, bourgeois Jacinta; both adore Jacinta's charming, selfish husband, the sybarite Juanito. Pérez Galdós steeps his story in scenes of working- and middle-class Madrid that are panoramic and intimate: the streets and reeking tenements, shops and stalls that open like mouths, the fashion trades, cafes where idlers thrash out politics, the pharmacy where Fortunata's sickly husband Maxi goes mad with jealousy, the convent in which the passionate

Fortunata is locked to repent her promiscuity, the twin beds where Juanito caresses Jacinta with lies. (Publisher's World)

Married to the retired magistrate of Vetusta, Ana Ozores cares deeply for her much older husband but feels stifled by the monotony of her life in the shabby and conservative provincial town. When she embarks on a quest for fulfillment through religion and even adultery, a bitter struggle begins between a powerful priest [Fermín, the Magistral] and a would-be Don Juan [Alvaro Mesía] for the passionate young woman's body and soul. Spain's answer to *Madame Bovary*, *La Regenta* wittily depicts the complacent and frivolous world of the upper class. (Penguin Classics)

The only full-length study of the classic serial is Sarah Cardwell's *Adaptation Revisited: Television and the Classic Novel* (2002). Cardwell starts from the assumption that adaptations of classic novels "form a distinct genre" (1), which she defines pragmatically on the basis of audiences' "commonly held" beliefs (2) and restricts her study to texts that are "unproblematically British" (3). The central contradiction of the genre is as follows:

On the one hand, it is clear that the programmes' emotive representations of the past and distinctive filmic, slow-paced style are part of their continuing appeal; on the other, the televisual context in which they are situated is characterized by its emphasis on its contemporaneity, presentness, and performativity. (Cardwell, 4)

Revisiting British criticism of the genre, Cardwell notes how it is often described as the "best" television (33), but this relies on a disavowal: "the best television is, it appears, television which appears to be non-televisual" (34). One critical argument for this attitude is the privileging of word over image: the move from verbal to visual representation is said to result in the audience's loss of the active imagination required of readers (36). Unsurprisingly scholars of English literature, who until recently dominated the field, also value the literary over the televisual (39).

　　Turning from criticism to theory, Cardwell identifies three main approaches: medium-specific, comparative, and pluralist. The medium-specific approach argues that "each separate medium . . . is unique and its unique nature gives rise to forms of artistic expression distinct from those in other media" (44). For Cardwell the argument for "ontological specificity" is attractive but deterministic, reducing textual features to a secondary, derived role (47). And its originator, curiously, relies on the written script for his analyses and cites Eisenstein, for whom Charles Dickens' literary language could be read for its "film-indications": verbal precursors to visual techniques such as shot size and montage (49). Abandoning critics' concern for "fidelity" and literary bias, "comparative" theorists sought rather to "explain equivalence" (or the failure to achieve it) in novel and film (52), addressing "non-linguistic" elements such as lighting and mise-en-scène, and focusing on "the kind of relation" set up between the two media (53). There is thus a "possibility of convergence" (58), with adaptation described as "transposition, commentary, and analogy" (63). The third mode of "pluralism" breaks with sustained comparison between novel and screen text in order to address both "film and television conventions and cultural and historical contexts" (70). Bourdieu's writings on cultural capital weigh heavily here. However, pluralist critics tend to reduce the aesthetic to the ideological: "the close analysis of style, tone, narrative structure, performance and so on is employed only in the service of making a wider political point" (71).

Cardwell's own approach (only apparently tautological) is to place "television adaptations in the televisual context" (77). BBC classic serials share "a particularly strong group style" expressed and recognized in content, style, and mood (78). Rejecting once more the ideological critique which sees the genre only as the perpetuation of elite literary culture, the maintenance of the distinction between "good" and "trash" television, and the fostering of reactionary nostalgia for a colonial past, Cardwell focuses on four aspects of televisuality that impact decisively but ambiguously on the genre of the classic serial. The first is temporality and presentness (83). Not only is TV transmission "never completed, always becoming," it also has "a peculiar actual or perceived relationship to real-life time" (85). The widespread use of direct address and of sound to attract the distracted viewer's attention heightens this sense of temporal and even spatial presence (86). The second aspect is performance. Even within period drama, TV's immersion in everyday life means that audiences are intermittently aware that their "imaginative engagement with the 'past' " is in fact a careful representation of that past, based on meticulously re-created props and costumes and, above all, performed by actors who "never wholly disappear beneath their roles" (89). The resonance of previous roles and real-life incidents (the example of Hugh Grant is given) reasserts the "contemporaneity" of period drama (91). This relates to the third element, of intertextuality. No TV show is an island and as the genre develops over time it makes perhaps as much reference to itself as to source texts (successive adaptations of Jane Austen share scenes absent in the original novel). Finally, then, the "televisual" must be expanded beyond mere broadcasting, embracing press and academy and affectively influencing everyday life (94).

In her case studies Cardwell notes marked formal differences between *Brideshead Revisited* (ITV, 1981) and *Pride and Prejudice* (BBC, 1995), coinciding generally with a drift from literary to a televisual culture (105). The period is the same as that I am studying in Spain, where *Fortunata y Jacinta* and *La Regenta* are also separated by fifteen years. But before addressing the programmes themselves along the lines advocated by Cardwell, I would like to extend the televisual in Spain to explore print accounts of the classic serial. As we shall see, they tend to collapse the political, social, and aesthetic.

Writing as they do from departments of Spanish Literature or *filología hispánica*, the few pioneer scholars of Spanish classic TV serials wholly neglect the televisual. In her meticulous study of Mario Camus's "cinematic reading" of *Fortunata y Jacinta*, Mercedes López-Baralt begins by citing the ontological specificity of literature and film, but goes on to adopt a "comparative" approach which allows for the "re-creation" or "translation" of codes from one medium to another (93), citing the origins of Griffith's cinematic narrative in the nineteenth-century novel. López-Baralt's preference for the verbal over the visual is reinforced by that of the director himself, quoted in an interview of the time as saying he preferred literature to film (95). Yet Camus was awarded the national cinema prize (Premio Nacional de Cinematografía) in 1985, five years after the screening of *Fortunata y Jacinta* and just one year after making his most successful film adaptation, *Los santos inocentes* (*The Holy Innocents*, 1984). Clearly the "best" television must be legitimated by other media, both the novel and cinema. It is not surprising, therefore, that López-Baralt's "translation of codes," supposedly comparative, is in effect evaluative, stressing inevitable "losses" (96). The first is that mentioned by Cardwell, the supposed "active participation of the imagination." The next is that of the narrator, who in Galdós's source text is the vehicle for an "intimate complicity" with the reader, for "Cervantine" perspectivism and ambiguity. In film theory, claims López-Baralt, even the distinction between first- and third-person narration (between subjective and objective points of view) is unclear. Additional "losses" are the "documentary" material in the novel (Galdós's minute description of the Madrid clothing trade), political events (the café discussion scenes are much reduced), the exploration of the unconscious (only Jacinta's dream in the Opera House is re-created) (98), and the rich colloquialism of Galdós's dialogue (101). Most serious, however, is the loss of psychological interiority, of Fortunata's "struggle" with herself. This is due to the miscasting of the insufficiently "sensual" Ana Belén as the fiery working-class heroine.

To her credit, however, López-Baralt adds to this sustained comparison between source text and adaptation a medium-specific appraisal of gains in translation. Galdós's ambiguity does not disappear entirely, but rather resurfaces in the image. The devout Guillermina Pacheco is cast and shot in ways which remind us of Goya's witches, thus coinciding with recent scholarly revisions of the character in the novel (97). Another "added element" is the music, whose main theme is shared by the non-diegetic orchestra of the score and the diegetic barrel organ that plays in the street below the characters (98). One invented sequence, an extended visit to the *zarzuela*, is held to be a welcome addition. Wardrobe and set design create a suggestive nineteenth-century "atmosphere," while the cinematography offers handsome "still-lifes" of fruit and poultry in the market (99). And if Fortunata's sensuality is repressed, the angelic Jacinta's is visually suggested through framing: seated on the bed she draws her husband close, her face level with his crotch (100). Here once more Camus's "reading" coincides with that of recent Galdosistas, who also champion Jacinta's repressed but fervent sexuality. Camus's interpretation of the two heroines is thus finally proclaimed "legitimate" (102).

In two articles, José Manuel González Herrán also carries out a sustained comparative reading of Clarín's *La Regenta* and Fernando Méndez-Leite's TV adaptation. Curiously, like the "medium-specific" critic cited by Cardwell, he pays great attention to the shooting script as an "intermediate text" between novel and screen. Like López-Baralt, González Herrán stresses the "fidelity" of the adaptation (still the ultimate good for literary critics) and thus focuses on the beginning and end of the series, the only moments in which a voice-over reads famous fragments of text over the image. González Herrán notes how even in this very special and uncharacteristic case (he treats no more than ten minutes in total of the four-and-a-half-hour running length), much of Alas's text is omitted and transposed into directions in the script. Thus although the final version does not re-create the opening scene of the novel (in which the canon Fermín de Pas surveys the fictional city of Vetusta from the top of the cathedral tower) it is still proclaimed "faithful" because it gives visual evidence of textual detail: a low-angle shot of the tower is overlaid by the swirling dust and trash which Alas had described as enveloping the city. González Herrán acknowledges that this absence is somewhat ironic, given that the scene in the novel (like the "film-indications" Eisenstein claimed to find in Dickens) was considered "cinematic" *avant la lettre*. After documenting more "losses" (the relative absence of such strongly drawn characters as the pedant Saturnino and flirtatious widow Obdulia), González Herrán comes to the modest conclusion that the script is indispensable to the study of literary adaptations as evidence for the intermediary process between source text and final programme.

González Herrán's second article goes no further beyond the comparative approach, simply juxtaposing the novel's famous ending with a shot-by-shot account of Méndez-Leite's version. If we look at the press coverage of *Fortunata y Jacinta* and *La Regenta*, however, we can go beyond the formal analyses of the medium-specific and comparative approaches to embrace the pluralist and televisual concerns for the ideological and historical.

On May 7, 1980, the day the first of ten hour-long episodes of *Fortunata y Jacinta* was shown on the then monopoly state broadcaster TVE, *El País*, the new daily paper, which had already established its implacable hostility to the medium, ran a lengthy report on the "four years and 160 million pesetas" it had taken to bring the novel to the small screen (Pérez Ornia, "Cuatro años"). Arguing that this is the most important production in the history of TVE, it notes that it will be scheduled in the popular "Grandes Relatos" strand, and can compete in "quality" and "dignity" with the American and British dramas that normally occupy that slot. While the report (which reads very much like a press release) stresses at the start that this Spanish series has been pre-sold to (unspecified) European and Latin American stations, it only confirms at the end that *Fortunata y Jacinta* is a co-production with France and Switzerland. The article also fails to mention that this required the casting of a French actor in one of the principal roles: François-Eric Gendron stars as the bourgeois philanderer Juanito. In spite of this incongruous internationalism (Gendron is crudely dubbed and conspicuously Gallic in physiognomy) the TV public constructed by the article is implicitly defined as a national body, undifferentiated even by region.

The bulk of the article stresses the sheer expense and expansiveness of the series in a barrage of statistics. There are 30 leading actors, 100 supporting players, and 3,500 extras. Shooting lasted for seven months (from May 14 to December 5, 1979) in authentic and historic locations throughout Spain (Madrid, Aranjuez, Toledo, Burgos, Seville). In addition 20,000 square metres of sets were erected at TVE's Prado del Rey studio, meticulously reproducing period versions of now changed streets and barrios of the capital, from the Plaza de Pontejos, where the wealthy Juanito and Jacinta live with the former's parents, to the squalid tenement in the Cava de San Miguel to which Fortunata returns to give birth and die. The literary advisor and the constructor of models are both cited with equal reverence, as is the composer of the original score. The technical crew of around 70 was made up of RTVE's own full-time workers. The great wealth of sets, 214 in number, are said to be proof of the "scrupulous fidelity" to both novel and period. Displaying the modesty typical of the cultural intermediary, Camus says that the verdict should be given by a literary specialist ("Galdosista"); and claims to be concerned as to whether audiences accustomed to high-speed car chases in Los Angeles will enjoy Galdós's characters and dialogue. The journalist makes only one cultural reference (identifying a supposed citation of Visconti's *Death in Venice*) and writes that viewers will be able to follow the series with Galdós's novel "in their hands." The programme will thus stimulate the audience to read and know the original even as it proves the professional competence of TVE's technical team.

It is clear from this piece that public service pedagogy is understood to lead mass taste and to promote literarity and, indeed, literacy. TVE's public ownership, manifest in its lavish display of resources, thus serves to articulate national identity in opposition to illegitimate foreign influences. At this period there is no sense that this public is differentiated or fragmented (that Catalans, for example, might not be quite so interested as Castilians in the minute re-creation of old Madrid) or that literary culture is elitist (that viewers lacking in cultural capital might be justified in preferring, on occasion, high-speed car chases to drawing-room dialogues). Much more problematic, however, is the relationship of the state to public broadcasting. The same journalist who welcomed *Fortunata y Jacinta* so effusively had just a few months earlier complained that "TVE scarcely produce[d] series" and was "permanently colonized" by foreign and especially US dramas (February 6, 1980). And a lengthy rebuttal from the Director-General a few days earlier had bitterly attacked *El País* for its coverage of the medium, which had repeatedly accused RTVE of political bias, corruption, and inefficiency. Claiming to voice the "reality" of the broadcaster, Arias Salgado (February 3, 1980) gives an unusually detailed account of the station's insufficient budget (considerably less than its French or Italian opposite numbers), its ageing plant, and its cumbersome commissioning system. How can the corporation plan ahead when it has had six directors in the last five tumultuous years? And the current production slate includes four prestige series: the escapist *Verano azul* (*Blue Summer*, created by TV auteur Antonio Mercero), *Fortunata y Jacinta*, the *Cervantes* mini-series, and an episode on Madrid for the international co-production *Grandes ciudades del mundo* (*Great Cities of the World*). Arias Salgado concludes by noting that the new broadcasting Statute had come into effect just the day before. He calls it a "constitution" for radio and television and pointedly refers to the "period of transition" through which RTVE has successfully passed. Public service broadcasting is thus directly parallel to the state, which, he implies, has gone through identical transformations with the coming of democracy.

The historical moment in which *Fortunata y Jacinta* was produced and consumed thus contributed markedly to the importance of its televisuality: RTVE was critically in need of the legitimation which classic literarity would bring it, especially from the dissatisfied elite readers of the new Socialist-affiliated newspaper. The middle-brow aesthetic of the classic serial is halfway between the legitimate culture of the nineteenth-century novel (its status reinforced at this time by still recent Francoist hostility to the republican and anti-clerical Galdós) and the mass culture that is identified with US imperialism. Traditional, temperate, and moderate, it thus serves as a form of cultural consensus in which the new nation can share without having to make that imaginative "leap" required when it watches British examples of the genre (November 25, 1980). On the same day that it announced *Fortunata y Jacinta* (May 7, 1980), *El País* lamented that the BBC's *Pride and Prejudice*, to be shown in the same slot, would be lost on Spanish audiences, unprepared for the subtle ironies of Austen's novel, "a small great tale" ("Un pequeño gran relato") (Conte).

But the clearest sense of the "presentness" of the classic serial is in columns written at the time by the most illustrious commentator on everyday life in the transition, Francisco Umbral. Returning repeatedly to the series, Umbral weaves it into his chronicle of contemporary Madrid. He writes first that Galdós has been thrown into the river, or sewer, of the *teletonta* ("stupid box"), while the budget would have been better spent on schools, so Spaniards could read *Fortunata y Jacinta* for themselves (May 15, 1980). He next relates the current heads of the two main political parties (Adolfo Suárez and Felipe González), bitterly confronted by the Socialists' motion of censure to the government, to Galdós's warring heroines (May 27, 1980). Finally he compares González's long march through "democracy, reform, Socialism, elections, [and] consensus" to a Galdosian noveletta, and the encounter between Felipe and his younger self to that between Fortunata and Jacinta (May 29, 1980). Made suddenly contemporary through the miracle of broadcasting, nineteenth-century fiction is here interwoven with twentieth-century politics in an affective influence on the everyday that only the collective and simultaneous experience of television can provoke.

Fifteen years later, when it was now the Socialist government not TVE which was mired in corruption scandals, the press reception of *La Regenta* was very different. Where *Fortunata y Jacinta*'s lavish production values were seen as key to its quality, *La Regenta* made rather a virtue of its modesty. On January 15, 1995, *El País* announced that Televisión Española was "seeking prestige with nineteenth-century realism" (Alonso). Unlike in the case of *Fortunata y Jacinta*, here the name of Fernando Méndez-Leite, credited with script, adaptation, and direction, precedes that of the novelist, although the occasion of the broadcast is given as the centenary of the literary "masterpiece." Described as a "mini-series" of three "chapters" (*capítulos*) of ninety minutes each, *La Regenta* is credited with a budget of 500 million pesetas. The director states that, given the series' serious ambitions, this is hardly a "super-production"; and the executive producer Eduardo Ducay says that the filmmakers had to "tighten their belts." Actor Juan Luis Galiardo, who plays Alvaro Mesía, the ageing Don Juan, claims the stellar cast had to shoot over twelve hours a day. Even the locations are low-cost. A single estate near Madrid had multiple uses for both interiors (Ana's bedroom) and exteriors (from Ana's garden to a wild forest). Costing only 100,000 pesetas a day, this location is, we are told, "more used by television production than film." (Conversely *Fortunata y Jacinta*'s expensively constructed sets were never used again.) Authentic and unmistakable locations such as the Cathedral of Oviedo were only used when necessary. The technical crew, freelancers who lacked TVE's job security, is said to number forty (as opposed to *Fortunata y Jacinta*'s seventy). The article fails to mention that the series was not an in-house production of TVE but made independently by Ducay's hopefully named "Classic Films."

On the first day of broadcasting, *El País* reported on the première in Oviedo at which the current Director-General of TVE had, like his predecessor in 1980, stressed the "international market" for the series and committed the channel to "the diffusion of culture and the production of quality products" (Alonso). As before, the key aim is "fidelity" to the novel, including not just plot but also "aesthetics and atmosphere." Singled out for special praise is the art direction by veteran Gil Parrondo, who is said to be the winner of two Oscars. In the TV listings that night *El País* stressed again the series' fidelity to its source novel, and noted that nowadays only "public television" was capable of making such great and welcome efforts.

Subsequent coverage focused on the battle for ratings. The second part of the series won "almost as high an audience" as the football match the same night (the first, on a highly competitive Tuesday, had beaten a sex talk show but succumbed to a sitcom on the private Antena 3) (January 20, 1995). The median audience for the three nights was given as almost six million viewers and an enviable 35.3% share (we remember that TVE's overall share that year was just 27.6%). Clearly "quality" products could still attract a mass audience in the age of media availability. The critical balance was more ambiguous. In his review Antonio Albert began by placing the series in a televisual context, acknowledging its intertextuality (January 18, 1995). Like *Fortunata y Jacinta* and other examples of the genre, he writes, *La Regenta* combined "spectacle and culture" and used the now familiar techniques: medium close ups, simple editing, meticulous but unoriginal art design, and an underplayed acting style. Carmelo Gómez as the tortured priest reminds the reviewer of a similar character in the trashy American mini-series *The Thorn Birds*. But, comparing *La Regenta* to Stephen Frears' feature-film adaptation *Les Liaisons Dangereuses*, the critic finds the series lacking in irony, identification with its heroine, and the "true drama" of internal passion. It has, rather, the minor virtue of being "correct."

What is striking here is the decline of literarity as the key criterion of quality. Even when Albert talks of irony, he refers not to the notoriously sarcastic authorial voice of the novel but to a recent period picture. The critic is highly aware of the presentness of nineteenth-century narrative (noting that public television must now entertain as well as educate), of the performance of its actors and technicians (which is compared to recent TV and film), and of intertextual reference. In other words he attends overwhelmingly to the series' televisuality. Moreover, what could once pass as legitimate culture (with Camus clinging to the coattails of Galdós) is now merely middle-brow. The aristocratic critic, confident of his own cultural capital, can afford to damn the conventions of the classic serial with faint praise: its style, mise-en-scène, and performance now seem too traditional, temperate, and moderate to merit the reverence due to artistic distinction.

Fortunata y Jacinta and *La Regenta*: close readings

Sally Faulkner has offered the most extended and convincing interpretations of the audiovisual adaptations of *Fortunata y Jacinta* and *La Regenta* (*Literary Adaptations*, 79–125). Contrasting film and TV versions and rejecting the "fidelity" criterion, she explores new themes like urbanism (the appeal to such spaces as staircases in *Fortunata y Jacinta*) and feminism (the negative consequences of Méndez-Leite's shift of focus from Ana to Fermín as the central character). She also offers a close analysis of a single sequence: Fortunata's disastrous wedding night, in which the predatory Juanito infiltrates the new marital home through transparent walls and phantom sliding bolts (102–3). Faulkner gives an exemplary comparative account, noting the convergence or otherwise of text and image, and privileging neither the aesthetic nor the ideological, in ways typical of the medium-specific and the pluralist approaches, respectively. Moreover, elsewhere in her book she twice refers to the middle-brow: scorned by intellectuals (13), and in Camus's film adaptations (24). She does not, however, discuss the classic serial as a TV genre.

In the readings that follow I explore rather the dynamic between literarity and televisuality, both of which are to be understood in the extended senses I have discussed above. Thus literarity is not reduced to the source novel, but embraces the pedagogy of public service television and the cultural competence of the viewer, affected as it is by class position and educational capital. While the literarity of the TV texts relies on external validation, the private pleasure of televisuality is produced internally through the performance of the medium itself and its affective effect on everyday life. We have seen from press coverage that between 1980 and 1995 the criteria for judging the classic serial in Spain seem to shift somewhat from the literary to the televisual. Cardwell has suggested this is also the case for influential examples of the genre made by the

BBC. The question to be answered is whether this trend can be identified in the aesthetics of Spanish classic serials in a national context where public service broadcasting (like the genre of the classic serial) is much less firmly established than it is in Britain. I concentrate on audiovisual elements such as lighting and mise-en-scène but on the understanding that some technical characteristics, such as shot size and length, have themselves been naturalized as "literary" through their long association with the classic genre.

The credits of *Fortunata y Jacinta* would seem to reinforce the most traditional, even fossilized, notion of literary authority. The sole image used is a sepia shot of Galdós and the first title, after the author, goes to the literary consultant. The ten-hour adaptation begins at the leisurely pace that will be preserved throughout. It is 23 minutes into the first episode before Jacinta is introduced (vapid Maribel Martín in bleached blonde hair and light blue gown) and 27 before we are given a brief shot of Fortunata (insolent Ana Belén in red dress and head scarf, as she eats a famously raw egg on a staircase) (Illustrations 4, 5). Belén, the unquestionable star of the series, will not be given any substantial dialogue until episode 5, again some 23 minutes in, when she recounts her back-story to a timid Maxi. This relaxed rhythm makes considerable demands on the viewer's concentration. Jacinta and Juanito, the intensive focus of episodes 1–3, simply disappear in episodes 4–5. The interlude in Las Micaelas (the convent to which Fortunata is confined in preparation for marriage to Maxi) runs over two episodes (5–6), as does the intermission in which Fortunata is protected by her elderly suitor Feijoo (7–8). In the last episodes, extended and inconsequential subplots are conscientiously depicted: the Anglomaniac Moreno Isla courts Jacinta and the chemist Ballester woos Fortunata, both without success (9–10). Even viewers who are, as *El País* recommended, following the series "with the novel in their hands," might be surprised that the two titular characters barely meet until their dramatic confrontation at saintly Guillermina's house in the ninth episode.

The adaptation's tolerance of discursiveness, digressiveness, and ellipsis is thus made to converge with that of the novel. And this ostentatious fidelity has serious implications for point of view. As in the novel once more, we are not privy to Juanito's affairs with Fortunata during the time that they take place. They are signalled rather by the vain investigations of his mother and his wife. Camus resorts to flashbacks, heralded by the conventional editing technique of the dissolve, to re-enact retrospective narration and memory. But, *pace* the academic critics, interiority is not always lost. Ana Belén's Fortunata is gifted with a rare voice-over for internal monologue. As she goes shopping and muses on the mixed prospect of marriage to Maxi, the now familiar footage of the picturesque market is reframed by her unaccustomed, non-diegetic speech. Or again, dreams by both female characters are re-created, conventionally set apart once more through close ups followed by dissolves. Antón García Abril's saccharine score drenches even the harshest action in lyrical nostalgia, its simple motif recurring each time the idle, lecherous, and charming Juanito returns to seduce his maltreated mistress.

4. Bourgeois Jacinta (Maribel Martín)

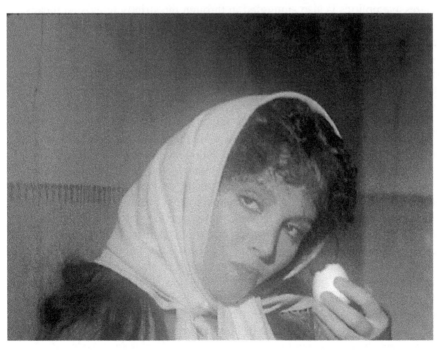

5. Proletarian Fortunata (Ana Belén)

But if the literary mood is predominantly nostalgic, the past serves (as Palacio argued) to re-evaluate the present. Period drama's potential for contemporaneity is made clear from the opening sequence. Camus cuts from Juanito frying eggs in his university lecture theatre (the first example of a chicken motif much loved by literary critics) to a student demonstration, shot in an authentic exterior, brutally broken up by the Guardia Civil. Watching in 1980, audiences could hardly fail to remember the recent history of long-haired student revolt in late Francoism and more distant, but still traumatic, memories of the Civil War (young demonstrators shout "¡Viva la república!"). Re-created on screen, such visually impressive sequences have an effect disproportionate to Galdós's brief and somewhat ironic verbal account (Juanito will never again express much interest in politics).

When Camus diverges from Galdós it is also to enhance "presentness." The lavish but claustrophobic bourgeois interiors suggest Juanito's parents are prisoners of their padded furniture. An empty love seat is placed pointedly in front of the dining table and the parents' marital bed is clearly unhappy (Galdós lengthily insists to the contrary). Muffled isolation is increased by the use of post-synched sound. Where Galdós's apartment is open to the varied and welcome urban noises of old, central Madrid, Camus's seems to be kept in quarantine. Audiences of the day were cued to respond to this implied critique of stuffy bourgeois repression: certainly they were well prepared for it by British imports since *The Forsyte Saga*.

Progressive politics is also smuggled in through the strictly televisual means of framing, camera movement, editing, and sound design. In repeated lateral tracking shots characters disappear momentarily behind market stalls, suggesting perhaps a critique of consumerism (Juanito's mother retains from the novel her weakness for shopping). Camus interrupts the main action at climactic points (as when Juanito meets Fortunata on the staircase) to give montage sequences of indigent street people sweeping up, making fires, or preparing food, sequences that are unrelated to the main action. Even the shooting style changes for working-class interiors, with a shaky hand-held camera re-creating the riotous drunkenness of Fortunata's aunt and company. Again, while Juanito confesses his love affair to Jacinta on their honeymoon, we hear outside their bourgeois hotel room strident working-class voices that, through a sound-bridge, signal a flashback to Fortunata's very different milieu. Camus thus suggests unobtrusively the economic interdependence of the aristocracy and the "fourth estate," a class conflict at once central to Galdós's text and attractive to such viewers as the Leftist readers of *El País*, known as *progres*.

Camus is not immune to the long takes and shot sizes familiar from the British classic serial. When Feijoo attempts to persuade Maxi to take back Fortunata as his wife the two men walk and talk in full length, hesitantly tracked by the camera once more, through a street shrouded in thick shadows, for an epic 125 seconds without a cut. But the camerawork refuses the wide shots of landscape and historical landmarks typical of UK classic serials of the *Brideshead* era. In the honeymoon sequence Burgos is shown in an unobtrusive low-angle shot of the Gothic cathedral at dawn, Seville by a brief shot of the Giralda illuminated at night. More typical of the exteriors is the scrubby waste-land on the fringes of the city by the new convent, a far cry from classic England's rolling hills and green pastures. Although city scenes are shot mainly on the lavish sets constructed at TVE's studio (whose upper floors are imaged in expert matte paintings), the built environment is strangely unfinished. Several times children are shown playing in streets that are only partly paved. The incomplete modernization of the capital, documented in detail by Galdós, is here unobtrusively enacted in sets that refuse to a large extent the popular pleasures of the picturesque.

As mentioned earlier, the production design of interiors seems calculated to provoke as much nausea as nostalgia: Camus tracks slowly behind the padded chair backs of the silent guests at the dinner following Jacinta's wedding; heavy draperies (whose colours often rhyme with the women's confining costumes) are so ubiquitous they even hang perilously over a roaring fire. And if the minutiae of nineteenth-century politics are indeed cut from the adaptation, Camus (like Galdós) pointedly shows how distant they are from women's real concerns in this predominantly domestic milieu. His camera tracks slowly behind Jacinta's upholstered behind as she leaves the men to their talk in the drawing room. The entrance of the new King Alfonso into Madrid is shown as a brief, but lavishly staged, procession, glimpsed by the women from a balcony. What little café discussion survives into the adaptation is evidently angled towards the twentieth-century viewer, mindful of the Civil War: "The country is full of rascals. No-one wants peace. They will destroy us" (episode 7).

But the "presentness" of the series is most clearly visible in performance. The casting of Ana Belén as Fortunata, dismissed by academics, establishes the modernity of Galdós: the actress was the quintessential female *progre* of the time, with an active and independent persona that carries on into her interpretation of Fortunata as a self-possessed working-class woman. The fact that Belén was herself born in Madrid's working-class neighbourhood of Lavapiés is not irrelevant. Movie fans might have remembered her from a recent, scandalous period role in Pilar Miró's *La petición* (*The Engagement*, 1976), where she played a young woman who literally fucked her partner to death. The indulgent screen time lent secondary characters such as Feijoo and Izquierdo (played, respectively, by veterans Fernando Fernán Gómez and Francisco Rabal) reveals greater fidelity to their star cachet than to the source text (especially as Rabal bears no physical resemblance to the original character). As *El País* remarked, of the main cast only Mario Pardo as Maxi was wholly unfamiliar to audiences. The lack of star profile here enhances some of the few moments of real viscerality in the production: Belén's Fortunata is strong enough to lift her skeletal husband like a rag doll and carry him to bed; Juanito's one-sided fight with Maxi is genuinely distressing. Here the immediacy of television viewing works in an uncomfortable way to enhance affective influence on the everyday.

An undoubtedly major example of a minor art (TV drama), *Fortunata y Jacinta* fills the profile of the middle-brow, as does its director. For although

Camus had begun his career with social realist dramas and was soon to be rewarded with major prizes, he had also condescended to provide vehicles for such extravagantly camp singers as teenage heart-throb Raphael and the ageing Sara Montiel (*Esa mujer* [*That Woman*, 1969] was much later cited by Almodóvar in *La mala educación* [*Bad Education*, 2004]). And one final feature of his production also has a problematic history. Publicity for the series called attention to the special effects credited to distinguished veteran Emilio Ruiz del Río. Called in Spanish *maquetas* or "models," the effects are in this case closer to matte paintings: elaborate masks placed in front of the camera to complete the image. Ruiz del Río's personal website (at www.iespana.es Tertre-Rouge/Films/Fortunata.htm) offers fascinating evidence of his meticulous work for *Fortunata y Jacinta* in re-creating such emblematic sites as the Plaza Mayor of the period, festooned with snow and trees. Ruiz del Río claims to have learned the technique first in Germany's UFA studios before applying it in Francoist studio-shot epics such as *Alba de América* (1951). The striking look that it gives the series is thus disconcertingly stylized, evoking as it does period cinema. As Bourdieu notes of the middle-brow, the popular aesthetic, in this case the taste for nostalgia, is thus modified by an explicit stylistic intention.

Of course Galdós himself was concerned with just this tricky transformation of the popular. Academics have explored his relation to *literatura de consumo* (Andreu). Let us look, finally, at how Camus interprets one of the most novelettish or melodramatic scenes in the book: the climactic moment when Jacinta hides in Guillermina's house while the "saint" interrogates Fortunata on her feelings for Juanito. The scene is surprisingly brief, only some four minutes long. As Guillermina and Fortunata begin to converse (in medium close up) the camera cross-cuts between them. What is striking, however, is the black gothic chair backs, seen nowhere else in the series, which loom ominously behind them. Camus uses deep focus to reveal Jacinta listening in from behind an opaque glass door behind Fortunata's left shoulder. The power of Fortunata's revelations (that Juanito sought her out, that she would not have been "bad" without him) is thus increased by the two women's spatial proximity within the frame. After Maribel Martín's normally placid Jacinta confronts her rival directly the scene is soon brought to an end. And it is, as in Galdós, interrupted anti-climactically by Juanita's mother, who is looking for her daughter. Temperate and moderate, Camus steers clear of excess and defuses dramatic tension. It is an ambiguous technique that could be read as evidence for either "literary" good taste or the typically televisual concern for everyday interaction.

In an address to GECA in 1995 (the same year the organization published the TV annual cited earlier), Fernando Méndez-Leite makes explicit his literary bias. When he first proposed serializing *La Regenta*, back in 1983, he suggested ten episodes of one hour each (the same length and format as *Fortunata y Jacinta*, which he does not mention) in order to produce a "literal and literary" serial which did not imitate the "classic" series of US and UK television (the two nationalities are strangely lumped together) (111). This "utopia" proved impossible, with the uncommunicative executives at TVE responding only that the project was "very long" and featured "too many priests." Méndez-Leite states that he was finally reduced to three episodes of ninety minutes each. Not only did this restriction require the excision of favourite characters and episodes, it also required the expansive, digressive, and temporally free-flowing structure of the novel (which he says is "non-cinematic" [116]) to be reduced to a "classic" plot: the exposition of characters and conflicts in episode 1, their complication in episode 2 (climaxing with Ana's barefoot procession through the streets of Vetusta on Good Friday), and their resolution in episode 3.

It is telling that Méndez-Leite seems to reserve the attribute "classic" not for the novel but for TV and film narrative (he claims not to distinguish between the two media [109]). And compared with the earlier *Fortunata y Jacinta*, *La Regenta* is clearly more visual than verbal. Rather than plumping placidly for a single image of the author, the credits unfold over a number of the handsome engravings made for the first edition and familiar to modern readers from the current Cátedra reprint. Indeed Méndez-Leite will re-create some of these images in his series (Obdulia coquettishly lifting her skirts free of a puddle, Fermín brooding ominously in the confessional). After *Fortunata y Jacinta*'s stately languor, *La Regenta* sets off at an indecently swift pace. The camera tilts down the black cathedral tower, momentarily swirling with trash that will never appear again in the squeaky-clean exteriors of the now restored historic centre of Vetusta–Oviedo. There is a quick cut to the handsome garden where Ana and her elderly husband Víctor (in an incongruously colourful waistcoat) make small talk with busybody Visitación. The two women walk briskly to the cathedral, as Fermín rehearses a sermon of papal infallibility to an adoring audience of his mother and servant (3 minutes). As in the novel, Ana and Fermín (Illustration 6) initially fail to meet (an elderly cleric fills in her back-story to the Magistral [9 minutes]), but they encounter each other in the sylvan promenade El Espolón (gloomily autumnal in the novel, here in glorious summer leaf [12 minutes]). Soon Ana is undressing in her bedroom, standing naked on the notorious tiger-skin rug (13 minutes), flashing back to her childhood and the primal "scene in the boat" with a youthful romantic companion (14 minutes), and shuddering in the first of many nervous attacks (16 minutes). It is an exposition which Clarín develops over five chapters and some three hundred pages. And although *El País* attacked the wordy dialogues of this adaptation, the first impression is rather one of movement. Characters walk hastily to and fro, captured in lateral tracking shots.

The accelerated rhythm might be attributed to Méndez-Leite's reduced budget relative to Camus's or, in a new and fiercely competitive environment, to the necessity to attract and sustain the attention of viewers tempted to change channels to Antena 3's sex talk show or sitcom. Certainly the clerical atmosphere (to which TVE executives objected) is rapidly eclipsed by Aitana Sánchez-Gijón's spectacular nudity. Méndez-Leite's camerawork converges

6. Ana and Fermín (Aitana Sánchez Gijón and Carmelo Gómez)

here with Clarín's insistently voyeuristic text. If the fluidity of time is not reproduced (the "scene on the boat" is the only flashback), the mobility of point of
view, which Méndez-Leite particularly prizes in the novel, is indeed depicted in
a heightened televisual technique. Apart from the first and last sequences,
voice-over is reserved for Ana as she reads impassioned letters she has written
to the Magistral. Ana, in uncinematic style, here addresses the camera directly.
The same set-up is used in her first confession to Fermín. Ana, in blue-black
mantilla and chalk white face, is shown in tight frontal close up, while Fermín,
bathed in ecstatic golden light, is seen from the side. Excising the novel's
exhaustive exploration of Ana's psyche (itself framed in ambiguous free indirect
style), Méndez-Leite trusts to the eloquent looks and gestures of his handsome
and intelligent leading lady.

La Regenta thus offers us the rich and potent visual pleasures of the traditional (indeed "classic") literary adaptation. The gowns are uniformly gorgeous
(Ana is robed in emerald green and mustard yellow satin) and the authentic
locations are expertly dressed (wardrobe and set are made to rhyme). When Ana
complains to the seductive Mesía that Vetusta is "so ugly", the viewer would be
hard pressed to agree. They are speaking in a plush theatre, all red velvet and
gold leaf, that bears no relation to the decrepit and freezing fleapit of the novel.
The gentleman's club (the "casino") and the Archbishop's palace are equally
lavish. Sensuous icons of the novel are lovingly shot in extreme close up: the

purple glove abandoned by the priest in Ana's garden, the red garter stolen and lost by Ana's maid Petra (proof of her sex act with Fermín), the rosebud chewed by Fermín on a fevered solitary walk, and the strawberry bitten into by an amorous Ana and sent as a gift for Mesía. The slimmed-down plot is thus compensated for by a pumped-up mise-en-scène. The insidious eroticism of Clarín's narration (which turns even a children's catechism class into a tour de force of precocious perversity) is converted into Méndez-Leite's sensual cinematography (far lusher than the claustrophobic *Fortunata y Jacinta*) and evocative live sound in such splendid but technically difficult locations as the Cathedral.

Typically, at the ball scene (a staple of the classic serial genre) our visual pleasure is greatly enhanced when Ana takes the floor in red and black (the other ladies favour beige and white) for an energetic gavotte with the Marques. In the novel she sits modestly until Mesía invites her to an ecstatic waltz. But Méndez-Leite refuses the *Brideshead* shots of country houses and rolling hills. The stately home that stands in for the Marques's summer residence, a notoriously cheap location, is shown only in the briefest of establishing shots as Ana walks towards the camera. And the scene where Fermín frantically searches for Ana in a rain-drenched forest is shot in the same location and with limited space, which precludes romantic wide shots. Méndez-Leite confirms his middle-brow approach here: we remember that, for Bourdieu, popular picturesque subjects such as landscape and folk dance (the latter also features in the TV *La Regenta*) are only acceptable if distanced by some clear aesthetic intention, in this case the refusal of that too showy visual pleasure often offered by the classic genre.

Performance style is also noticeably restrained or "literary," in the extended sense. Overbearing characters such as Visitación, endlessly pealing with laughter in the novel, here appear more sly and subtle, evoking (as *El País* remarked) the courtly duplicity of *Les Liaisons Dangereuses*. The degenerate acolyte Celedonio is here not obviously effeminate. But to focus on performance is, as Cardwell shows, to return inevitably to the televisual. In a display of generic intertextuality two accomplished character actors from *Fortunata y Jacinta* return in *La Regenta*: María Luisa Ponte (doña Lupe) as the devout doña Petronila, and Manuel Alexandre (Estupiñá) as a drunken Santos Barinaga. Viewers welcome them like old friends, recognizing the increasing intertextuality of the later classic serial. Movie buffs would also remember Julio Medem's more recent *La ardilla roja* (*The Red Squirrel*, 1993; released just two years before *La Regenta*), in which Carmelo Gómez (Fermín) played a homicidal maniac and Cristina Marcos (Ana's maid Petra) a sardonic lesbian. Certainly Gómez's "contained fury" and "sober intensity" (said by Chris Perriam to be major characteristics of his persona [88, 90]) give added resonance to his role here as the repressed but passionate priest. If Méndez-Leite's professional insecurity is typically middle-brow (he confesses that he has been unable to sustain a movie career [110]), then his ability to cast film stars like Gómez and Sánchez Gijón in the main parts of his series lends it and him additional cultural capital.

La Regenta's art direction (by double Oscar winner Gil Parrondo) also heightens the programme's cachet, separating the "best" of television from indiscriminate trash. But so does Bingen Mendizábal's musical score. Where Antón García Abril provided a sickly soundtrack for *Fortunata y Jacinta* that relied on a small number of readily identifiable themes, Mendizábal pens a symphonic score in the spirit of the period whose orchestral leitmotifs are hard to pin down. The visual pleasure of the cinematography is thus somewhat qualified by the atmospheric but abstract soundtrack. And the contemporary associations of casting and dialogue (in Victorian Vetusta, as in 1990s Spain, liberals and conservatives are equally corrupt) are undercut by music that is so clearly rooted in the nineteenth-century.

Let us look at how these dynamics work in a single sequence: Ana's famous procession through the streets of Vetusta in Holy Week. The scene begins with an extreme close up of the erotic focus in Clarín's own version: the bare feet on the paving stones. Fortunately Aitana Sánchez Gijón (unlike her character in the novel) is in no danger of injury, as the well maintained streets of modern Oviedo lack the sharp stones and filthy puddles of Vetusta. The procession is then shown from the point of view of the characters watching from a balcony above. The rich costumes and float are spread out for their and our pleasure (the real-life *cofradía* or religious association took part in the sequence, apparently oblivious to its sacrilegious intent). Unlike in the novel, Fermín is marching beside Ana, her purple robes rhyming with his now familiar gloves: as his triumph cannot be told by the narrator, it must be shown visually. Fermín looks up to Mesía, who gazes steadily back. The eye line match (a standard technique of continuity editing) here establishes the rivalry between the two suitors with clarity and economy. The iconography of the *paso* and *nazarenos* (float and penitents), overfamiliar to Spanish audiences, is here undercut by the swelling soundtrack of Mendizábal's restlessly probing musical phrases. There is a tricky, even precarious, balance here between the popular and the elitist which is typical of both the middle-brow and the classic TV serial.

Niche nation

It took me five weeks to re-read the two novels, but only five days to watch and annotate the two classic serials. It is not clear how many of those Spaniards who have no professional interest in Galdós or Clarín can make the considerable investment in time that is required in getting to know their literary works. Certainly such a commitment would come into conflict with the ever increasing time all classes devote to television. It seems possible that the good people of Oviedo who collaborated so willingly with Méndez-Leite were not fully aware of the source novel's merciless parody of provincial life. Perhaps they were pleased, however, by the adaptation's aestheticized vision of their city. Certainly the series, with its strict aversion to vulgarity, must have seemed well deserving of a première at Oviedo's historic theatre.

It is not clear how the "success" of such a project is to be measured. Writing in *El País*, respected novelist Antonio Muñoz Molina noted (February 1, 1995) that, for a quality press obsessed with ratings, *La Regenta* had suddenly become not one of the best Spanish novels of all time but a "partially failed" programme in the current TV schedule, eclipsed by sporting events and sitcoms. Interestingly, however, Muñoz Molina does not simply defend "quality" against "quantity." Clarín's novel, he writes, emerges as a secret and obstinate "best seller," when sales are accumulated over the course of a century. It is a commercial strategy also employed by the newer medium of DVD. TVE's "Series Clásicas" brand (a name invented for the video reissues) ensures that the classic serials of Spanish television, made under diverse conditions and over several decades, will be in circulation for the foreseeable future. The latest hit talk show may not be so lucky. It is a phenomenon also noticed by *The Economist* (May 7, 2005), which reports a shift "from mass market to niche nation": a "long tail" of small-selling specialist cultural products can be more profitable to the merchant than a short list of best sellers aimed at the lowest common denominator. Even specialists in management strategy are attempting to incorporate the subjective factors of "taste" and "quality" into their objective models of performance in the cultural industries (Hadida).

John Corner has noted "three types of badness" often attributed to TV: mis-selection, misrepresentation, and mis-knowing (109–10). We have seen that the literary adaptation has been accused of all of these: choosing to retain or excise the wrong elements of a novel, using imagistic brevity to betray narrative complexity, and debasing the perceptual or cognitive experience of reading. Yet we have also seen that in the case of Spain the genre has attempted to serve Palacio's broad aim of revising the present on the basis of the past and thus renewing the associative fabric of society. This is a continuation of public service as social good (or "pedagogy"), which has not totally disappeared in the age of media abundance. Moreover, comparison with the influential UK originals shows that the Spanish classic serial as genre has distinct characteristics, avoiding both facile nostalgia and decorous irony: there are no *Brideshead*-style architecture and landscape shots in *Fortunata y Jacinta* and *La Regenta* and little Austenian understatement. Both series, in their different ways, depict a nineteenth-century Spain in which rural and urban settings are a site of struggle. There are clear implications for both the tragic first half of the twentieth-century and the tragicomic post-Franco era, when democratization coincided with persistent charges of corruption.

We have seen that TVE was also frequently accused of internal corruption and external influence. But any corporate study such as this one reveals that programming, whether it is founded on in-house or independent production, is relatively autonomous in relation to the institutional settings in which it is developed: television "authorship" displays "occupational complexity and contingency" (Corner, 76–7). Hence Camus's *Fortunata y Jacinta*, a genuine super-production with a clearly progressive perspective, could be made by a still reactionary TVE before the Socialists had come to power; and Méndez-Leite's artistically ambitious *La Regenta* could still be produced for a state broadcaster now hostile to its length and subject matter ("too many priests") and caught in a bitter battle for ratings. As TVE's annual had suggested in 1980, the relative commercial success of both series proved that audiences need not be turned off by cultural programming if it is presented in an appropriate form. Nonetheless, the aesthetic differences between the series reveal a clear shift from a "literary" to a "televisual" frame of reference, in the expanded senses of the terms I suggested earlier.

Re-creating the famous last sequence of *La Regenta*, Méndez-Leite's camera tracks slowly backwards through the huge handsome space of Oviedo Cathedral. The unconscious Ana, whose lips have just been not just kissed but licked by the toad-like Celedonio, is placed at the very centre of the marble floor's chequer-board pattern. It is a camera movement, a location, and a set-up that in its stately aestheticization could not be more characteristic of the classic serial, the TV genre most associated with public service broadcasting. But if media critics reject such programming as "literary" or "middle-brow," perhaps invoking Bourdieu's "aristocratic" bias which prefers even the unaesthetic to self-conscious "quality," we risk rejecting out of hand a significant proportion of the production of European television together with a neglected segment of its audience. Standing patiently at the crossroads between social class and cultural taste, the classic serial deserves more sympathetic and generous examination.

Fortunata y Jacinta (TVE 1, 1980)

Director: Mario Camus
Scriptwriters: Mario Camus, Ricardo López Aranda
Art direction: Emilio Ruiz del Río
Original music: Antón García Abril

Cast
Fortunata: Ana Belén
Jacinta: Maribel Martín
Maximiliano Rubín: Mario Pardo
Juanito Santa Cruz: François-Eric Gendron
Don Evaristo Feijoo: Fernando Fernán-Gómez
Mauricia: Charo López
Doña Guillermina: Berta Riaza

La Regenta (TVE 1, 1995)

Director: Fernando Méndez-Leite
Scriptwriter: Fernando Méndez-Leite
Art direction: Gil Parrondo

Original music: Bingen Mendizábal

Cast
Ana Ozores: Aitana Sánchez-Gijón
Víctor Quintanar: Héctor Alterio
Alvaro Mesía: Juan Luis Galiardo
Don Fermín de Pas: Carmelo Gómez
Doña Paula: Amparo Rivelles
Petra: Cristina Marcos

Works cited

Alas, Leopoldo ["Clarín"]. *La Regenta*. Ed. Juan Oleza. Madrid: Cátedra, 2004.

Andreu, Alicia G. *Galdós y la literatura popular*. Madrid: Sociedad General Española de Librería, 1982.

Bourdieu, Pierre. *Distinction: A Social Critique of the Judgement of Taste*. London: Routledge, 1996.

Cardwell, Sarah. *Adaptation Revisited: Television and the Classic Novel*. Manchester and New York: Manchester University Press, 2002.

Casey, Bernadette, Neil Casey, Ben Calvert, Liam French, and Justin Lewis. *Television Studies: The Key Concepts*. London: Routledge, 2002.

Corner, John. *Critical Ideas in Television Studies*. Oxford: Oxford University Press, 1999.

Ellis, John. *Seeing Things: Television in the Age of Uncertainty*. London: I. B. Tauris, 2002.

Faulkner, Sally. *Literary Adaptations in Spanish Cinema*. London: Tamesis, 2004.
—— "Spanish 'Middlebrow' Cinema?" (unpublished paper).

GECA. *El libro de la tele: anuario de la televisión en España*. Madrid: Temas de hoy/GECA, 1995.

Giordano, Eduardo, and Carlos Zeller. *Políticas de televisión*. Barcelona: Icaria, 1999.

González Herrán, José Manuel. "Finales de novela, finales de película: de *La Regenta* (Leopoldo Alas, 1884-85) a *La Regenta* (Fernando Mendez-Leite, 1994–95)." In Norberto Minguez Arranz (ed.), *Literatura española y cine*. Madrid: Compás de Letras/Complutense, 2002, pp. 43–64.

González Requena, Jesús. "Las series televisivas: una tipología." Jiménez Losantos and Sánchez-Biosca, pp. 35–54.

Hadida, Allegre. "Defining and Measuring 'Performance' in the Film Industry: an Art and a Business, Really?" Unpublished paper given at Cambridge University Film Seminar, May 5, 2005.

Jiménez Losantos, Encarna, and Vicente Sánchez-Biosca (eds). *El relato electrónico*. Valencia: Filmoteca Generalitat Valenciana, 1989.

López-Baralt, Mercedes. "*Fortunata y Jacinta* según televisión española: la lectura cinematográfica del clásico galdosiano por Mario Camus." *Anales Galdosianos*, 27–8 (1992–3): 92–107.

Méndez-Leite, Fernando. "Adaptación y puesta en escena de *La Regenta*." *Espacio SGAE Audiovisual* (April 1995): 109–23.

Palacio, Manuel. *Historia de la televisión en España*. Barcelona: Gedisa, 2001.

Pérez Galdós, Benito. *Fortunata y Jacinta*. Ed. Francisco Caudet. Madrid: Cátedra, 2000.

Perriam, Chris. *Stars and Masculinities in Spanish Cinema. Oxford Studies in Modern European Culture*. Oxford: Oxford University Press, 2003.

"Profiting from Obscurity: What the 'Long Tail' Means for the Economics of E-Commerce." *The Economist* 7 May 2005: 83.

RTVE. *Anuario*. Madrid: RTVE, 1980.

SGAE. *Informe sobre hábitos de consumo cultural*. Madrid: SGAE, 2000.

Electronic sources

Albert, Antonio. "La virtud de la corrección." *El País*, January 18, 1995; May 9, 2005. <http://www.elpais.es/articulo.html?d_date=&xref=19950118elpepirtv_5&type=Tes&anchor=elpepirtv>.

Alonso, Sol. "Televisión Española busca prestigio en el realismo del siglo xix." January 14, 1995. *El País*, May 9, 2005. <http://www.elpais.es/articulo.html?d_date=&xref=19950114elpepirtv_3&type=Tes&anchor=elpepirtv>.

Arias Salgado, Fernando. "La realidad de Radiotelevisión Española." *El País*, February 3, 1980; May 9, 2005. <http://www.elpais.es/articulo.html?d_date=&xref=19800203elpepieco_5&type=Tes&anchor=elpepieco>.

Conte, R. "Un pequeño gran relato." *El País* 7 May 1980. 9 May 2005. <http://www.elpais.es/articulo.html?d_date=&xref=19800507elpepiage_1&type=Tes&anchor=elpepigen>.

González Herrán, José Manuel. "Tres comienzos de *La Regenta*: la novela (Leopoldo Alas, 1884–1885), el guión cinematográfico (Fernando Méndez-Leite, 1989–91), la serie de televisión (Fernando Méndez-Leite, 1994–95)." <http://www.cervantesvirtual.com/servlet/SirveObras/12258305308923728432091/index.htm>.

"La segunda parte de *La Regenta* logró casi tanta audiencia como el fútbol." *El País*, January 20, 1995; May 9, 2005. <http://www.elpais.es/articulo.html?d_date=&xref=19950120elpepirtv_4&type=Tes&anchor=elpepirtv>.

"Los Mallen", historia turbulenta de una familia." *El País*, Nov. 25, 1980; May 9, 2005. <http://www.elpais.es/articulo.html?d_date=&xref=19801125elpepiage_7&type=Tes&anchor=elpepigen>.

Muñoz Molina, Antonio. "La Regenta y éxito." *El País*, February 1, 1995; May 9, 2005.   <http://www.elpais.es/articulo.html?d_date=&xref=19950201elpepicul_14&type=Tes&anchor=elpepicul>

Penguin Classics. Synopsis of *La Regenta*. May 9, 2005. <http://www.amazon.com/gp/product/product-description/0140443460/ref=dp_proddesc_0/002-1138538-0886463?%5Fencoding=UTF8&n=283155>.

Pérez Ornia [*sic*]. "Cuatro años y 160 millones de pesetas para llevar 'Fortunata y Jacinta' a Televisión Española." *El País*, May 7, 1980; May 9, 2005. <http://www.elpais.es/articulo.html?d_date=&xref=19800507elpepicul_13&type=Tes&anchor=elpepicul>

———. "TVE apenas produce series." *El País*, February 6, 1980; May 9, 2005. <http://www.elpais.es/articulo.html?d_date=&xref=19800206elpepiage_1&type=Tes&anchor=elpepigen>.

Publisher's World. Synopsis of *Fortunata y Jacinta*, May 9, 2005.

<http://www.amazon.com/gp/product/0140442774/002-1138538-0886463?v=gl
ance&n=283155>.
Ruiz del Río, Emilio. Personal website. May 9, 2005. <www.iespana.es/
Tertre-Rouge/Films/Fortunata.htm >.
Umbral, Francisco. "Isidoro." *El País*, May 29, 1980; May 9, 2005.
<http://www.elpais.es/articulo.html?d_date=&xref=19800529elpepisoc_1&type
=Tes&anchor=elpepisoc>.
————. "Tácito." *El País* May 27, 1980; May 9, 2005. <http://www.elpais.es/
articulo.html?d_date=&xref=19800527elpepisoc_5&type=Tes&anchor=elpepis
oc>.
————. "Tirarse al Duero." *El País*, May 15, 1980; May 9, 2005. <http://www.
elpais.es/articulo.html?d_date=&xref=19800515elpepisoc_2&type=Tes&anchor
=elpepisoc>.

3

Chronicles of a Village: Francoist Newsreel, Feature Film, and Television (*Crónicas de un pueblo* [*Chronicles of a Village*, 1971–4]; *Cine de barrio* [*Neighbourhood Cinema*, 1995–])

From trace to sigh

Spain is not now notably rural. According to *The Economist*, in 2004 France, Italy, and the United States had a less urbanized population (216, 146, 166, 234). But, as is well known, city dwelling came late to Spain, when the hunger of the 1950s and the economic boom of the 1960s led to rapid depopulation of the countryside. Television had early implications for the city/country divide. By 1964 research suggested that, of the US imports then dominant, urbanites favoured the gritty crime drama *The Untouchables*, while villagers preferred the gentler *Dr Kildare* (Palacio 63). The first reliable statistical survey reported in 1966 that 51% of those living in the largest cities owned a television set (more than those who had access to hot water) and 66% considered TV essential; the figures for the smallest towns were just 5% and 38%, respectively (64). Curiously 60% of the urban population and 35% of the rural declared themselves to be regular viewers (66). The reason for this apparent anomaly is that country people watched television communally: so-called "tele-clubs" had been set up by the government in 1964. By the end of the decade they numbered three thousand and were considered by the regime to be sites of political agitation (60). The second half of the 1960s saw a change in viewing tastes with the arrival of a lower-class audience, which preferred domestic programming to imports (71).

It is worth remembering, then, that TV has not always been consumed privately; and that it has not always been thought to be the opium of the people. The question arises, however, of the relationship between the new medium and the earlier visual media from which it evolved; and of the possibility of a distinct Francoist aesthetic across those media. In this chapter I examine newsreel (the form of cinema which, through its regularity and impermanence, most closely anticipates aspects of television); Francoist series drama (the genre that most closely interacts with everyday life in the period); and the scheduling of Francoist feature films on post-Franco television (the clearest and most disturbing sign of nostalgia for the Dictatorship). I focus on the theme of ruralism, which, because of the demographic changes sketched above, becomes the quintessential marker of historical change between old and new Spains.

Ángel Llorente's scholarly account of art and ideology in Francoism (which focuses on the 1940s) already suggests some themes that will be taken up in studies of visual culture in later decades of the regime. Llorente notes how the militant anti-fascism of the scholarship of the 1970s gave way to indulgent and partial "postmodern revisionism" in the 1980s (15). Scholars either reduced art to cultural policy or, conversely, decisively separated the two (17), both approaches condemned by Llorente. He proposes rather that the art of autarchy was hardly "homogeneous" (divided as it was into the three categories of "official," "minority-elitist," and "majority") and that the connections between these categories were at some times congruent and at others contradictory (18). Likewise Francoist theory of art, such as it was, oscillated between utopia, banality, and libellous attacks on modernism (33). The ideal fusion of fascist art, linking choreography, liturgy, verticality, and ideology in the monument or the mass demonstration, was rarely achieved or even attempted (19). If regime philosopher Laín Entralgo had proclaimed Franco, along with Hitler and Mussolini, the "creator of a style," that style was confused (54).

Even in architecture, held to be the most important visual art, there was no official programme to be carried out and no formal definition of a Francoist aesthetic (73). An initial "imperial" architecture proved evanescent, while monumentalism coexisted with pre-War rationalism, and official public buildings shared no common style with private home design. Unlike in Nazi Germany, economic realities meant that plans to transform the city into a great monument went unrealized (79). Likewise, although the Falangists proclaimed muralism and history painting the new media (as in Germany once more) both went undeveloped (187). Llorente suggests that the ideological agrarianism of the Falange expressed itself in the vernacular style used to rebuild devastated villages, but this vision of a "traditional" or "essential" Spain is more an attempt to return to a pre-capitalist past than a nostalgic look back at the rural world (82). In easel painting and printmaking, rural scenes were reduced to the heroic landscape of symbolic ruins, such as Zuloaga's *El Alcázar en llamas* (*The Alcázar in Flames*), which cites El Greco's version of Toledo and its surroundings (195) and Antonio Cobos's cover for the magazine *Reconstrucción* (a church tower rising over a ruined village) (217). The obsession with ritual and symbol noted by José Carlos Mainer (cited in Llorente, 35) is evident.

In his monumental study of Francoist film of the following decade, Carlos F. Heredero also suggests that culture cannot be reduced to an instrument of the regime. Tracing the period from the eclipse of autarchy to the dawn of developmentalism (*desarrollismo*) (27), Heredero argues that there is indeed evidence of culture against the grain (*a contracorriente*) (34), and of *posibilismo* when faced by all-pervasive censorship (59). Heredero's is an exemplary study of visual culture as institution (of the film industry and its varied professions and discourses) and as genre (from religious and child-star pictures to farces and melodramas).

As Llorente does for art of the 1940s, Heredero stresses that film of the 1950s was not homogeneous or uniform, no prisoner of the regime (15). Indeed he cites "contradictions" between the Francoist apparatus of propaganda, the film industry, and the material reality of the period. These contradictions allow us to glimpse "cracks" or "furrows" ("grietas," "surcos") which in turn leave "traces" ("huellas") on celluloid. Heredero's chosen period is framed by two contradictory years. 1951 saw such diverse films as *Alba de América* (the last of the historical epics), *Surcos* (*Furrows*, the mature expression of a Spanish version of neorealism), and *Esa pareja feliz* (*The Happy Couple*, the first shoots of "regeneration") (16); 1961 saw Berlanga's *Plácido* (a film of his maturity) and Buñuel's *Viridiana* (a "raid" which led to a renewed crack-down in the regime's film policy) (17–18). These dissidents did not, however, attract audiences from traditional genres; and over the decade the *costumbrista* comedy, populated by rural immigrants to the city, gave way to the romantic comedy (known as *rosa* or "pink" in Spanish), set in a female and professional milieu (20). Citing film historian Román Gubern, Heredero argues for closer attention to the complex relation between artistic message and lower-class (or "popular") audiences (22).

Gubern also wrote the prologue to a very different volume on the popular culture of the Dictatorship: Terenci Moix's nostalgic account of Francoist song and cinema, *Suspiros de España* (*Spanish Sighs*, 1993). As we have seen in the case of previous critics, Gubern argues that the *copla* and its film should not be condemned because it was used by the regime for propaganda purposes (Moix, 12). Rather it is to be read as an "itinerary": "la evolución de los gustos y de las modas . . . de las estrategias de la expresión de la afectividad . . . el reencuentro con nuestra memoria personal y con la cultura popular de nuestro país" ("the evolution of tastes and fashions . . . of the strategies for expressing emotion . . . the re-encounter with our personal memory and our country's popular culture," 13). Moix himself claims that, as revealed in the voices and faces of memory, the message of popular song of the period is "ambiguous," alternately conservative and progressive. Its language can be both banal and literary, and it betrays "rural roots" which have been "pulled out" of modern Spain (15). Moix praises the "flavour" (*sabor*) of the *copla* or popular Spanish song, expressing as it does the life experience and memories of three generations (16). Where once it was criticized for obscuring social reality, now it stands revealed as a valuable document; where once it was vulgar (*hortera*) now it can be re-evaluated (17).

Stars of song and cinema, the *folklóricas* celebrated by Moix are thus "weather vanes" spinning with the changing winds of the times. One key example here is Carmen Sevilla, dubbed by Moix "the smile of Spain," who went from the kitsch *españolada* of the fifties to the *destape* (disrobing) of the seventies (139). She began as a "girl next door" (albeit with castanets and a flamenco train), an exemplary young lady who even had a spiritual director (139). Her wholesomeness thus contrasted with the fiery gypsy temperament of rival Lola Flores or the disturbing sensuality of Paquita Rico (142). But the novice nun in *Hermana San Sulpicio* (*Sister San Sulpicio*, 1952) would find herself posing as a French maid in a backless uniform in *La cera virgen* (*Virgin Wax*, 1971) (150, 154). Retiring to a country retreat in the early 1980s (Moix calls her "bucolic"), she returned to the limelight on television in 1991 where she presented a game show with such stunning incompetence that viewers wondered if her gaffes were deliberate. For the movie buff Moix, Sevilla's "sentimental chronicle" thus ends in "televisual absurdity" (158). Still he looks back fondly on Carmen's smile in a time when smiles were sorely needed.

Moix does not comment on one photo reproduced in his large-format album: a fresh-faced toothy Carmen Sevilla is firmly shaking hands with the ageing weak-chinned Franco (23). But if Moix's coffee table book is knowingly indulgent in its nostalgia, it suggests an important corrective to the previous scholarly works we have examined. Where Heredero's "trace" is material and institutional (the filmic residue of contradictions in the Dictatorship's visual regime), Moix's "sigh" is immaterial and evanescent (the memory of fragile personal experience). The fundamental difference between the two is thus that of objective conditions versus subjective dispositions. Gubern puts it well once more when he says we should study "el proceso de reelaboración de las tradiciones culturales y populares . . . para seducir a sus potenciales espectadores asegurándose su lealtad" ("the process of reworking cultural and popular traditions . . . in order to seduce potential viewers and ensure their loyalty," cited in Heredero, 23). But as Moix suggests in his comments on the sad fate of Carmen Sevilla, the main medium for this working through of popular tradition in which viewers are seduced into loyalty is not cinema but television. Conversely, in an earlier period TV might also be seen as an arena for the political act in which the masses are both actors and spectators. This, Llorente claims (48), is one of the many (unfulfilled) aims of Francoist aesthetics.

The most detailed account of Francoist television of which I am aware comes in Lorenzo Díaz's richly illustrated study of five decades of programming, *La televisión en España, 1949–95*. The second part of Díaz's volume picks up from Heredero's account of film in the fifties with the new "developmentalism" of 1962–75. Noting the central demographic change of the period (the arrival of "bumpkins" [*catetos*] in the city [218]), Díaz focuses on the great figures of this "golden age": "luxury" scriptwriters Jaime de Armiñán, Adolfo Marsillach, and Antonio Gala (who were to make their names in cinema, theatre, and literature, respectively); and spectacular presenters or producers such as Miguel de la Quadra (bare-chested envoy to the Amazon [413]), Valerio Lazarov (who introduced the zoom to Spanish studios [422]), and Félix Rodríguez de la Fuente (originator of the nature series *El hombre y la tierra* [*Man and Earth*, 434]). Díaz devotes special case studies to the "sociologist" Antonio Mercero, who created the series-drama-cum-comedy *Crónicas de un pueblo* in 1971, and "anthropologist" Luis Pancorbo, the high-brow foreign correspondent who reported on *Otros pueblos* (*Other Peoples*) for still parochial Spaniards. I return to Mercero, the only producer-director to remain successfully active from the Dictatorship to democracy, later in this chapter.

Díaz, frequently ironic or caustic in his commentary, has no hesitation in talking of "quality television" at this time (440). And he wonders aloud how "la televisión franquista huérfana de libertades y rigurosamente vigilada por el aparato del Régimen produjese productos de calidad" ("Francoist television, deprived of freedom and rigorously controlled by the regime's apparatus, could produce quality content"). One example he notes is an "excellent" documentary on such a troublesome topic as García Lorca's Granada, broadcast in 1969. As we shall see, TVE, which had moved into its new studios in Prado del Rey in 1964 and had successfully pursued international prizes in 1967–8, offered surprisingly varied schedules in the early 1970s. We can now explore these political and aesthetic conundrums in relation to that most televisual of film genres, the newsreel.

NO-DO

So durable was the Francoist newsreel NO-DO ("Noticiarios y documentales cinematográficos" or "Film News and Documentaries"), that beginning in 1943 it outlived the regime itself, with a final bulletin in 1981. This huge archive of weekly newsreels and documentaries is newly accessible in the monumental study by Rafael R. Tranche and Vicente Sánchez-Biosca, which comes with a videotaped two-hour selection of footage from four decades. Like Llorente, Tranche laments that as time passes and memory of the Dictatorship recedes revisionism becomes attractive. He attacks a "sentimental dimension" acquired by NO-DO, which he blames in part on television (15). In the 1990s TVE scheduled a number of documentary series which Tranche calls "pseudo-historical" and "pseudo-sociological," drawing on the rich archives of NO-DO, which had come to be housed in the state broadcaster itself. He condemns this as an "alibi" for the regime (16). Ironically, given the Dictatorship's love of anniversaries, TVE's worst offender is a documentary broadcast in 1993 for the 50th anniversary of the newsreel, which Tranche brands "syrupy" (almibarado). Here, he writes, the story of NO-DO is presented as interchangeable with the history reported by NO-DO (in Spanish the distinction is between "historia" and "Historia"). Anecdotal and clichéd, this TV programme lends legitimacy to the past simply because it is past.

Like Heredero and Díaz for cinema and television, however, Tranche claims that newsreel was no mere "vehicle" of the regime. The development of NO-DO has to be placed in its political context; and its history is not parallel to that of the regime, from which it was relatively independent (17). Unlike Nazi Germany and Fascist Italy, Francoism was relatively uninterested and inefficient in its use of propaganda (18). As in the case of, say, architecture once more, this was for two reasons: technical and financial limitations and ideological "confusion" (the regime favoured, at once and alternately, traditionalism, religiosity, and militarism). Tranche cites the words of historian Juan Pablo Fusi, for whom it was not so much a question of systematic indoctrination as "ideological demobilization": Spain was made to "adjust to" or "settle down with" (*acomodarse a*) Francoism. But just as Heredero sees "cracks" in the cinema of the regime which reveal the "traces" of historical process, so Tranche argues that newsreel serves as a "microsociology of the everyday" through which we see glimpses (*atisbos*) of another reality: frightened faces, desolate landscapes far removed from the "great events" of History (19, 21). He suggests we "cool down" (*enfriar*) the sentimental dimension of NO-DO and assume a critical distance.

In the second half of the study Vicente Sánchez-Biosca offers a formal reading that supplements Tranche's historical account. For Sánchez-Biosca, Francoism's "mythographic" style is often combined with kitsch and banality (141). And, ironically for newsreel that claims to depict changing events, NO-DO is notable for its timelessness (243). Just as TV would later keep the calendar for the nation, NO-DO offers a "cyclical" version of time. It celebrates the yearly round of anniversaries for the regime (the Victory Parade, the commemoration of the death of José Antonio) and the Catholic festivals (Christmas, shown as a time for children, and Holy Week, the essence of Spanish mysticism). Sánchez-Biosca writes:

> Un tiempo cíclico, ajeno a acontecimientos turbadores y mirando un pasado remoto y legendario . . . ; un pasado imperial, mítico e intocable. . . . El presente no circula, pues algo cayó en la ingravidez con el triunfo de la cruzada: el pasado selectivo constituye el espejo mítico que se ritualiza a cada momento . . . los años se suceden siguiendo hitos prefijados que emergen de ese pasado y convierten el presente en una ceremonia . . . inerte de aquél.
>
> (277)

> A cyclical time, incompatible with disturbing events and focusing on a remote and legendary past . . . ; an imperial, mythical, untouchable past. . . . The present does not circulate, since something fell into weightlessness with the triumph of [Franco's] Crusade: the selective past makes up a mythic mirror which is constantly ritualized . . . the years pass following pre-established milestones which emerge from the past and turn the present into a static ceremony of that past.

In this weightlessness and inertia the processions of Holy Week become interchangeable with Franco's inauguration of yet another power station or reservoir. The celebration of the supposed "millennium of Castile" in 1943 is the "epiphany" (283) of this conversion of the present into static, imperial ceremony.

In the spaces of Francoism time does not pass: "ataviados con sus trajes típicos . . . o celebrando una romería o procesión, los pueblos de España son presentados . . . como encarnación de la entraña española . . . sinécdoque . . . de la totalidad" ("tricked out in their folk costumes . . . or celebrating a pilgrimage or procession, the villages of Spain are presented . . . as the embodiment of Spain's inner being . . . a part . . . that stands in for the whole," 278). And if the regime's calendar has its fixed landmarks, then its geography has idealized "places of memory" (449): the resonant ruins of the Alcázar of Toledo, the sober monumentality of El Escorial, and the overwhelming scale of El Valle de los Caídos. Still, writes Sánchez-Biosca, there is evidence in NO-DO of change within permanence (279). As the decades roll slowly on, a solemn visit to the Valle can be preceded by a festive country jaunt; and by the 1960s Christmas is associated with unaccustomed consumerism and Easter shown as a time for tourism (279, 573). NO-DO's endless journey through the "authentic" and "folkloric" villages of Spain gives way to a series of sites presented as ideal for leisure activities (279). And there is a greater detail in the attention to the singularity of popular traditions (the commentary begins to note the "weathered faces" of Galician fishermen [572]). In spite of itself, then, NO-DO offers "flashes" or "cracks" (*destellos, fisuras*) of modernity (572, 573).

Let us look at how the newsreels themselves coincide with the textual account given of them by Tranche (who was responsible for the selection of items on the videotape) and Sánchez-Biosca. The footage is clearly chosen to enhance the cyclical view of Francoist time. Indeed NO-DO comments on that same repetition: the first bulletin (1943) offers a message from the Caudillo from the palace of El Pardo. Twenty years later NO-DO returns to the palace, citing itself, and has the ageing dictator congratulate the newsreel on its longevity. Striking, however, are the new details of the 1963 version, intended to evoke everyday life: now books are piled up everywhere in the grand rooms and Franco's "personal telephone" is shown in close up. In other bulletins NO-DO repeatedly reports on itself, giving exhaustive accounts of its news-gathering process.

Gymnastics is also obsessively repeated. In the first bulletin children exercise in rural landscapes where just recently (we are told) their fathers fought. Now peasants are shown bringing in the harvest by hand (1943). In the same year modestly dressed girls and bare-chested boys march through villages and across sierras singing patriotic songs. An item on "reconstruction" shows ruined buildings (1943), but one called "Spanish folklore" stresses the "primitive charm" of Galicia: girls in traditional dress pose placidly or dance decorously against landscape shots of the sea or hills (1944). Elsewhere the countryside is the setting for repeated rituals. On the seventh anniversary of the death of José Antonio, founder of the Falange, mourners process to the Escorial (1943); sixteen years later they carry his remains through the bleakly impressive Castilian landscape to El Valle de los Caídos (1959). A thousand women exercise in front of the Escorial once more, a chilling vision of Fascist mass monumentalism strangely undercut by the small-scale display of domestic labours shown later in the same bulletin (Franco's rapacious wife Doña Carmen wears an incongruously extravagant hat) (1944).

While the camerawork is rudimentary in these early newsreels, often limited to some shaky pans, the editing is curiously gimmicky with shots linked by a wide range of showy wipes and irises. The lack of live sound, however, contributes to the sense of airless inertia noted in NO-DO by Sánchez-Biosca: we never hear the lapping of that picturesque Galician sea; the song of the bare-chested boys is not in synch with their martial movements.

As the years pass and victory parades proceed with monotonous regularity, changes become visible within this permanence. In 1943 the treatment of Christmas had been moralistic: audiences were warned that the spirit of the holiday lay not in the poultry displayed in the market (which few Spaniards could afford in any case) but in the small figures of a child's nativity scene. Women sent packages to the División Azul, fighting with the Nazis on the Eastern Front. By 1959 this charitable focus has disappeared. Children write letters to the Three Kings asking for presents, which are displayed somewhat ominously against a black background. January 1967 is pure consumerism: trendy young women try on the latest styles in the department store sales. Television sets are reduced to bargain basement prices.

Even the countryside is not immune to modernity. In 1963 Spain is the "ideal country for tourism" (although all we are shown is the queues of Citroens at the border). In 1962 "a day in the country" shows women fishing in a river outside Madrid as men cook paella, each with equal incompetence. The moral is predictable: the sexes should stick to their own. Franco's summer holidays change in their treatment. In 1961 he is shown relaxing on a northern beach with his grandchildren; in 1974 he fishes for salmon in Galicia and Asturias. The commentary focuses with unaccustomed gloom on the contrast between the beauty of the landscape and the poverty of the fish stock. The new use of colour complements the "beautiful and varied geography" still praised by the voice-over.

Most fascinating, however, is a mini-narrative from 1967 on rural winners of the sports lottery. We see a tractor driver in Alicante informed of his good fortune at his workplace, as is a petrol service station attendant. A chicken farmer is so shocked he drops his eggs. After each man is shown at work, we see the group celebrating in the village bar. In Jaén farmers beat olive trees with sticks. In an unusually lengthy interview with one of them, the NO-DO journalist reveals that the villager has literary ambitions and asks if he would rather have won the Nadal Prize. The briefly famous farmer struggles to improvise an acceptable reply in correct formal Spanish. The sound, now of course recorded live, highlights the pathos of the segment. It is a clear moment of "crack" or "gap" in the airless, inert repetition of NO-DO, breaking through the habitual banality. Here we witness for a moment the historical trace of the dictatorship: frightened faces, desolate landscapes, ruined lives. It is an uncomfortable glimpse of the everyday, reminiscent of reality television, that we will also see in late-Francoist series drama.

Crónicas de un pueblo (Chronicles of a village, 1971–4)

Las historias cotidianas de un pueblo ficticio de Castilla. Una lección sobre El Fuero de los Españoles ideada por la mano derecha de Franco, el Almirante Carrero Blanco.

La serie a pesar de su carga ideológica, consiguió un rotundo éxito en la
pequeña pantalla, llegando a competir con los telefilms americanos números
uno en audiencias durante muchos años.
La escala jerárquica estaba muy definida, como ya lo explicaban los antiguos
libros de texto, las autoridades del pueblo: el alcalde, el cura, el cabo de la
guardia civil y el maestro.
En esta serie ocurría lo mismo, ellos eran la voz cantante del pueblo con el
alguacil que unía a las autoridades con el resto de ciudadanos.
La serie se rodó en Santorcaz (Madrid) en la ficción era Puebla Nueva del Rey
Sancho.
Todo muy bien pensado ideológicamente como por aquel entonces mandaban
los principios del Movimiento. (teacuerdas)

The everyday story of a fictional village in Castile. A lesson on the Statute of
the Spaniards conceived by Franco's right-hand man, Admiral Carrero
Blanco. In spite of its propagandistic dimension, the series was a resounding
success, even managing to compete with the American series that were
number one with Spanish audiences for many years. The social hierarchy was
very clear. As the old textbooks still suggested, the authorities in the village
are the mayor, the priest, the Civil Guard corporal, and the schoolteacher. In
this series it was just like that: they called the tune in the village, with the
bailiff serving as intermediary between the authorities and the rest of the
inhabitants. The series was shot in Santorcaz, in the province of Madrid,
which was called "Puebla Nueva del Rey Sancho" in the show. Everything was
well planned from a propaganda point of view, as the principles of the
Francoist movement dictated at that time.

Lorenzo Díaz calls Antonio Mercero, the creator of *Crónicas de un pueblo*
(1971–4), "the master of situation comedy." But he also writes that Mercero has
portrayed Spanish society better than academic sociologists, giving an exceptional "daguerrotype" of the Spaniards who emigrated to the city in the 1960s
and 1970s (456). The only Spanish director to have won an Emmy (for *La
cabina* [1972], a political allegory of freedom and captivity), Mercero created
hit series in the dictatorship (*Crónicas*), the Transition (*Verano azul* [*Blue
Summer*, 1981–2]), and full democracy (*Farmacia de guardia* [*All Night
Chemist*, 1991–5]). Díaz claims that Mercero's shows inspired nostalgia even at
the time of showing: all Spaniards who were "lost in the city," he writes,
dreamed of Puebla Nueva del Rey Sancho, the mythical village in which rural
types lived idyllically together (457).
    There could, however, have been no more brutally propagandistic intent than
the commissioning of *Crónicas de un pueblo*. According to Díaz, Mercero says
simply that the series was born "for political reasons," in order to explain the
then recent *fuero*, or Francoist decree, to the massed audience. As director and
often screenwriter of a "lyrical and human story" he was disturbed by the political necessity of having to fit in explicit dialogue such as "As the article number
so and so of the *fuero* says." Still, he claims, the "human" tone lent this
"typology" of the Spanish villager credibility (particularly in the central figure
of the teacher, reminiscent of Antonio Machado). And this was the first time the

rural world was treated on TV. Díaz confirms this identification of the audience with the fiction, however didactic: we were all from villages, he writes, and *Crónicas de un pueblo* was a breath of fresh, rural air, especially when compared with the US TV movies then still prominent on TVE's schedules (458). Mercero makes one final observation on credibility: although the regime's brief was so specific as to insist that the Mayor be played by a young and handsome actor, the rest of the ensemble cast were supporting actors who viewers were unlikely to recognize (Illustrations 7, 8, 9).

Although Díaz notes that Mercero began as a film director (his most recent feature to date was *Planta cuarta* [*The Fourth Floor*, 2003]), he does not note that Mercero, a graduate of the official film school, is known for his early work for NO-DO. Mercero's own official website (Mercero) lists 18 short documentaries produced by the state newsreel from 1968–78. While some of the titles sound traditional even folkloric or touristic (*Viaje por Cuenca* [*Journey through Cuenca*, 1969]), Mercero's NO-DO segments are still remembered for their pioneering use of sound: thus a football match was scored to a minuet by Boccherini (*Ballet futbolístico* [*Football Ballet*, 1971]) or a traffic jam shot like a bullfight (*Difícil "faena"* [*A Difficult "Pass"*, 1974). As we shall see, this technical experimentation carries over unexpectedly into his work for popular television made in the same period.

TVE's schedules of the early seventies, we remember, were full of prestige projects or novel formats: documentary series took Spaniards to the Amazon, talk shows were hosted by *progres* with dangerously long hair and loud shirts. The season of 1970–1 saw "quality" products from novelist Antonio Gala and film director Josefina Molina (Díaz 448); 1971–2, work by Pilar Miró and the lavish RAI biopic of Leonardo da Vinci (450); and 1972–3, Mercero's own multiple prize-winning *La cabina* and Fernando Fernán Gómez's controversial *Juan Soldado* (*Johnny Soldier*, 451). TVE's outgoing popular success had been *La casa de los Martínez* (*At Home with the Martínezs*), a magazine show re-creating a middle-class family home complete with maid, cook, and celebrity guests. In this peak period of development and expansion (for Spain as for Spanish television) it is thus surprising that *Crónicas de un pueblo* should have been such a success, with both audiences and critics. Its sheer parochialism and domesticity must have been conspicuous in schedules now devoted to cosmopolitan modernity. Clearly it was the sentimental, nostalgic dimension (Díaz's "breath" of rural air, Terenci Moix's "sigh") which first struck a chord with newly urbanized viewers.

The success of the series is all the more surprising given its transparent didacticism, which, as creator and critic acknowledge, seems shocking today. In the course of the series we are informed that, according to the *fuero*, a Spaniard has a right to privacy in his own home ("El amor y una manzana"/"Love and an Apple") and a duty to report offences such as robbery ("Las hebillas de oro"/"The Golden Buckles"). Citizens can be obliged to take part in emergency labour, as in the case of fire-fighting ("Hierbas para guisar un cordero"/"Herbs to Cook a Lamb"), and enjoy the "right to work" ("La oveja negra"/"The Black

7. The Mayor (Fernando Cebrián)

8. The Teacher (Emilio Rodríguez)

9. The Postman (Jesús Guzmán)

Sheep"). In addition the state will offer credit to small businessmen, thus avoiding recourse to loan sharks ("Una apuesta divertida"/"An Amusing Bet"). This theme of the dignity and necessity of labour, assisted if necessary by the regime, recurs in perhaps the majority of the twenty episodes re-released on DVD.

Sometimes these morals are so over-explicit (often in episodes directed by Mercero himself) that contemporary audiences would have no difficult disregarding them if they so pleased. Titles and dialogue even seem, occasionally, to highlight this process. In one episode called, transparently, "A Story with a Moral" ("Cuento con moraleja"), the young mayor complains that the older teacher is turning the whole village into a classroom. Elsewhere the didactic intent is more integrated (the mayor notes there was no need to compel willing villagers to put out the fire) or flatly contradicted by the context (the grumpy old man invoking the right to privacy is in fact intent on preventing his daughter's marriage to an impoverished suitor who courts her through the traditional grille). Implicit morals are perhaps more insidious. The authority of mayor, teacher, and priest is unquestioned and episodes invariably end with the reconciliation of class and generational conflict. Individualism and dissidence are to be tamed. The "black sheep" is a rancorous ex-convict reconciled to the village when he is offered a job in the local bar (in a transparently symbolic subplot, children kidnap a black lamb and paint it white so it will be accepted by

the majority). A wine trader who refuses to pay taxes sees the light when his
neighbours, paid out of the public purse, refuse to offer services such as refuse
collection (the street sweeper) or paternal advice (the teacher) ("Cuento con
moraleja"). A habitual beggar is integrated into the work force (according to the
teacher: "We are complicit in his anti-social behaviour"). But social tensions
can come from the top as well as the bottom: a snooty new boy in school, son of
an architect, is tricked into participating in class by canny village kids who
pretend to be stupid ("El rebelde"/"The Rebel").

This organic community seems uncannily isolated. The only contact with the
(unnamed) city is the bus, whose service is often disrupted to comic or dramatic
effect. Outsiders are almost invariably malign. A big city lawyer, played in a
rare cameo by veteran film star Alfredo Mayo, arrives in a huge American car
and attempts to take land from a shepherd who has no formal title to it, for use
as a waste dump (the *fuero* informs us that the shepherd cannot be evicted ["El
señor influyente"/"The Influential Man"]). Two trendy young girls in a
broken-down sports car carry out a robbery, frustrated, once more, by a shepherd ("Rififi en Puebla Nueva del Rey Sancho"/"Theft in Puebla Nueva del Rey
Sancho"). A pair of sinister hippies (one wearing a star of David round his neck)
beat up the bailiff, who is placidly taking a siesta in the countryside ("Las
hebillas"). A "professor" from the "Central University" turns out to be a thief
intent on robbing the village church (locals rumble him when he is unable to
distinguish between medieval and baroque painting ["La noche de los
arqueólogos"/"Night of the Archeologists"]). This fear of the outside is occasionally satirized, as when the children, hearing the Civil Guard announce that a
dangerous foreign criminal is on the loose, identify him wrongly with a harmless local businessman ("Juanito y sus detectives"/"Juanito and His Detectives"). The community, often shown in crowded group shots, must defend itself
from external influence as well as internal individualism.

This sense of timelessness, familiar from four decades of NO-DO, recurs in
Crónicas de un pueblo's stress on festivals: the annual village fiesta, a wedding
between the mayor and the chemist, and Christmas, the children's holiday par
excellence, all figure as the main themes of episodes. And again, as in NO-DO,
cyclical time intersects with resonant, idealized places of memory. Episodes
often begin with landscape shots of the millennial Castilian meseta, so beloved
of Francoist aesthetics and ideology. The village itself is dense with icono-
graphic associations: in long shots from the fields outside, the ancient church
tower rises above the lower houses like the steeple in the engraving on the cover
of *Reconstrucción*.

The similarity is apt because the visual or televisual aspects of the series
clearly contradict the ideology expressed so blatantly in the scripts. Shot
entirely on location with live sound and a large number of local extras, *Crónicas
de un pueblo* plays more like ethnographic documentary than sitcom (there is no
laughter track). The landscape is often bleak and actors are bundled up against
the bitter cold or sweating in the fierce sun. Opening montages suggest a rural
Spain that has been unchanged since the Civil War: the shepherds' life is hardly

idyllic and tiny, black-clad ladies pick their way down unpaved streets. The series concept often calls attention to this underdevelopment. In "La escoba"/"The Brush" the bailiff is ashamed at having to sweep the streets. When he refuses to do so, the whole village pitches in. But this explicit moral of communal action is undermined by the lengthy shots of the ruinous infrastructure: village streets are clearly pitted with holes and choked with dust. Or again, when the bus driver wishes to buy a lorry ("El camión"/"The Lorry") the overt message is one of development: the state will lend him the capital to carry out his dream. But what stays in the mind is the opening shot of the truck abandoned in a barn by its previous owner, with chickens roosting on top. Clearly the village named with humorous incongruity "New Town of King Sancho" (the last King of that name ruled Castile in the thirteenth century) is more ancient than new. Even at a narrative level it is hard to integrate modernity into village tradition. The teacher struggles gamely to introduce "modern" group-teaching methods into his old-fashioned classroom (there is also much discussion of a new and well equipped school, which we never see); an episode in which an enterprising young man drills for water in a barren hillside is full of desolate shots of impoverished homesteads; the comic postman (played by an actor with over fifty minor credits in Francoist film) is often shown leading the school kids in idiosyncratic gymnastics (surely a parody of NO-DO). But they never get the athletic facilities discussed by the town council.

Location is reinforced by casting. The supporting players, here promoted to top billing by Mercero, share a very specific physical type: weathered faces, poor teeth, and emaciated frames. The teacher, on the other hand, is noticeably overweight. In group scenes the cast blend in perfectly with the extras. Often the camera will, say, track up the aisle of the church, focusing on impassive, care-worn figures which offer clear traces of bitter hardship under the regime. Village streets and faces alike are mute witnesses to history. For modern viewers the look is shockingly similar to that of a rural film shot at the same time but set thirty years earlier: Víctor Erice's *El espíritu de la colmena* (*The Spirit of the Beehive*, 1973).

Shooting style encourages this documentary effect. Some episodes boast long unbroken takes or sequence shots more typical of art movies than TV. "La peseta de Dionisio"/"Dionisio's Penny" has an impeccable moral of respect between social classes: the bus driver mends the car of a bourgeois visitor out of pure solidarity and requests only symbolic payment. But the opening sequence pointedly contrasts the old, communal bus (with black smoke belching from behind) with the comfortable car driven by a businessman with his fur-coated wife and flirtatious hippy daughter. When finally they arrive in the village, we are treated to a two-minute shot in which the bus pulls up in the foreground in the central square; the broken-down car is pushed into frame in the background by the visibly exhausted bourgeois family; the bus driver argues with the postman as the father argues with the bailiff; and the attractive daughter walks off into the village to the delight and consternation of local youth. Another sequence shot of over three minutes occurs soon after, where the teacher asks kids to gather round him and explains, once more, the "dignity of work." As he does so, one child actor seems to fall over and the teacher asks him to "take care."

Such a shooting style enhances both the impression of documentary realism of the series (almost unknown in cinema of the period) and its implicit respect for the everyday life of the rural poor (who are dignified by the camera's patient, familiar attention). Sometimes the plot simply comes to a halt and the camera records *vérité* footage. In the fiesta episode a village woman teaches a child to beat a lamb's carcass with a branch in order to enhance the meat's flavour. The episode ends with lengthy group shots of anonymous villagers dancing, their figures and faces once more distinctively rural and uncinematic. Typically also, what in NO-DO would have been folkloric or picturesque is here fully integrated into the particularity, even tragedy, of everyday life. A boy dressed up in folk costume is teased by his peers for wearing a "skirt"; the fiesta is disrupted by a fierce forest fire in which one character is burnt. We are far indeed from the pedagogic moralism that inspired the regime to commission the series.

Let us look more closely at two episodes which would appear at first to reconfirm the cyclical and static regime of timeless memory encouraged by the regime. As the series developed over three years and 113 half-hour episodes, the lack of romance was clearly felt to be a problem. In "La media naranja" (literally "Half an Orange", figuratively "His Other Half") the handsome mayor is finally engaged to the pretty chemist. In a typically transparent symbol, literal oranges also figure in the subplot, where a small boy is shamed for littering the streets with peel. What is striking, however, is the linking of the subjective story of personal romance with the objective narrative of rural development. The mayor summons the chemist (who is also a councillor) to the "river bank," a traditional site for courting. This sets tongues wagging in the village. The setting is hardly romantic, however. The season is frigid mid-Winter and bare trees frame a polluted stream festooned with discarded rubbish. The mayor intends to discuss water purification with the young woman. In spite of the fact that they are constantly interrupted by nosy neighbours, the couple do finally confess their love for one another. Where first the priest, referring to rural depopulation, had noted that he performed more funerals than weddings, now a village gossip says the couple were brought together not by the traditional matchmaker but by a water purifier.

This episode seems to reconcile Heredero's historical "trace" of the past (the objective legacy of underdevelopment and neglect) with Moix's "sigh" of rural nostalgia (the subjective memory of rural romance). It is a compromise that continuing TV drama, parallel as it is to the lives of viewers, is uniquely able to provide. But it is important to insist that the "micro-sociology" of *Crónicas de un pueblo* (its minute attention to the times and spaces of rural life) is not overtly sentimental. Continuing his experimentation with soundtrack, begun with NO-DO, Mercero uses a bewildering variety of music, often incompatible with the visuals, and never appeals to the facile seductions of folkloric *copla*.

In spite of its title ("El viajero de la sonrisa"/"The Traveller with the Smile"), one Christmas episode is equally ambivalent. A mysterious stranger approaches the town. First he encounters a shepherd in a bleak field, disconsolate because villagers no longer buy his lambs for the holiday meal. Then the men of the village refuse to sing at Midnight Mass, arguing that now church is just for women. Even the school teacher, normally a model of Machadian irony, is disconsolate, remembering the death of his child. All ends happily with the whole village participating in Midnight Mass as the angelic visitor smiles over them. There are prominent shots of the nativity scene which, as we have seen, is the stock-in-trade of NO-DO's version of the holidays. Yet the pervasive melancholy of the episode and its unambiguous references to disconcerting social change (the decline of traditional husbandry, tradition, and religion) suggest once more that television, even under a dictatorship, can give surprising and moving glimpses of historical reality. This is a vision of Francoism that is, of course, rendered much more complex when seen on contemporary TV screens.

Cine de barrio (Neighbourhood Cinema, 1995–)

El alegre divorciado (1976)

Ramón y Socorro, propietarios de una taberna en Madrid, son un matrimonio cincuentón. Su hijo Carlos se encuentra en México, país en donde va a contraer matrimonio con Gloria, hija de un importante hombre de negocios mexicano. A la boda van a asistir Ramón y Socorro. Al llegar a México, Ramón se entera de que en éste país existe el divorcio. (todocine)

The Gay Divorcé

Ramón and Socorro, the owners of a bar in Madrid, are a fifty-something married couple. Their son Carlos is living in Mexico, where he is engaged to be married to Gloria, the daughter of an important Mexican businessman. Ramón and Socorro travel to be at the wedding. When they reach Mexico, Ramón finds out that divorce is legal there.

¡Se armó el belén! (1970)

Las aventuras y desventuras de un sacerdote de mediana edad y un poco chapado a la antigua, que atraviesa un suburbio de Madrid para imponer a sus feligreses sus personales percepciones. (adictosalcine)

What a Carry On!/Setting up the Nativity Scene

The adventures and misadventures of a middle aged priest who's a bit on the old fashioned side. He goes around in the outskirts of Madrid trying to impose his own personal views on his parishioners.

Grandes amigos (1967)

Tras la muerte del padre de Nino, él y su madre se verán obligados a abandonar el pueblo donde vivían e instalarse en Madrid. Allí, Nino hará todo

lo posible por ganarse la amistad de los niños de la escuela contando con la
ayuda del maestro, del titiritero con el que viven y de una milagrosa figura del
Niño Jesús que concede al niño todo lo que pide. (Culturalia)

Great Friends

After the death of Nino's father, he and his mother are forced to leave the
village where they used to live and move to Madrid. There Nino does all he
can to make friends with the kids in his school, with the help of the teacher,
the puppeteer they live with, and a miraculous statue of the Christ child which
grants Nino whatever he asks for.

Cine de barrio is TVE's long-running and top rated Saturday afternoon show,
which book-ends a feature film of the Francoist era (generally from the 1960s or
1970s) with studio discussion. Beginning on the minority second channel in
1995, it was soon transferred to the majority first channel and was anchored
until 2004 by the unctuous José Manuel Parada. In its hour-long introduction to
the often obscure feature, *Cine de barrio* also shows extracts from NO-DO and
specially shot documentary inserts from locations in the capital or provinces.
The main attraction, however, is the *tertulia* or group discussion, which is often
graced by surviving stars of the period and by Parada's long-time sidekicks, an
Argentine pianist (until 2000) and a near silent middle-aged female assistant
(until 2003). The studio set, under Parada's regime, mimicked a private home,
with comfortable chairs and sofa, while the animated credit sequence showed
the whole family (grandmother, adults, and small children) gathering round the
television set in anticipation of the show. Much disparaged by the press, *Cine de
barrio* remains a unique example of the complex relationship between newsreel,
feature film, and television and of the uncanny survival of the Francoist
aesthetic into an indulgently nostalgic democracy.

The show can thus be read as another example of the postmodern revisionism
that lends legitimacy to the past simply because it is past and which we have
already seen in the cases of visual arts and television documentary. And
spurning the rare and culturally distinguished dissident films made by auteurs
of the period (such as Berlanga or Buñuel), it tends to choose long lost examples of popular genres now scorned: religious and child-star pictures, farces and
melodramas. Frequently the theme of the featured film is that of rural migration
to the city or the misadventures of *paletos* (country bumpkins) in the capital.

Cine de barrio firmly places itself in the line of Terenci Moix's *Suspiros de
España*: its host is lavishly indulgent to now elderly *folklóricas* and they in turn
return the compliment. Rather than dismissing it out of hand, however, I would
argue (as Gubern does of Moix) that *Cine de barrio* takes its readers on a
journey through evolving tastes and fashions or strategies of affect. Certainly it
stages a very explicit encounter with personal memory and national popular
culture, acknowledging the rural roots of both producers and audience. *Cine de
barrio* gives some evidence of what I have called, after Heredero, "trace" (the
material evidence of the past): Parada is formidably knowledgeable of Francoist
cinema, if indiscriminate in his passion. But it engages much more with that

immaterial and evanescent register I called (after Moix) "sigh": a subjective air of nostalgia which has clearly seduced contemporary viewers into loyalty. Sugary and sentimental beyond compare, *Cine de barrio* could never be called quality television. But it offers a micro-sociology of the everyday (of the relationship between myth, kitsch, and banality) which strikes a chord with viewers, if not critics.

Analysis of a four-minute sequence taken from a Christmas edition of *Cine de barrio* (December 18, 1999) will give a taste of what it feels like to watch this unique programme. The sequence begins with location shots of minor celebrities (so called "friends" of the programme and its host) singing traditional *villancicos* (carols) at a party. We then cut to the studio, where the host and his regular sidekicks (the male pianist and female companion) are festively dressed. Addressing the camera directly, the host pitches the boxed sets of videos marketed under the brand name *Cine de barrio*. This sales pitch is illustrated by a clip from a feature starring celebrated child star Marisol. This is not shown free to air, but is only available for payment. There then follows a clip from the featured film of the day, *El alegre divorciado*, starring the late Paco Martínez Soria, arch *paleto*, and vivacious, plump Florinda Chico: the latter is trying on a transparent negligée to the consternation of her husband. During an interview shot on location at the now elderly Chico's home, the camera lingers on her memorabilia, as our host flatters the star: surely she was as attractive as she was *simpática*? The collage effect of the editing suggests a free flow between past and present, harmless nostalgia and shameless commercialism.

Let us examine, briefly, three films shown in successive weeks over that most historic of anniversaries, the new millennium (synopses are given at the beginning of this section). By coincidence these features follow an itinerary that goes back in time, revealing contradictory accounts of the town/country divide. *El alegre divorciado* (*The Gay Divorcé*, 1976; shown December 18, 1999) is a *costumbrista* comedy co-produced with Mexico, directed by Pedro Lazaga, the prolific maker of such pictures, including ten years earlier the self-explanatory *La ciudad no es para mí* (*The City is Not For Me*). The opening credits play over classic establishing shots of Madrid (Cibeles, the Castellana, the Metropolitan building), before we cut to the street where short, fat, and ugly Paco Martínez Soria is carrying suitcases to a taxi. Modernity seems ubiquitous as he and Florinda Chico arrive in a gleaming Barajas airport and fly for their first time to Mexico City. Here once more the bourgeois interiors of their wealthy son and postcard shots of the centre or of touristic Xochimilco suggest leisured consumerism. A jaunt to Acapulco is full of airy modern beach houses and bikinied babes. The broad humour derives, of course, from the placing of Martínez Soria in such a context. Although he is attracted by that most modern of conditions, divorce, he embodies in the coarseness of figure, voice, and gesture the unrepentantly rural traditions of popular Spain. Constantly frustrated and humiliated (forced to wash the dishes when he is unable to pay the bill in a swish night club, almost drowning in pursuit of those bikinied babes, and showered with paint at his son's wedding), Martínez Soria shows that cosmopolitan modernity is no match for parochial domesticity, a fitting moral for a show called *Cine de barrio*.

The context in which the show places this feature is, however, striking. We are shown not just the respectful interview from the home of veteran Chico (she shows us a photo signed by the King), and an undated NO-DO segment of Christmas in Madrid, but a location report from Martínez Soria's own *pueblo* (home town) Tarazona, where the historic theatre contains a shrine to the local hero, including such relics as his spectacles. In connection with the theme of the film, we are given a report from the Madrid association of separated people: middle-aged and elderly suitors shyly play chess or dance together. Members of the association talk of rebuilding shattered lives and of working to change Spanish law. They are treated with some dignity by the young female interviewer. There could be no clearer example of TV joining hands with cinema to strengthen social bonds in city and country alike.

One week later, on Christmas Day, Parada screened *¡Se armó el Belén!* (*What a Carry On!/Setting up the Nativity Scene*, 1970), a *costumbrista* comedy also starring Martínez Soria, but in a very different milieu. Director José Luis Sáenz de Heredia, a notorious rightist, had made the most famous propaganda film of the regime, *Raza* (*Race*, 1942). Exteriors are here shot in Alcobendas, a bleak new industrial town north of Madrid, where Martínez Soria plays a lovable priest, born in the country, who is here caught out by social change. Scolded by his superiors for not keeping up with the times, he sells the parish church's traditional images and invites the local long-haired youths to a disco on site. This misguided attempt at modernization misfires: hooligans start a fight. But salvation comes through television. Martínez Soria visits TVE's gleaming new studios at Prado del Rey and persuades them to broadcast a live nativity scene from his neglected town. When predictable chaos ensues and is seen around the nation, the priest is unexpectedly taken up by his once neglectful flock. Even the Leftist doctor admits that "men are more important than ideas and we can understand each other through the heart."

In the studio discussion of the film Parada repeats this line of dialogue, noting how different the political situation was then. The actor who played the doctor claims that in spite of his own beliefs, director Sáenz de Heredia employed a gang of revolutionaries and anarchists on the set. Jesús Guzmán (the skinny postman in *Crónicas de un pueblo*, who has a supporting part in *¡Se armó el belén!*) comments on the working conditions of the day where actors needed a certain number of speaking parts to get a union card. There is a phone interview with a one-time starlet, now living in Mexico, who remembers that she always rushed to the cinema with her mother, afraid of missing the NO-DO. Political, professional, and personal histories mingle in reminiscence. Parada is wearing a silver shirt for the holidays and a nativity scene sits on a table behind his right shoulder.

The next Saturday is January 1, 2000. In honour of the new millennium *Cine de barrio* has attracted a special studio guest: Sara Montiel, the greatest of all *folklóricas*. Sarita (as she is still familiarly known), frozen faced through surgery or botox, puffs on a cigar. She unsteadily recounts that it is now 43 years since she became a global star (not just in Spain, she insists). The inevitable NO-DO segment shows preparations for New Year's Eve in the Madrid of the 1950s. The announcer pompously enumerates the foodstuffs he claims lucky citizens will enjoy. Back in the studio Parada says this clip proves that nothing has changed: we thought that by 2000 we would all be living in outer space, but in fact we are the same Spaniards as years ago. Cue the undistinguished weepie (Sarita's description) *Grandes amigos* (*Great Friends*, 1967), a film of popular piety which seems to belong to a different century, not just a decade, from those shown in previous weeks. The director this time is Luis Lucia, known for his sentimental musicals with hugely popular child stars such as Joselito and Marisol. The little known and hugely irritating Nino stars here, taking up some three precious hours of the schedule on one of the most prestigious days in broadcasting history.

Grandes amigos (the title refers to the child and Christ) begins with a rural idyll, shot in distant Jadraque, Guadalajara. Little Nino lives with his black-clad widowed mother (inevitably called María) and the family donkey by the railway line, where his mother operates the level crossing. Following an errant ball he discovers a statue of the child Jesus, hidden in a cave during the Civil War. When the mother is thrown out of her job, she, the child, and Jesus set off for the city on the donkey (Jadraque's ancient castle can be seen on the hillside behind the road). Arriving in the Castellana and Cibeles once more they are roundly abused as *paletos*. They head for a working-class barrio on the outskirts, a cross between a wasteland and a building site. The relentlessly cheery Nino is cruelly teased by savvy urban kids, but hides his disappointment from his saintly mother and confides only in the child Jesus. A kindly teacher, whose beard gives him more than a little resemblance to the adult Christ, supports Nino by saying that he too was born in a village and feels no shame in his origins. The character is similar to the schoolmaster in *Crónicas de un pueblo*. Coincidentally, the actor who would play the TV teacher just three years later turns up in *Grandes amigos* as a good-hearted lorry driver.

While *El alegre divorciado* is wholly secular (albeit roundly condemning divorce in the final reel) and *¡Se armó el belén!* shows the pressures facing the church in a rapidly urbanizing society, *Grandes amigos* (made just a few years earlier) claims that popular piety can survive the transition to the city, just as the beloved donkey can still be happily housed in an urban outhouse. The claim may be unconvincing, but it adds a further layer of reminiscence to that brutally swift experience of urbanization that would have scarred older viewers of *Cine de barrio*. Focusing in its first reel on that perfect place of memory that is the rural village (complete with historic monument on the hillside), *Grandes amigos* would seem to confirm host Parada's claim, so in synch with the cyclical time of Francoist newsreel, that nothing in millennial Spain has changed. Yet the evidence of viewers' eyes will surely tell them that even movie stars are not immune to the passing of time and that the visions of Spain presented by the regime are inconsistent, even contradictory.

Repetition and recognition

In 2004 José Manuel Parada fell from grace. After taking the provincial *Cine de barrio* on an unlikely Mediterranean cruise, a budget-busting location shoot, he was sacked by TVE, who installed *folklórica* Carmen Sevilla as his replacement. Sevilla's continuing incompetence (what Moix called her "televisual absurdity") revealed that to embody film history is not the same as to present it on television; and that "heartwarming" ("entrañable"), the adjective invariably used of and in *Cine de barrio*, is no easy affect to pull off in a studio. As if ashamed of the domesticity of the original format, TVE stranded Sevilla in a cold new set, more stylish and less familiar to faithful fans.

The generation who enjoy *Cine de barrio*'s journey through the history of emotion have lately been neglected by schedulers in search of younger, urban audiences. Television in Spain has thus returned to its historical origins. As we have seen, it was to the cities that TV sets first came in the 1960s and in the early 1970s programming still aimed for "quality." Current demographic trends continue to reinforce this urbanization of Spanish population and television: Santorcaz, the ancient village of *Crónicas de un pueblo*, had just 616 inhabitants in 2003 (Santorcaz); Alcobendas, the new industrial town where Paco Martínez Soria played a rural priest at odds with modernity, now boasts of its proximity to Madrid's Barajas airport and has a population of 104,026 (Alcobendas).

Even given the modest cultural capital of its large target audience, the poor quality of the features chosen for the *Cine de barrio* strand remains puzzling. Why would viewers sit through *Grandes amigos* on the day of the millennium, even when accompanied by the heartwarming host Parada and genuine diva Montiel? I would suggest that it is precisely because these films are generic (typical *costumbrista* comedies or sentimental child pictures) that they serve as a stimulus for a generalized nostalgia for cinema in the Dictatorship. Indeed, discussion on the show is often about the experience of movie-going (arriving with your mother in time for the NO-DO). *Cine de barrio* is thus a working through (in Gubern's Spanish "re-elaboración") of popular cultural traditions. The familiarity of such films, unexceptional in any way, is also appropriate for the medium of television, which, unlike cinema, puts a premium on repetition and recognition. *Cine de barrio* might be read as an alibi for the conservative Partido Popular, as NO-DO was for the regime, ideologically demobilizing the masses. But if it prizes consensus over conflict (arguing that people should communicate with the heart not the head), then surely this is because older Spaniards remain aware of the true, tragic cost of such conflict. And consensus need not mean forgetfulness. If it did, why devote three hours every Saturday to memorializing the past?

TV nostalgia can prove airless. Certainly *Cine de barrio*'s studio is claustrophobic. But I have argued that the show reveals how the past remains embedded in the present and can even, with the millennium, be projected into the future. Actors and directors are also repositories of memory. A secondary or character player like Jesús Guzmán (the postman in *Crónicas*, a lugubrious pool player in *¡Se armó el Belén!*) embodies a reassuring continuity when seated on *Cine de barrio*'s sofa. And if TV is enmeshed with Francoist film, then it provides the opportunity for continuing careers as substantial as those in cinema. Antonio Mercero, creator of *Crónicas*, deserves fuller study as a true TV auteur, whose favourite themes (especially that of childhood) recur over thirty years in a wide variety of political, historical, and narrative contexts. Scholars have endlessly interrogated a small corpus of feature films on the rural topic (*Surcos* [1951], *Bienvenido, Mr Marshall* [1953]). Their conclusions might well be modified if they addressed popular television such as *Crónicas*, which played so much larger a part in Spanish national life.

There are thus continuities both within and across media in the period. The schoolchildren of *Crónicas* are the young grandparents of those in the period drama *Cuéntame*, TVE's hit of the millennium; and they are the cousins of the little girls in *El espíritu de la colmena*, an art movie whose look is not so different from the television show that is contemporary with it. Places of memory are enriched by repetition. The bare hills and fragile streams of Castile's countryside and the bars and barns of its villages recur in newsreel, popular feature film, and series drama alike, although it seems unlikely that even the Caudillo could find a fish in *Crónicas*'s polluted brook. If there is a Francoist aesthetic that cuts across media, then, it cannot be reduced to the ideology of the regime or to the political positions of producers: *Crónicas*, commissioned as propaganda, provides clear evidence of underdevelopment; even Sáenz de Heredia's *costumbrista* farce finally proves sympathetic to Leftist professionals. I would argue, however, that TV is more likely to provide examples of those cracks or furrows that scholars have claimed to find in the visual arts, cinema, and newsreel of the regime. To watch *Crónicas* for the first time is to feel oneself transported in a time machine in an apparently unmediated fashion. And, unlike popular cinema of the period, it needs no dose of sugary nostalgia to make it palatable. The live sound and grainy 14mm stock produce a potent reality effect that is more innovative, both in technique and narrative, than equivalent Spanish cinema. Moreover TV's intolerance for the monumental and the massive make it more structurally immune to fascist visual rhetoric than other visual media: the little school house fits better on the small screen than the Valle de los Caídos.

The specificity of television and the intimacy of its history thus make it more closely linked to national life in the late Francoist period than any other medium. While cinematic *paleto* Martínez Soria was jetting off to Mexico, the televisual country folk of Puebla Nueva del Rey Sancho could barely make it by bus to the nearby city. This trace of historical circumstance, etched on the faces of TV actors and extras alike, is complemented or supplemented by the "sigh": the fragile evolution of affect as coded in representation and lodged in memory. It is an emotional charge or commitment that is not to be dismissed out of hand and is uniquely engaged by the TV text's relation to the everyday.

Crónicas de un pueblo (*Chronicles of a Village*, **TVE 1971–4**)

Creator: Antonio Mercero
Executive producer: Ramón Crespo
Directors: Julio Coll, Antonio Giménez Rico, Miguel Lluch, Miguel Picazo, Antonio Mercero
Scriptwriters: Juan Farias, Víctor Jorge, Antonio Mercero

Regular cast
The Teacher: Emilio Rodríguez
The Priest: Francisco Vidal
The Mayor: Fernando Cebrián
The Postman: Jesús Guzmán
The Bailiff: Antonio P. Costafreda
The Chemist: María Nevado
Dionisio: Rafael Hernández

Cine de barrio (*Neighbourhood Cinema*, **TVE2 and TVE1 1995– **)

Regular performers
Host: José Manuel Parada (1995–2004)
Pianist: Pablo Sebastián (1995–2000)
Assistant: Eva León (1999–2003)
Host: Carmen Sevilla (2004–)

Works cited

Díaz, Lorenzo. *La televisión en España, 1949–95*. Madrid: Alianza, 1994.
Economist, The. *Pocket World in Figures: 2005 Edition*. London: The Economist/ Profile, 2004.
Heredero, Carlos F. *Las huellas del tiempo: cine español 1951–1961*. Valencia: Filmoteca, 1993.
Llorente, Ángel. *Arte e ideología en el franquismo (1936–1951)*. Madrid: Visor, 1995.
Moix, Terenci. *Suspiros de España: la copla y el cine de nuestro recuerdo*. Intro. Ramón Gubern. Barcelona: Plaza y Janés, 1993.
Palacio, Manuel. *Historia de la televisión en España*. Barcelona: Gedisa, 2001.
Tranche, Rafael R. and Vicente Sánchez-Biosca. *NO-DO: el tiempo y la memoria*. Madrid: Cátedra/Filmoteca Española, 2000.

Electronic sources
Adictosalcine. May 28, 2005. <http://www.adictosalcine.com/ver_pelicula.phtml? cod=8267>

Alcobendas. May 28, 2005. <http://www.alcobendas.org/contenidos_estaticos/datos_basicos_de_alcobendas.htm>.

Culturalia. May 28, 2005. <http://www.culturalianet.com/art/ver.php?art=13926>.

Mercero, Antonio. May 28, 2005. <http://iespana.es/antoniomercero.htm>.

Teacuerdas. May 28, 2005. <http://www.teacuerdas.com/nostalgia-series-cronicas pueblo.htm>.

Santorcaz. May 28, 2005. <http://www8.madrid.org/gema/datsocio/datos136.htm>.

Todocine. May 28, 2005. <http://www.todocine.com/mov/00126923.htm>.

4

The Urban Sitcom: Community, Consumption,
Comedy (*Aquí no hay quien viva*
[*No-one Can Live Here*, 2003–])

From needs to choices

For the period 2000–2005, Spain had the lowest fertility rate in western Europe and the seventh lowest in the world, just ahead of the collapsing demographies of the ex-Soviet republics (*Economist, Pocket World*, 19). The average number of people per household fell to 3.2 (*Economist, Pocket World*, 217). Unsurprisingly the family was in a state of flux. One academic commentator on Spain writes of the "new diversity of . . . modern models" of the family: democratic, single parent, dysfunctional. After the decline of the authoritarian patriarchal family "duty has given way to reciprocal forms of cooperation based on choices as well as needs" (Jordan, 79). According to census data, 65% of households were now nuclear families, 12% single people, 10% single parents with children, 7% extended families, and 4% unrelated people cohabiting (Jordan, 80). What is striking is that elderly people tend to remain in their homes for as long as possible and, unlike in northern Europe, there is little unmarried cohabitation. Family formation is postponed, contributing to the low birth rate.

Demography thus intersects with housing. With home ownership very high, Spain has the lowest proportion of renters in the European Union, at just 20% (Jordan, 112). The great majority, some 84% in urban areas, live in flats or apartments. These homes are relatively small by European standards and have "high levels of noise pollution, lack of light and space [but] far higher levels of contact with neighbours." Surprisingly, perhaps, most Spaniards express satisfaction with their living arrangements, even though commentators see "growing segmentation [and] more widely separated wealthy and impoverished residential zones," previously atypical of Spanish cities.

On November 6, 2002 the *Wall St Journal* noted that over the past twenty years real-estate prices had risen faster in Spain than in any other European country (Vitzthum). While the population density for the nation as a whole was only 80 per square kilometre (comparable to the impoverished states of sub-Saharan Africa), the density of Madrid was, at 21,000 per square kilometre, exceeded only by Tokyo. The *Journal* noted the negative effects of these prices not just on the birth-rate, but also on labour mobility (and thus stubbornly high unemployment) and indebtedness.

It is not clear, however, that population density is socially negative. As early as 1978, Spanish scholars writing on the social structure of their cities identified urbanization itself with density, defined as the enrichment and complication of flow of interpersonal relations (Martín Moreno and de Miguel, 103). The re-densification of Anglo-American cities has become a common goal of town planners and theorists. Richard Rogers, architect of the Pompidou Centre, called in *Cities for a Small Planet* for a sustainable city which would be "diverse [but] also compact . . . focus[ing] and integrat[ing] communities with neighbour-hoods and maximis[ing] proximity" (169). Speaking from the experience of sprawling, low-density London, he argues that citizens must learn to live closer to their neighbours.

Urban redevelopment, such as that proposed by Rogers, is often criticized by academics as socially regressive and culturally superficial. But in the case of Spain or Catalonia, once more, some commentators have contested this attack on renovation as gentrification and privatization. Antonio Sánchez has said of Barcelona's "magic mirror" (the redevelopment of the port area) that it should be read not as "narcissism," but as "the rediscovery of public space and collective identity" (294). He asks hostile scholars to take a holiday from ideological critique.

Students of urban television in the UK and US have often spoken in terms of identity. In *Sensing the City through Television*, a study of five English-language drama series, Peter Billingham addresses identity in the categories of class, ethnicity, gender, and sex, discussing both the representation of the city and "ideological context." Yet, in keeping with the emphasis on density and interpersonal relations identified above, pioneer scholars of Spanish or Catalan urban TV fiction have focused rather on community. Hugh O'Donnell writes that Barcelona-based *telenovelas* (his term) respond critically to the "wide-spread delegitimation in official political discourse of notions of community and solidarity [in favour of] increased consumption, entrepreneurship and [economic] success." Such programmes provide:

> A cultural space where values [of community and solidarity] are not only kept
> alive but even . . . celebrated. They create imagined communities which . . .
> are simultaneously conservative in their melting away of class barriers . . . and
> progressive in their narrative defence of the values of solidarity, mutual
> respect, and sharing and in the openness to and tolerance of difference. (303)

In the context of the "normalization" of the Catalan language, clearly TV fiction will have an especially charged load in the process of community creation. But, as we shall see, the ideological ambivalence claimed by O'Donnell for Barcelona *telenovelas* is also attributed by US media scholars to that most flexible of fictional formats, the sitcom.

In 2005 *The Economist* published a special supplement "A Survey of Consumer Power," arguing that the long-time catch phrase of marketing ("the customer is king") was now true. If consumers "exercise ever more choice"

(16), however, it is increasingly difficult for producers to gain their attention. When asked what they did while they last watched television, US viewers replied that they listened to the radio (9%), read a newspaper (38%), surfed the internet (17%), or spoke on the phone (54%) (9). Unsurprisingly some media scholars, less favourable to consumerist competition, have a more sceptical view of such "choices." In *European Television in the Digital Age*, Stylianos Papathanassopoulos puts forward the commonly held view that the commercialization of media leads inevitably to a decline in quality (18):

> A television culture led by market forces tends towards the maximization of profit and the minimization of financial risk, resulting in imitation, blandness, and recycling . . . European public broadcasters have argued that commercial broadcasters tend to broadcast a high proportion of cheap imported content, particularly in the start-up phase of their activities and to invest less in original productions. (19)

We will see that this reliance on foreign programmes and second-hand content was not reconfirmed by Spanish commercial broadcasting after it became fully established in the 2000s. But Enrique Bustamante, perhaps the best known of Spanish TV scholars, argues nonetheless for the economic precariousness of private television, claiming it has seven inherent problems: the dominance of offer over demand (with consumers only able to choose from what is presented to them) (73); the unpredictability of audience results and of advertising income (74); the inflation of production costs; the difficulty of maintaining a proper cost/benefit relation (75); the length and cost of the economic cycle; and the poor remuneration of independent producers (76). Bustamante backs up these problems supposedly endemic in private television (which, we remember, was introduced in Spain only in 1990) with problems exacerbated by competition between channels. Competition, he claims, accelerates the inflation of costs and the fragmentation of audiences (79); it puts pressure on income (with channels forced to offer discounted tariffs) and adds uncertainty to the advertising market; and it increases the need for capital and the costs required to fulfil new government regulation, itself inspired by concern about the effects of competition (80).

In his discussion of production, Bustamante gives an account of the economic model of what he calls "fiction" (113). He notes the extreme competitiveness of the US model, with thousands of ideas pitched, tens of pilots planned, and most of the tiny number of series to reach the screen failing in the first season. He also sketches the US production process: the centrality of the executive producer to the artistic vision; the swift rotation of directors; the division of labour in scriptwriting (synopses, "Bible," workshops), and the use of teams of writers to cope with an accelerated rhythm of creation (114). Bustamante writes that Europeans have studied the collective lessons of Hollywood but have put up strong resistance to them: their television is based rather on a model of individual authorship derived from a cinematic tradition.

In the preface to the second edition of his best selling book, Bustamante casually dismisses TV content, claiming that he is professionally required to watch new formats and programmes so "toxic" they require vigorous exercise to get out of his system (v). But some British TV scholars are not so hostile to commerce and consumption. In *Seeing Things* John Ellis discusses the development of differentiation in commodities. Since the 1970s, he writes, mass markets for standardized consumer products have given way to a "wider range of differing products and differing versions of the same products [for] consumers who are more discriminating" (63). Commodity production thus "provid[es] people with the means of establishing their distinctiveness from each other rather than their commonality with each other." He goes on:

> [The market] presents consumers with choices, linked to a sense of self and self-worth, where once they had needs, generated by the struggle to survive and live comfortably. (63)

This "increased choice" of media "availability" (perhaps analogous to the choices that have recently replaced duties in Spanish families) was mainly targeted at the new "huge and relatively prosperous urban populations" (64). In the current time of media "plenty," however, the possibilities of choice can become burdensome. "Time famine" and "choice fatigue" were once mitigated by traditional broadcasting, which suspends choice by offering the "fait accompli" of the network schedule (this is Bustamante's dominance of offer over demand) (174). In the 2000s broadcasting still, writes Ellis, has "valuable brands" but they tend to be in "routine or mundane areas of programme making" that converge with everyday life (such as decorating and cooking shows in the UK). Ellis thus predicts that high-cost genres such as drama will "tend to disappear to subscription-based services" (174). It is an economic logic also echoed by Bustamante. The difference is that for Ellis consumerism and commerce are not implacably opposed to community. Rather, the reality-based programming suddenly dominant in schedules is evidence of a certain mode of televisuality that is itself communal: the collective "witness" and "working through" of social and personal issues.

We may now look at a TV genre which seems both particularly vulnerable to economic pressure and particularly sensitive to social change: the situation comedy. Although academic commentators have sometimes stressed the lack of development in the genre and its "stability" in form and content (Mills, 63), brief notices in the English-language trade press chart a number of changes as well as continuities over the past fifteen years. In 1990, *Hollywood Reporter* wrote that American comedy was "in a rut" dominated, unlike the UK, by "family concepts" (November 1: 11). But by 1995, *Spectrum* wrote that British sitcoms were suffering from a lack of good writers and that UK private broadcasters had sacrificed comedy for drama series (Winter: 6). In 1997, *Box* wrote that the British sitcom had "lost its sense of humour just as the Americans had discovered theirs" (April/May: 60). In 1997, *TV World* asked "what makes the most successful comedy exports?" (August/September: 31) while *Broadcasting and Cable International* replied that there was a "rise in local comedy and sit-com shows on a global scale" (October: 52). Yet, according to *TV World* in the same year, even French broadcasters were "adopting similar strategies to the US and UK to create successful international sitcoms" (December: 37). By 1998, *Broadcast* lamented "the fall from favour of the British sitcom . . . out-rated by 70s repeats" (August 21: 14), while *TV World* noted "the absence of good comedy shows in Europe and the US" (October: 63) and *Television Business International* claimed that "crossovers or formats for comedy are not often successful as each culture has a different viewpoint" (October: 51). In the same month, *Sight and Sound*'s TV column noted one attempt by the BBC to learn a production lesson from the US: the first use of a live audience for feedback in a British sitcom (34).

The end of the millennium saw a number of references to the decline of or crisis in the genre (*Television*, December/January 1998–9: 24; *Sight and Sound*, March 1999: 32; *Television*, August/September 1999: 24). Five years later, with the ominous boom in reality programming, the sitcom was newly defined as "scripted comedy" and its "prospects for the future" seemed even more precarious (*Broadcast*, January 23, 2004: 18). Yet the UK launch of *Joey*, a critically unsung spin-off of the urban sitcom *Friends*, could still be the highest-rated programme ever on a national channel (*Broadcast*, February 18, 2005: 10). Clearly "cost-conscious comedy" (*Television*, May 2005: 4) was not yet dead.

It is instructive to compare this industry account of the decade with an academic survey of the US. In her collection *Critiquing the Sitcom*, Joanne Morreale notes that although the 1990s began with ABC's family oriented comedies topping the ratings, soon the genre offered a critique of the "idealized nuclear family" (247) with *The Simpsons* and *Seinfeld* (which began in 1989 and 1990, respectively). NBC aggressively courted the "young, white, urban, unmarried, upscale" audience, with characters often presented within dysfunctional workplace "families" (248). *Will and Grace* (1998) added the first gay protagonist in network sitcom. Cable also sought the "desirable demographic" with shows such as *Sex and the City* (1999): "young, sophisticated, urban viewers, who appreciate parody and complexity of representation but who are potentially lured away from television by new media forms" (249). Repeating the trade press narrative, Morreale writes that as the millennium approached, the sitcom "waned." "Family viewing" was now inconceivable, as in the US "families rarely watched television together" (250).

Morreale traces the rise of the "urban" US sitcom ("with complex characters that faced complicated situations") back to the early 1970s:

> These new sitcoms added elements of drama to the sitcom form. The humour was character-based rather than a consequence of characters facing absurd situations. Moreover, sitcoms became a forum for examining social problems and issues, which were perhaps easier to confront in the context of humour [such as] death, alcoholism, and divorce. . . . Storylines often continued from

show to show and the characters developed over time. The sitcom began to tackle difficult topics and to adopt the serial form previously the domain of the soap opera. (152)

Beyond this historical account, which consistently identifies the "quality demographic" with the urban audience, *Critiquing the Sitcom* discusses familiar social factors in Anglo-American TV studies ("family, gender, class, race, ethnicity" [xi]), seeks to decode ideology ("the way that people think, act, and understand themselves and their relationship to the social order"), and stresses the ambivalence of the genre ("progressive messages are struggled into conservative texts, and vice versa" [xix]).

How does this industrial and critical context map onto Spanish sitcom? Lorenzo Díaz, a practitioner as well as a scholar, is one of the few Spanish commentators to write, however briefly, on comedy as a distinct genre within "fiction." He notes that 1997–8 saw a boom in locally produced series that embraced all national channels (189) and signalled a shift in audience tastes away from quiz or variety shows. The Spanish audience was no longer "amorphous" but was more smart and selective in the face of increased choice (190). He claims that one specialized group of consumers favoured sitcoms with a family setting. Díaz himself had contributed to the teleplays of one top-rated show of the period, *Hostal Royal Manzanares*, starring the veteran and much loved clown of Francoist film comedy Lina Morgan, dubbed by Díaz "the queen of deep Spain" (149). At a time when, as we have seen, the English-language trade press suggested that sitcoms were becoming increasingly local, Díaz also claims that the success of this show, much attacked by critics, was due to its parochial nature: what could be more specific to Spain than the common or garden Madrid guest house in which the show was set? This comedy of manners (*comedia costumbrista*), however coarse it appeared to non-devotees, worked perfectly as long as the familiar, impish Lina remained true to her traditional image: it flopped when producers put a mobile phone in her hand, a fur coat on her back, and a handsome young suitor on her arm.

In spite of this tendency to conservativism (of both form and content), some commentators have vindicated the pleasures of comedy, without appealing to ideological critique as justification for their interest. John Corner has written of the potential of sitcom for expressing a "social dimension," even "social change":

> It would not be exaggerating to say that the pleasures of television comedy have contributed greatly to the formation of nationally specific affective orders and to changes in these. Such orders provide norms for guiding [viewers as to] what is a matter for laughter and what is serious, beyond a joke. These in turn are based on the deeper structures of sentiments and feelings which underpin cultural and social values. . . . the way in which certain themes move into, and out of, the realm of the comic (including public issues such as the portrayal of occupational groups and private issues such as those to do with sexuality) is very much a television-guided process, even if it also

involves television reflecting broader shifts and trends in the culture of
humour. (97)

One notable example of such shifts in the realm of the comic, both public and
private, is the increase in gay and lesbian characters in US shows. This trend
was noted in a 2005 article in *El País*'s weekly supplement, which compares the
American programmes with their few Spanish equivalents, such as Antena 3's
sitcom *Aquí no hay quien viva* (*No-one Can Live Here*, 2003–) and Tele5's
late-night comedy talk show *Crónicas marcianas* (*Martian Chronicles*,
1997–2005). Even here, however, there is proof of the national specificity of
affective orders: the humorous reality make-over show *Queer Eye for the
Straight Guy* flopped when the format was transferred to Spain.

Before turning to a corporate study of Antena 3 (the channel that launched
both *Aquí no hay quien viva* and the Spanish *Queer Eye*), I would like to address
the sometimes overlooked question of narrative structure in television drama,
with special attention to sitcom. In her lecture collection *Storytelling in Film
and TV,* Kristin Thompson argues against academic theories of "flow" and in
favour of "close aesthetic analysis" of television (3). She contends that there is a
"classical television" narrative which shares much with its classical film equivalent, such as consistency of character motivation (22) and linear causality (23).
One technique she had previously identified in film also recurs in the new
medium: the "dangling cause" – "information which leads to no effect or resolution until later in the film" (19). This temporary suspension of a narrative line
is, however, particularly important in television, where plots are consistently
broken up by commercial breaks and gaps between episodes and seasons.
Television exposition, then, is structurally prone to redundancy (31) or
dispersal, intended to keep intermittent or inattentive viewers up to date.

This repetition need not, however, imply a lack of complexity: the typical
twin narratives of sitcom (known by writers as "A plot" and "B plot") are often
"causally connected" (32); and screenwriting manuals recommend there should
be a "cliffhanger" before each ad break (31). In the US, then, one-hour shows
have four acts, each with its own crisis and climax, with half-hour shows
divided into two acts (42), focused on a "turning point" (43). Cable shows on
subscription channels which are free of ads appeal to looser narrative structures.
Sex and the City's "acts" are of varied length, but the turning point is still
signalled by editing: a conspicuous fade, wipe, or dissolve (52). Mafia drama
The Sopranos may have three or four acts, with one or two plot strands complete
in each episode and as many as five or six stretching across episodes (53). Such
multiple story lines, which go back to quality urban dramas of the 1980s such as
Hill Street Blues, give a sense of "density and realism" (57).

The "story arc" across the season gives added complexity (59): "A show's
runner arcs a season's worth of shows like a writer structures a script" (61).
There will be a season opener, a "first act" ending (coinciding with a US
holiday), a midpoint during "sweeps week" (when advertising rates are set) and
a closer which will hope to bring back the audience in the coming autumn. In

such circumstances the redundancy of dispersed exposition is a necessity, although manuals warn that "recap is fraught with hazards" (68). Such formal complexity (both within and across episodes) is of course meant to be invisible and is not generally noticed by the viewer. This, Thompson writes, is why there has been little formal analysis of storytelling in TV (71). We shall see later how a team of writers arc a narrative across a season of *Aquí no hay quien viva*, the most popular Spanish sitcom of the 2000s. But first, returning from the aesthetic to the industrial, I give a brief corporate study of *Aquí no hay quien viva*'s broadcaster Antena 3 and its independent producer Miramón Mendi.

Antena 3/Miramón Mendi: corporate profiles

Who we are

Currently, ANTENA 3 is the first Free TV and Commercial Radio Communications Group, listed on the Spanish Exchange Market. The Company operates in different sectors of activity through, among other companies, ANTENA 3 (TV), ONDA CERO (radio) and MOVIERECORD (advertising in commercial theatres).

Among the shareholders of ANTENA 3 group there are multinational companies from the contents and communications sectors, such as the Planeta, De Agostini and RTL groups, apart from Banco Santander Central Hispano.

ANTENA 3 was incorporated as a company in 1988, and was awarded one of the three Private TV licenses tendered in Spain. The channel became the first private TV offer available to Spanish viewers – its regular broadcasts started on 25th January 1990 – and soon it started its development as one of the references of the audiovisual Spanish market.

Recently, in Spring 2003, the Company started a new phase with the incorporation of the company Kort Geding, owned by the Planeta and De Agostini groups, into its shareholding. The new shareholders appointed a new management team, who immediately implemented a strategic plan, the first objective of which was the flotation of the Group. This materialised on 29th October 2003, when ANTENA 3 group made its market debut in the Madrid Stock Exchange. (Antena 3, "Who we are" [original document in English])

Aun siendo en esencia una productora de televisión, describir nuestro ámbito de influencia empresarial es una tarea difícil de perfilar, dada la diversidad de opciones que se abren constantemente en un mundo del espectáculo cada día más supranacional. Miramón Mendi nace en un principio orientada a satisfacer ciertas necesidades del mercado español como fue la producción de programas de entretenimiento en un entorno de abierta y sana incipiente competencia.

Respondiendo a las nuevas corrientes que se han sucedido a lo largo de nuestros 18 años de existencia profesional, Miramón Mendi ha evolucionado hasta llegar a cubrir campos tan ricos y diversos como: La organización de eventos televisivos puntuales como la Gala de la Hispanidad en Nueva York, Miami y Puerto Rico, Galas del Día del Padre, Día de los Enamorados, Gala de la Primavera, Festival de la OTI 1994, etc.

La promoción, registro y difusión de géneros tradicionales como el Teatro, la Opera y la Zarzuela. La provisión de servicios indispensables para nuestro mercado (luz y sonido profesional, decorados, vestuario, catering, etc.).
Y así como la representación de nuevos y consagrados valores artísticos . . .

(Miramón Mendi)

Although we are basically a TV production company, it is hard to define the limits of our business activities, given the diversity of options constantly opening up in a show business which is increasingly transnational. Miramón Mendi was originally intended to fill gaps in the Spanish market, such as the production of entertainment shows in a newly open and healthily competitive atmosphere.

Responding to the new trends which have taken place in our 18 years of existence, Miramón Mendi has evolved to cover such diverse and varied fields as: the organization of one-off TV events such as the Hispanic Galas in New York, Miami, and Puerto Rico, Galas for Father's Day, Valentine's Day, for Spring and for the OTI [Hispanic Song] Festival in 1994, etc.

The promotion, recording, and screening of traditional genres such as plays, opera, and *zarzuela* [Spanish operetta]. The provision of indispensable resources for our market (professional lighting and sound, sets, wardrobe, catering, etc.).

We also serve as the representatives of both new and established performing stars . . .

On June 18, 2003 *The Economist* published a report on entertainment ("Special Report"). Under the heading "Lights! Camera! No Profits!" it argued that the "biggest failing of the industry" was the "mismanagement of creativity" (11). Executives had become so focused on distribution (new media) that they had neglected content and failed to make products audiences wished to see in any medium. Moreover this increased competition from distributive "windows" had led to soaring costs and the growing power of artists to demand inflated salaries (12). The conflict between industry and aesthetics, habitual in the sector, had thus become newly acute in the first decade of the new millennium.

In Spain broadcasters and content-providers faced particular problems. On November 6, 2004 the heads of national TV channels submitted to electronic interrogation by readers of *El Mundo* ("Los responsables"). Maurizio Carlotti, CEO of Antena 3, Spain's first private channel, defended his company against the charge of "trash TV" (*telebasura*), arguing that each channel has its own "editorial project" and that the public service contribution of private television is in its contribution of "pluralism" and the "chance [for viewers] to choose." He repeated twice that the audience targeted by Antena 3 is a "family" one and stressed the channel's innovative programming: 44 new shows in the last 15 months, including the late-night talk show starring Catalan comic Andreu Buenafuente. If we look back at the turbulent history of Antena 3 revealed by the trade press, however, we can test the hypotheses of Papathanassopoulos and Bustamante sketched earlier, namely that market forces lead to bland or borrowed programming and that competition increases production costs and promotes financial instability.

In February 1989, *Cineinforme* (8–9) interviewed Antena 3's grandly titled "director of international relations," Luis Ezcurra Carrillo, a year before transmission began. He said that the origin and philosophy of the channel was in its successful radio operation, which gave it a base in news. Transferring these skills into TV, the group aimed to imitate the speed and flexibility of US television (he cites CNN as a model) and to avoid the "defects" of European channels: letting some fashionable auteur direct a series of 29 episodes which no-one watches. Antena 3 will have greater respect for the ratings (8). The majority owner was at that time the proprietor of *La Vanguardia*, the conservative Barcelona daily. The executive claims that feature films will not form a great part of programming, with foreign product limited to some 30% of the schedule and (according to legislated quotas) 45% devoted to Spanish and EU content and 15% to in-house production (9). Stressing the break with public television, Ezcurra notes that the channel is attracting job applications from professionals who wish to return to Spain, having worked in Latin America, and is actively discouraging TVE workers. The average age of his personnel is 29.

Two years later *Television Business International* stresses the "different programming philosophies" of the new private networks (December 1990–January 1991: 39). Since the end of monopoly state broadcasting, ratings and share are now taken seriously, as are sponsorship, barter, and counter-programming. TVE is "bid[ding] aggressively for product" and all stations are having swiftly to learn the "techniques of scheduling and marketing to maximize the value of their purchases." By May 1994, *Cineinforme* wrote that Antena 3, promoting itself as the generalist alternative to TVE, had got off to a "shaky start" (9). But with a change of management it now held second place in the ratings and was known for its news: a debate between the leaders of the Socialist and People's Parties had attracted 11 million viewers. As for programming, *Cineinforme* mentions only Antena 3's acquisition of US films and series and its successful workplace sitcoms: *Farmacia de guardia* (*All Night Chemist*, created by veteran Antonio Mercero) and *Lleno por favor* (*Fill It Up*, starring long-time film favourite Alfredo Landa).

The most detailed corporate report is published by the British *Moving Pictures* (January 1995: 51–64) and written by noted film scholar and journalist John Hopewell. In this "broadcasting fairy tale," Hopewell begins by focusing on the channel's audience. After the channel made its debut to the lowest market share of any national station, new management arrived in June 1992 and Antena 3 "powered into domestic production, carved out an upscale, youthful demographic, and by 1994 ran neck-and-neck with TVE1" (51). While the state broadcaster's audience remains bigger, the commercial channel's audience is "better": bigger spending, young (48.7% under 34), and upper to middle class (63.55%). Moreover Antena 3's audience is urban: "22.2% living in towns with a population of 500,000 or more (contrasting with 17% for TVE1)." While previously a mix of earnest news and current affairs and bought-in game shows (such as *Wheel of Fortune*) had turned off audiences and advertisers, the new turnaround came through changes in programming and an emphasis on Spanish production, especially sitcoms (52). Although these comedies sometimes feature old-time movie stars like Landa and Lina Morgan, the concern was also to "mould an upscale demographic" (56). Here feature films were vital, as the channel's high percentage of 15–45-year-olds coincided with the age demographic of those who attended cinemas (62).

Beyond the broadcasting of features (and the ownership of Movierécord, the cinema advertising brand which has long irritated filmgoers in Spain), the group "plung[ed] headlong into the theatrical film industry" (*Screen International*, September 8, 1995: 40). José Manuel Lorenzo, the new Director-General, said that Antena 3 would produce ten feature films in 1995 with a total spend of $10 million. And in 1999 it was the first private channel to sign an agreement with the Spanish federation of audiovisual producers (FAPAE), supporting the local film industry (*Cineinforme*, July–August: 18). This was hardly disinterested, however. A recent law had obliged TV channels to devote 5% of their income to local film and TV production. By 2002 finances remained problematic. Antena 3 won audience but lost money with the rights to the soccer World Cup (*Cineinforme*, July: 108) and it was not surprising that in the same year it broadcast the highest percentage of advertising of any channel (27.06%). Antena 3 continued to complain vigorously about the "unfairness" of competition from TVE, which, uniquely in Europe, was a public service broadcaster both subsidized by the government and bidding aggressively for advertising (Finanzas.com, August 20, 2004).

Moreover, new government regulation, motivated by the fear of a decline in standards through commercial competition, kept on coming. After protocols on programme content (1993), classification for minors (1999), and advertising (2002 and 2003), a new voluntary code to regulate content in relation to children was signed in 2004 ("Código"). This provided for a draconian child-protected zone that extended from 6 am to 10 pm, thus leaving few time-slots free for adults. The classification system was based on that already existing for cinemas, with recommended cut off points at the ages of seven, thirteen, and eighteen; while the four areas of content cited by the criteria were social conduct, violence, conflict, and sex. The specificity of Spain shines through at some points nonetheless: programmes recommended for all ages can include nudity (as long as it is "innocent"), and sex education is prescribed for the under-sevens. Under-eighteens are to be protected from shows that display "intolerant" attitudes in a positive light, as from those that promote "extreme thinness" and sadomasochism (held to be a "degradation of human dignity"). This voluntary code, signed by all free-to-air national stations, is especially important for Antena 3, given its repeated commitment to the elusive "family audience," a claim somewhat undermined by its equally reiterated quest for a "quality, urban demographic."

We can compare the objective narrative of the trade press with Antena 3's own self-depiction in recent annual reports (*Informe anual*, 2001–4), a valuable source for the study of corporate mentality. In 2001 the then Chairman, Luis Blasco, wrote that there had been tremendous competition for both viewers and advertising in a shrinking market (5), whose instability was caused by the "disloyal" competition from the (unnamed) rival public broadcaster (6). In the light of poor financial results, Blasco was reduced to praising the channel as "commercial and familial" (a curious combination), while CEO Ernesto Sáenz de Buruaga claimed Antena 3 as a space in which Spanish society could exercise its "creativity" (11). In spite of the continuing decline in advertising revenue and audience share by generalist channels (20), Antena 3 claimed, citing research by the independent source GECA, to be "the most valued by the public" (25). Amongst its varied offer, the report cites US import *The Simpsons* (said to be intended for children, although it is popular with young adults); a Latin American *telenovela*, *Yo soy Betty la fea* (*I Am Ugly Betty*, targeted at "housewives"); and major feature films ("for men"). The only domestic show highlighted is the workplace crime drama *Policías* (*Police Officers*). It is not surprising, then, that the director of content notes that programming has been "stable" in 2001 (32) and that the only prize cited for the channel is for news (38).

Things are not so different the following year, when Blasco speaks once more of the economic downturn and the costs of digitalization (4). World Cup soccer is a welcome example of event or prestige programming, but the group has required "restructuring" for increased profitability (6). A new logo features a three-colour fan device, hopefully described as "optimistic" (10). Prizes go to animation, quizzes, and news (13), and the only "fiction" mentioned is the ailing dance drama *Un paso adelante* (*A Step Forward*), which has been nursed into a second season (32).

In 2003 a new corporate regime brings yet another logo: a day-glow orange balloon. On the cover a young man (a single parent?) is shown playing on the beach with three young children, a fitting image for a "family" channel which seeks to keep up with the times. The new chairman, José Manuel Lara Bosch cites renewed profitability due to a boom in the advertising market (5). The new CEO, Maurizio Carlotti, claims to have "rationalized" the schedule and "revised" relations with content providers, thus enhancing quality control and reaching an "attractive" target audience (9). Antena 3 is, we are told, now amongst the most profitable companies in the European audiovisual sector, as shown by its recent flotation on the stock market (10). The secret of its success is that it is a "content-factory" (20), with audiences showing "spectacular" growth under the new regime to reach a 19.5% share (25). The channel's dominance on Sunday (said here to be the day of greatest consumption in Spain, although other sources cite Thursday) is due to the "surprise" hit of the year: urban sitcom *Aquí no hay quien viva*, which reaches a 32.00% share, or over five million viewers (30). The only other programmes highlighted are the major movies favoured by male viewers, both Spanish (*Torrente 2*) and North American (*Mission Impossible 2*) and quality drama imports such as *24* (33).

Finally the 2004 report, bathed in incandescent corporate orange, crows over the best financial results in the channel's fifteen-year history and the biggest increase in audience share in Spain (9). The report also stresses the "European" background of the company's executives and investors (14) and the youth of its staff, whose median age is now 36–40 (20). Prizes go once more to cult US imports (*The Simpsons*, *Sex and the City*, *24*) and the only local show rewarded is once more *Aquí no hay quien viva*, as "best series" (30).

Crosscutting between the trade press and the in-house corporate materials we can now see if the general observations of media scholars cited in the previous section of this chapter coincide with the particular case of Spain's first and most popular private TV channel. We have seen that, as Papathanassopoulos suggested, Antena 3 did in its start-up phase rely heavily on imported content, in spite of government quotas for foreign shows and a commitment to serious current affairs. As time went on, however, and bought-in programming failed to deliver an attractive audience, the channel rejected second-hand content and invested heavily in local production, focusing on high-risk feature films and sitcoms. It is thus hard to argue, with Papathanassopoulos, that commercialization led in this case to a decline in quality or that market forces, anxious to maximize profit and minimize risk, resulted in bland or recycled programming.

The same mixed picture emerges in relation to Bustamante's critique of private TV. Antena 3's corporate history, with its frequent regime changes, clearly confirms the structural instability of the Spanish television ecology, in which competition heightens the unpredictability of both costs and benefits. But the inflation of production spend and the uncertainty of advertising revenue (not to mention the burden of complying with mounting regulation) need not result in "toxic" content. Rather, as *The Economist* suggested, consumers are kings, exercising their choice to select rare innovative programmes which can in turn transform the economic prospects of a channel.

The situation is rendered more complex, however, in that the national networks are dependent on independent producers for that vital content. Antena 3 rapidly increased its proportion of indie production from 8% in 1997–98 to 15.1% in 1999–2000 (Bardají and Gómez Amigo, 61). But, given its demographic profile, it would appear most unlikely that its saviour would be the small-scale Miramón Mendi, which in 2000 produced only two shows and 153 hours compared with reality pioneer Gestmusic-Endemol's twenty shows and 1,697 hours (Bardají and Gómez Amigo, 65). Helmed by veteran José Luis Moreno, Miramón Mendi had made no fiction series before *Aquí no hay quien viva* and was notorious for producing the cheesy (or in Spanish, *casposo*: literally "dandruffy") variety shows that appealed to older viewers and featured the senior stars who are also represented by the company. The jewel in its crown is *Noche de fiesta* (*Party Night*), a pot pourri of musical numbers, quizzes, and crudely written sketches, which has long been an unwelcome feature of the down-market Saturday night schedule on TVE1.

What Miramón Mendi brought with it, however, was its state of the art production and post-production facilities (based in studios outside Madrid and including lighting, sets, and wardrobe). It also had valuable international experience, having produced gala events in collaboration with networks in Europe, Latin America, and the US. We can now explore this unusual partnership of network distributor and independent producer with reference to the concept and history of the urban sitcom that saved Antena 3 and became Spain's most popular programme: *Aquí no hay quien viva*.

Aquí no hay quien viva (*No-one Can Live Here*, 2003–): production history

NUEVA SERIE DE ANTENA 3 PARA EL PRIME TIME DEL DOMINGO

El Domingo 7 de septiembre [de 2003] se estrenó la comedia "*AQUÍ NO HAY QUIEN VIVA*," producción de Miramón Mendi para Antena 3 y que narra la vida de una comunidad de vecinos y los problemas que surgen por la convivencia en grupo.

"*Aquí no hay quien viva*" es una tele-comedia ambientada en un edificio de viviendas en el núcleo urbano de una ciudad cualquiera. Sus protagonistas son los vecinos, un grupo de personas tan divertido como heterogéneo.

En estos tiempos de bonanza para este género, se han hecho infinidad de tele-comedias sobre familias y lugares de trabajo diversos, pero no sobre un edificio de viviendas. Este es, desde nuestro punto de vista, uno de los atractivos de esta serie: resaltar cómicamente la problemática de la convivencia en grupo.

"*AQUÍ NO HAY QUIEN VIVA*" pretende lograr la complicidad del espectador de dos formas: por un lado, cualquiera que se siente delante del televisor puede sentirse identificado, ya que todos en mayor o menor medida hemos vivido situaciones curiosas, estresantes o cómicas en nuestras comunidades de vecinos; y en segundo lugar, porque esta tele-comedia, por su estructura, satisface ese componente oculto de voyeur que todos llevamos dentro: "¿Qué estará haciendo el vecino?"

Es, en definitiva, una comedia que explora las miserias humanas del día a día desde un punto de vista original, realista y divertido. ("Aqui")

NEW SERIES FOR ANTENA 3 FOR PRIME TIME SUNDAY

On Sunday September 7 [2003] the sitcom *No-one Can Live Here* was premiered. Produced by Miramón Mendi for Antena 3, it tells the story of a shared apartment building and the problems that arise from living together.

No-one Can Live Here is a sitcom set in a block of flats in the centre of any city. Its stars are the residents, a group of people who are as funny as they are diverse.

At the present time when this genre is so popular, countless sitcoms have been produced about families or workplaces, but not about an apartment building. From our perspective this is one of the most attractive things about the series: it calls attention in a comic way to the problems of living together in a group.

No-one Can Live Here aims to make viewers involved in two ways: first of all, anyone sitting in front of his set can identify with the show, as we have all experienced odd, stressful, and funny situations in our own apartment

buildings; secondly, this sitcom's set-up plays to the hidden voyeuristic tendencies we all have inside: "What can the neighbours be up to?"
To sum up, it is a sitcom which explores the everyday miseries of human life from an original, realistic, and humorous perspective.

In his corporate profile of Antena 3, published for the network's fifth anniversary (*Moving Pictures*, January 1995: 51–64), John Hopewell deals at some length with the sitcom genre. Noting that classic film comedies from the 1960s and 1970s were rating successes, Hopewell reads Antena 3's early "drive into domestic production" as a "continuation" of these popular features (52). The "formula" to these sitcoms, set in the workplace or shared home, is that "they chart an effective social map of Spain, ironizing gently, but consciously, at the typical Spanish character glitches of the types who live around them." They are not cheap to produce, however, given the increasing costs of "above-the-line" creative talent: actors turned into stars by TV "naturally" demand star-fees when renegotiating their contracts. Nor do veterans like Lina Morgan come cheap. Scheduling is also a concern (56). It is more expensive to produce home-grown shows than to buy in US imports, but the former serve to "tie in" and "tie down" viewers. In the 1994–5 season Antena 3 stripped sitcoms every night from 9.30 to 10 pm, thus encouraging comedy fans to stay with the channel's offer. But even successes need "fine-tuning." The main character of *Farmacia de guardia* (the family sitcom which was the channel's greatest hit and inspired the explosion of local production on private TV) was initially provided with an elderly father, who was soon pensioned off in favour of younger cast members.

Six years later the new independent production companies complain, however, of the difficulty of getting new shows on commercial screens. The young creators of a new comedy format (albeit based on the US evergreen *Saturday Night Live*) claim that their show was mishandled by private network Tele5: erratically scheduled and not allowed to find its audience, it was pulled after just three weeks (Colom Esmatges). Moreover it played against TVE 1's strong comedy line up: a sitcom starring the ubiquitous Lina Morgan followed by a "classic" film comedy of the kind that had inspired earlier Antena 3 sitcoms. If networks had recently learned, as *Television Business International* advised, to maximize their revenue through scheduling then it was to the detriment of the independent producers on which they now relied for most of their fiction content.

Aquí no hay quien viva is thus a rare case indeed of an unheralded programme from unknown young creators which unexpectedly established itself as the most popular show in the nation. Yet *Aquí no hay quien viva*'s concept clearly coincides with some social changes we saw earlier. An urban comedy par excellence, *Aquí no hay quien viva* stresses the density, proximity, and sociality still typical, albeit under threat, of Spanish cities. It focuses on six households in a shared apartment building, significantly known in Spanish as a *comunidad* ("community"), drawing its look in part from a well known comic book, *13, rue del Percebe*. The households of the first season are as follows: an unmarried straight couple (failed architect Roberto and posh girl Lucía); two female friends (Alicia, a would-be TV star, and Belén, a waitress in a burger bar); a "consumerist family" (prissy Juan, pushy Paloma, and their children teenage Natalia and young José Miguel); a separated man (Armando) with his mother (Concha) and daughter (only Concha survived into the second season); two elderly sisters, one unmarried (Vicenta) and one abandoned by her husband (Marisa); and a gay couple (lawyer Fernando and journalist Mauri). The picture is completed by the feckless caretaker, Emilio, and manager of the local video store, Paco (Illustrations 10, 11, 12).

The set-up thus stresses urban diversity (of age, class, and sexuality) but also the recent break-down in the patriarchal family. All but one of the households is made up of new elective families, which, however conflictive, are based more on desires than duties, more on choices than needs. This flexibility will also enable characters to move in and out of the building as season follows season. As both Morreale and Corner have suggested, comedy here proves itself to be particularly sensitive to social change, especially in the incorporation for the first time in Spain of two regular gay characters. Treated with some dignity, this couple confirm how new forms of affective structure can move into media visibility. Moreover, the large number of characters points to an ensemble show which, unlike its counterparts in the US, is based more on community than identity. *Aquí no hay quien viva* was planned from the start as a choral comedy. While there were six *Friends*, five *Simpsons*, and four female protagonists in *Golden Girls* and *Sex and the City*, the innovative opening credits of this Spanish sitcom showcase over a dozen "neighbours" with equal billing.

In a lengthy feature in the Christmas 2003 issue of *El Mundo*'s magazine (Rodríguez), Alberto Caballero, one of the thirtyish creators, stresses the uncertainty of their show's production process. The speculative script spent five years in limbo, before Antena 3's then director of content finally read the spec script and approached Miramón Mendi's José Luis Moreno, who confesses that the success of the show is a "mystery" to him. Moreno lives, we are pointedly told, in a 5000-square-metre mansion on the outskirts of Madrid and also happens to be Caballero's uncle. During the property boom of the 1990s Caballero and co-creator Iñaki Ariztimuño did field work, interviewing real-estate agents, administrators, and lawyers and drawing on their own rich experience of renting and sharing apartments around the city. Living together, they say, is the source of "inexhaustible plot lines." But the pair also drew on British and American sitcoms, familiar to Spaniards: *George and Mildred* for the ogre-like landlady; *Married with Children* for the hooligan sensibility; *Golden Girls* for the older female characters, and *Frasier* for the witty dialogue. The production process was also imported from the US, with Caballero serving as script coordinator or "runner" for a team of young writers. *El Mundo* reprints a lengthy extract from the show's "Bible": the psychological profiles of no fewer than seventeen characters. The industrial labour process clearly paid off. By the twelfth week (November 23, 2003) the show had reached a 40% share and a rating of

10. The posh couple, Roberto and Lucía (Daniel Guzmán, María Adánez)

11. The consumerist couple, Juan and Paloma (José Luis Gil and Loles León)

12. The gay couple, Fernando (left) and Mauri (Adrià Collado and Luis Merlo)

8,970,000 viewers. This became the biggest audience of the year for a single episode of Spanish "fiction," beating even the veteran period drama *Cuéntame cómo pasó*. The journalist writes that the Cuesta family (the highly coloured chairman of the association and his wife and kids) are now on first-name terms with the more sober Alcántaras.

   Success brought its problems to the independent producers. According to *El Mundo*, Antena 3 commissioned successively: four initial episodes; a first season of 13; and two holiday specials for Christmas and New Year's Eve, when three of the actors were invited to ring in the New Year in Madrid's Puerta del Sol (as the child in *Cuéntame* had been asked in a previous year). In the second season the length of episodes grew from around 40 minutes (already twice the length of a US sitcom) to 60 minutes (filling, with commercial breaks, an extended one-and-a-half-hour slot). Hence the unusually swift rhythm: each sequence lasts one page (one minute) before jumping to the next flat (the next parallel plot strand). Transitions between the six domestic sets are effected by three communal spaces: the staircase, entrance, and mail boxes. Elsewhere, in an interview with his local paper, Ariztimuño gives more detail on the show's production line, which is as fast as its caffeinated scripts (Oliveira Lizarribar). Two episodes are made in tandem, with shooting and editing for seven days each and then two days on sound and post-production. During this fortnight the writers fine-tune the original gags on set and write the scripts for the next two episodes. It is not clear how the executive producer, who boasts of thirty-five years experience in show business, could help with such newly intensified modes of production. In *El Mundo* Caballero claims that this is the one Spanish show where the writers are in charge.

The nature of *Aquí no hay quien viva* is clearly determined by the unforgiving TV production process, here enhanced by adopted US models of division of labour. Yet, according to *El Mundo*, even Spanish housing administrators are fans of the series, claiming it is a "reflection of Spanish society." Comic fiction, we are told, can barely keep up with reality: one real-life press ad read "Building for sale, with or without residents." The Spanish "buyers' mentality," which sees renters as an "extinct species," is clear in the show's cooperative building of home owners who occasionally sublet.

On the other hand, in contemporary Madrid 130,000 elderly people now live alone, with eighty dying alone each year. Fernando Tejero, who plays the rodent-like caretaker, reports that in real life one old neighbour in his building offered to pay someone to have coffee with her. *El Mundo*'s property correspondent claims that Madrileños live "anonymously" and are in danger of missing their own real-life "series." The article ends by noting that the flat owned by the gay couple, valued in one episode of the series itself at 36 million "old pesetas," would in fact be worth 41 million in Madrid's central barrios of Chueca and Lavapiés.

We can see from this detailed press coverage that *Aquí no hay quien viva* is thus a curious combination of domestic and foreign, traditional and modern. It both harks back to a now endangered sense of community and looks forward to continued rapacious consumerism, focusing on the booming property market. This tension is confirmed in the account of the shoot also given by *El Mundo*: as the ensemble cast of Miramón Mundi's hip urban comedy attempt to tape their special holiday episode they are interrupted by noise from the studio opposite, which is staging the "dandruffy" New Year's Eve gala of variety show *Noche de fiesta*. This is the product differentiation of Ellis's media regime of "availability" with a vengeance: highly diversified production takes place quite literally under the same roof.

We have seen that, *pace* Papathanassopoulos and Bustamante, the competition of commercial television does not necessarily drive down quality but rather can increase demand for good local programming, such as *Aquí no hay quien viva*. The two media scholars were correct, however, in stressing the unpredictability of financial results: Antena 3 had little hope for the innovative *Aquí no hay quien viva* and only picked it up for a full season when it broke through the 25% share barrier. But, in spite of successive management shake outs, Antena 3's durable corporate aims proved to be in tune with their new hit show. The channel claimed from the start a strength in news and current affairs (a concern echoed by this sitcom's avowed topicality) and in feature films (many of the cast were familiar from movie comedies). But Antena 3's pioneering sitcoms are here given a tilt away from the general "family" audience to the specialist "quality" demographic. It is significant that, in spite of its huge audience, the show has always aired at around 10 pm, as the lengthy "child protected" time period comes to an end. As we shall see, *Aquí no hay quien viva*'s plots tend to focus on the four areas of TV content held to be problematic: social behaviour, conflict, sex, and even (comically distanced) violence. The "tolerance" and "dignity" with which the show portrays its diverse urban cast is, however, fully in line with the voluntary code on content only recently signed by Antena 3.

Aquí no hay quien viva's increasingly mainstream success did not save it from the perils of cut-throat competition. In the second season Antena 3 moved it from Sunday to Wednesday, aggressively counterprogamming against Tele5's popular family comedy *Los Serrano*. And the third season began without the show's most popular actress. Loles León, one of Almodóvar's more extravagant *chicas*, had demanded a star-fee the budget conscious producers refused to give. It seems likely that Miramón Mendi's safe profile in traditional shows was essential in first getting an innovative new project on the air. Once it was established, however, *Aquí no hay quien viva* attempted to square the circle of "family" and "quality," to reconcile needs and choices, community and consumption. We can now see how this contradictory cohabitation leaves its trace in the aesthetics of individual episodes and across a season.

Aquí no hay quien viva: the second season

> Aquí, aquí, aquí no hay quien viva,
> aquí no, aquí no.
>
> Todos los días son así
> no podía imaginarlo cuando vine aquí.
> Solo buscaba algo de paz
> me despierto cada día en medio de un huracán.
>
> Aquí, aquí, aquí no hay quien viva,
> aquí no, aquí no.
> Aquí, aquí, aquí no hay quien viva,
> aquí no, aquí no.
>
> La casa sobre mi se derrumba,
> al portero no le puedo encontrar.
> Los vecinos me vigilan y escuchan,
> no aguanto en este lugar.
> Mete en una coctelera,
> un tren, un terremoto y un volcán.
> Y tendrás esta escalera.
>
> Aquí, aquí, aquí no hay quien viva,
> aquí no, aquí no . . .

No-one can live here, here, here
No, not here.

Every day is the same
I couldn't have guessed when I first came.
I was just looking for some peace
And I wake up every day in the middle of a hurricane.

No-one can live here, here, here
No, not here.
No-one can live here, here, here
No, not here.

The house is falling down around my ears,
I can't get hold of the caretaker.
The neighbours are spying and snooping on me
I just can't stand this place.
Put into a blender
A train, an earthquake, and a volcano.
And you'll get this building.

No-one can live here, here, here
No, not here . . .

The lyrics to the theme tune of *Aquí no hay quien viva* suggest, with comic exaggeration, the struggle to survive everyday life in the Spanish city. The song is performed (like all the incidental music) by the significantly named "Vocal Factory." It is a jaunty piece of *a capella* that invokes both African American harmonizing and retro Barbershop stylings. This knowing urban hipness also appears in the show's graphic style, which employs a signature yellow (not so far from Antena 3's corporate orange) with psychedelic lettering and daisy motifs.

In the vertiginous credit sequence the camera descends swiftly from outer space (a satellite whizzes by) to a light-speckled globe (Madrid is prominent). It comes to earth in a generic city and, careering through urban towers, stops short in front of a mustard yellow four-storey building. The walls pull back as in a doll's house to reveal the regular cast lip-synching to the theme tune, straight into the camera. It is a self-conscious beginning which will recur in the frequent knowing gags about TV incorporated into the dense and lengthy scripts. Every episode is knowingly titled after the fairy-tale formula: "Erase . . ." ("Once upon a time there was . . .").

In the final show of series one (December 31, 2003; 3,278,000 rating, 26.7% share), Antena 3 had taken advantage of the fact that New Year's Eve fell on a Wednesday to move their hit show to its new night. They also scheduled it an hour later than normal at 11 pm so it would lead straight into the live broadcast from Madrid's Puerta del Sol in which *Aquí no hay quien viva*'s stars rang in the New Year. It is hardly surprising that this episode should revolve around a staple of the holiday: the grapes traditionally eaten at midnight, which the caretaker's father attempts to sell to the residents for an extortionate price. In this festive setting the gay theme becomes newly prominent. The homosexual couple, now out to all their neighbours after the first season's comic concealments, invite the whole building to a party. The old ladies coo over the men in their "little gay love nest," while pushy housewife Paloma (played by Loles León) is so excited she says she must have taken "a gay pill." The couple fear their enthusiastic neighbours will ask to be fed "gay cheese" (and they've completely run out). Clearly coming out can have disadvantages other than homophobia. Paloma also claims she "could have been a 'chica Almodóvar' " (León has in fact played supporting roles in ¡Átame! [Tie Me Up! Tie Me Down!, 1989] and Hable con ella [Talk to Her, 2002]). In another filmic reference, the caretaker Emilio is lured into participating in a porno shoot in the building, a set up not dissimilar to Torremolinos 73 (2003), a then current feature film starring the same actor, Fernando Tejero.

If this self-conscious parody and complexity of representation were intended to tie up and tie down the desirably urban demographic for Antena 3, the wider success of such a media-literate strategy seemed uncertain. Aquí no hay quien viva's creators were right to fear the new time-slot, in which they were counterprogrammed against Tele5's popular family sitcom Los Serrano. Share fell rapidly in the first few weeks, to rise only in the second half of the season as Emilio's long heralded wedding approached. It seems, then, that the series' runner did indeed know how to "arc" his season across the fourteen episodes, which played from March 31 to June 6, 2004. While occasionally the plots were tied into much-anticipated current events of that spring (notably the marriage of the Crown Prince of Spain), elsewhere the supposed "actuality" of the show was somewhat out of synch: the episode in which the residents elected a new chairman (the Spanish presidente has evident political overtones) did not air until June 9. This was fortunate given the terrorist outrage that coincided with the real elections held some three months earlier. Unlike Tele5's 7 Vidas (a sitcom Aquí no hay quien viva resembles in its urban setting and queer content), Antena 3's prize show makes few party political gags.

As the new season developed the twin themes of community and consumerism came to the fore. In the first episode (March 24, 2004; 6,805,000 rating, 37.1% share) a new family called the Guerras (needed to fill out the now extended running time) are introduced. They have reluctantly downshifted from a house in the suburbs to this inner city apartment building. The nervous New Age mother, Isabel, says that the welcoming committee looks like "something out of a Berlanga film" (the comic ensemble is indeed not dissimilar). The main plot device here is an excess charge required of residents in order to paint their building's crumbling façade ("Isn't beauty on the inside?" asks one miserly old woman). Meanwhile the gay couple split when lawyer Fernando gets a well paid job in London (his lover Mauri's English is limited to "Bush gin tonic parking"); and feckless Emilio accepts a bribe from another man to give up his girlfriend, the mousy Belén (She: "You think our love is worth only 5000 euros?"; He: "You're right. I should have asked for more.") Of the seven or eight crosscut narrative strands in this episode, it is the gay Mauri's plotline which stands out. He is given a rare location sequence at the airport (he has planted metal implements in his lover's luggage to prevent him passing security) and in a unique downbeat scene with no comic sting at the end returns to his now empty flat in silence.

The empty flat (the broken relationship) is a prime example of Thompson's "dangling cause," which can be used to fuel future plot twists. Episodes 2 (March 31, 2004; 6,572,000 rating, 34.0% share) and 3 (April 14, 2004; 6,580,000 rating, 35.1% share) provide Mauri with a succession of substitute objects for his handsome boyfriend: a big black dog ("You said he was a puppy"), a broken down car (sold by Andrés Guerra, the new con-artist resident), and the caretaker's slimy father (who invokes "solidarity with the aged" to get inside the liberal gay man's comfortable home). This third episode is perhaps the most explicit about consumerism. Loles León's housewife is conned into setting up her own business ("Paloma Urban Fashion") and turns her flat into a sweatshop using her elderly neighbours as slave labour. When her dresses fail to sell, the conman who has taken her money (Andrés once more) spouts business jargon: her brand is "elite" and she must take care not to "saturate the market." Rather she should "diversify" into a man's line and fragrances. Claiming, typically, that "things don't exist until they're on TV," Andrés encourages Paloma to slip her bizarre collection, all ostrich feathers and sequins, into a legitimate fashion show. Loles León, resplendent in gold and purple, proclaims herself "the great hope of Spanish fashion."

The line is typical of a vein of self-deprecating national humour that runs through the season. In the fourth episode (April 21, 2004; 5,991,000 rating, 29.3% share), the sex war continues with men and women competing in a basket ball competition. When the caretaker, in an effort to impress his new fiancée Rocío, fails to make a long shot, his lugubrious father tells him he messed up "big time, like a real Spaniard." And subsequent episodes indulge in ironic references to contemporary social problems such as urban violence and street crime. In episode 5 (April 28, 2004; 5,747,000 rating, 28.7% share) an elderly resident is mugged outside the building and the neighbours set up a "citizens' patrol." But when sexy model Alicia is also attacked on the street, all Juan (the "chairman" of the building) can think of doing is to give the mugger his own wallet and watch to make him go away. "Now you see," he shouts after him with self-righteous and illogical impotence, "that crime doesn't pay." In another plotline, reminiscent of Alex de la Iglesia's feature film *La comunidad* (2000), the neighbours fight over a stash of money they have come across. When a crime syndicate kidnaps the caretaker's unpopular father, the residents, already planning their windfall purchases, demand a vote on the matter before agreeing to pay the ransom. Community and consumerism are in constant comic conflict.

Two consecutive episodes juxtapose individualist commerce and collective responsibility. In episode 6 (May 5, 2004; 5,507,000 rating, 27.7% share) the neighbours set up stalls outside the building selling junk on the street. Competition is fierce. When deceitful Andrés pretends to court an elderly resident in order to get a painting for free, she sells it to him instead. Breaking off the feigned romance, she says: "I'll always have the memory." He replies bitterly: "Not to mention the 1000 euros." In the next episode (May 12, 2004; 5,474,000 rating, 27.9% share) the residents stage a hunger strike, claiming the electricity company is at fault for a power surge. Anti-capitalist rhetoric in public ("No corporate excesses!") is juxtaposed with selfish betrayals in private (individuals soon sneak off for salami, leaving their comrades in the lurch). As in episode 8 (May 19, 2004; 5,620,000 rating, 28.9% share), in which residents frantically outbid each other when an empty flat is put up for sale, solidarity is no match for greed. Confirming the Spanish obsession with property ownership, the latter episode also makes extended reference to local laws of inheritance.

The theme of TV itself returns in the next two episodes where wealthy young Lucía first installs a satellite dish without permission (May 26, 2004; 6,188,000 rating, 31.8% share) and then makes a home video of herself having sex with partner Roberto (June 2, 2004; 5,316,000 rating, 30.2% share). In the former episode there is a nice inversion of gendered viewing habits. Macho Roberto becomes hooked on a tacky Latin American *telenovela*, which he charges his neighbours 20 euros to watch (*Aquí no hay quien viva* is always precise about monetary values). The discourse on television here is counterpointed by references to cinema: Roberto spoils Lucía's attempt to watch a well known recent feature film on TV ("Kidman's a ghost and they're all dead") in order to get back to his soap. Meanwhile Mauri and his new lesbian room-mate Bea try to get back together with their respective ex-partners only to find the latter kissing passionately on the sofa (Mauri's ex has become a woman). The couple console each other by saying they can always sell the rights of their story to Almodóvar. The rest of the building waits mesmerized for the cliffhanging climax of the *telenovela*, even neglecting the belated First Communion party Paloma has laid on for her son ("He had a spiritual crisis when he saw [Catholic spokesman] Father Apeles on TV"). When Lucía pulls the plug on the satellite dish at a vital moment, the residents are obliged to pay Paco, the video store guy, 300 euros for a precious taped copy.

In the next episode rabid audiovisual consumerism is also prominent. The male friends (who call themselves "the committee of wise men," parodying the group established to regulate Spanish television) pay a prostitute to initiate geeky Paco into sex by feigning romantic love with him. In order to break the ice the prostitute engages him in discussion on his favourite classic cinema (there is an erudite reference to *Stagecoach* here). Meanwhile the sex video the young couple have made is mistakenly returned to the store in a *Mary Poppins* DVD case, only to be borrowed by the old ladies. Warming to the unexpected "extras" ("This must be the director's cut"), they insist they have the right to 24 hours rental when the reluctant stars ask for their home movie back. Consumerism thus extends to sexual relations, and not just on DVD. In parallel plotlines cynical Andrés encourages the hen-pecked Juan to have an affair ("Marriage is a motorway – sometimes you just have to pull off and fill up at a service station"). Sexy Alicia (whose extreme thinness surely contradicts Antena 3's voluntary code) boasts of how romantic she is, going on long walks with one guy while having meaningless sex with another. Individual choices (in love as in television) take precedence over collective needs.

Confirming Corner's suggestion of televisually-guided social change, the improvisation of new life styles dominates episode 11 (June 9, 2004; 5,376,000 rating, 30.9% share), nominally about the elections for chairman of the residents' association. The lesbian and gay flat-mates (Mauri and Bea) decide to have a child by artificial insemination. Rapid-fire discussion of their new kind of "large family" (two fathers and two mothers) leads to the mock-consumerist conclusive argument: "More presents [for the child] at Christmas!" Bea will later complain passionately about Spain's demographic crisis and reliance on immigrant workers for population growth (she's really just angry that the public health service will not pay for her fertility treatment). Meanwhile the New Age neighbour Isabel has been elected chairwoman and takes away the communal TV aerial: the four hours Spaniards spend watching television could be better spent "relating to one another." A day without television proves so terrible that the old chairman, Juan, is encouraged to mount a coup d'état. He addresses the assembled residents from his tiny balcony, claiming to be working for a "more just, modern, and supportive *comunidad*." His wife Paloma congratulates him: that's the way to manipulate the masses.

The last two new episodes of the season (episode 14 was a clip show of edited highlights) feature that most consumerist of community events, a wedding, in this case between caretaker Emilio and postwoman Rocío. The focus is at first on the dress: the jealous girls have already tried to sabotage the wedding by encouraging Rocío to choose an unattractive gown (good fashion sense is indispensable in the show). Parallel hen and stag nights (June 16, 2004; an impressive 6,490,000 rating and 35.7% share) lead to unexpected reversals. The boys don drag to check up on the girls' visit to a sex club that features male strippers, while the leather-clad dominatrix hired for their own party ends up teaching them her secret recipe for lentils (traditional home cooking par excellence). Sex and domesticity intermingle. At the wedding itself (June 23, 2004; 5,170,000 rating, 35.5% share), the marriage ceremony is crosscut with the queer insemination plot: Bea is now pregnant and Mauri proudly tells his boyfriend, briefly returned from London, "We are going to be fathers." Daringly, the show risks disappointing its fans at the season's climax. The wedding does not take place, when Rocío realizes Emilio still loves his ex, Belén. As if fearing the hostility of the sophisticated (and unmarried) youthful audience to the wedding episode, that time-honoured ratings device, *Aquí no hay quien viva* is unusually explicit here in its stress on modernity and social transformation. Bea notes "the family is changing" and Mauri, in a typical film reference, looks forward to "three gays and a baby." Rarely has the juggling of "quality" and "family" proved more adept.

From these plot synopses it is clear that *Aquí no hay quien viva* draws on the US tradition of urban sitcoms that dates back to the 1970s: it incorporates elements of drama, addresses social issues in its continuing story lines, and, for all its expertly paced farce, is strongly character-based. It is significant that of the excellent ensemble cast, the two who won "best acting" prizes for 2004 were those whose roles permit most pathos: Malena Alterio's Belén and Luis Merlo's Mauri, who are both abandoned by their boyfriends at the start of the season. But while some plot strands are reminiscent of American shows (the artificial insemination story line featured in both *Friends* and *Will and Grace*), the televisual form is distinctly Spanish. The hour-long running time and seventeen regular characters permit far more narrative strands per episode than the A plot/B plot favoured by US network shows. It is also impossible to identify clear "acts" of whatever length, each structured with their own complication and climax. As mentioned earlier, the plot unit is, rather, the short single scene, lasting around one minute. These scenes are linked by swish pans from one window to another or jerky fast-motion shots up the staircase. There is also no consistent use of external establishing shots to signal a return from an advertising break. Indeed Spanish networks reserve the right to go to commercials whenever they please. This, then, is a formal structure looser even than the HBO shows studied by Thompson such as *Sex and the City*, which are free of the rigid requirements of US network scheduling.

While *Aquí no hay quien viva*'s scripts do employ multiple dangling causes, and plot strands are logically connected (with predictably hilarious results), there is little redundant exposition. "Recap" is generally limited to the pre-credit sequence where, typically, the "committee of wise men" reminds characters and viewers of salient plot points from last week and earlier. But in general the show makes some demands on viewers' tolerance for narrative density and complexity. This characteristic is, typically, satirized in the sitcom itself. When gay lawyer Fernando, supposedly absent in London for most of the season, enquires about the climactic wedding of which he was hitherto ignorant, housewife Paloma replies: "Your problem is that you've missed too many episodes!" Paloma's insistence that she is indispensable to the building also seems to echo actress Loles León's much publicized salary negotiations with the producer, which would end unhappily with her character in a coma after falling from a window.

Narrative complexity, prized by the desirable demographic weaned on the speed and flexibility of new media, is complemented by spatial density. The show has an unusually large number of permanent and interconnected sets: the six different flats, the caretaker's home and video store, the entrance hall, staircase (on four floors), and street. Characters not only meet in the liminal, communal spaces but also catch sight of each other through windows that open onto a central patio. Living close indeed to their neighbours (as Richard Rogers recommended), they find that opportunities for voyeurism are constant (as Miramón Mendi's initial concept suggested). There is thus a clear link between social practice (the close *convivencia* of diverse citizens in Madrid) and aesthetic form (the quick-cut encounters of TV farce). It is significant that, in contrast to the Spanish cast, the relatively homogeneous protagonists of *Friends*, *Frasier*, or *Sex and the City* barely know their neighbours.

While *Aquí no hay quien viva* stresses from the start the inconvenience or embarrassment of enforced cohabitation (the crass residents who ask the male couple for "gay cheese") and freely addresses social problems (such as prostitution and street crime), it cannot contemplate the urban solitude and alienation which is also the lot of some elderly Spaniards. It seems that this would endanger another key aspect highlighted by Miramón Mendi's series concept: the "identification" of viewers with the highly coloured and densely populated households. One other issue is also, in Corner's terms, considered improper source material for comedy, or beyond a joke: racism. While everyone comments on the attractiveness and intelligence of the caretaker's fiancée (who is a major character in some ten episodes) no-one appears to notice that she is of African descent. Homosexuality is more easily incorporated into the narrative and the building (lesbian Bea is soon given a privileged slot in the credit sequence) and the social problems of gays are frequently rehearsed. However, the new ethnic diversity of Spanish cities can be addressed through casting but not comfortably articulated in the scripts.

I would suggest, then, that the crazy farce of *Aquí no hay quien viva* offers a certain social map of urban Spain (as Hopewell claimed for earlier Antena 3 comedies). And it is one which is intensely local, but not parochial (several actors are heard speaking excellent English). But what is nationally specific about the affective order displayed in this sitcom would seem to be the uncanny persistence of community even amongst rampant consumerism. Comedy thus serves both to reconcile contradictory social trends and to address itself to multiple and diverse demographics.

TV's magic mirror

The loss of Loles León did not appear to affect *Aquí no hay quien viva*'s continuing success. The ensemble comedy was founded from the start more on community than on individuals. This is clear even from the expert art design. While normally costume serves to differentiate characters from one another, here the look is relatively seamless. Even old maid Vicenta dresses up in day-glow tops with prints of Josephine Baker or Aztec pictograms. While the consumerist family's flat features some floral prints and the gay professionals' home boasts a Rothko reproduction, the saturated colours of the sets are all of a piece and highly reminiscent of the Almodóvar who receives occasional name checks in the scripts.

If individual actors and sets are submerged into a collective cast and studio, then it is not clear that *Aquí no hay quien viva* follows the European tradition of individual authorship in sitcom production. Although the team-written scripts are highly consistent, the show cannot be attributed to the single signature of either its veteran executive producer or its youthful creators. Rather, as I suggested in my study of corporate mentality and production history, the show's sensibility, which is "winning" in both senses of the word, seems due to a process of collective development that extended over a period of years. *Aquí no hay quien viva* thus confirms Alvarado and Buscombe's observation in their pioneering empirical study of television authorship that "the production process [is] of such complexity and involve[s] so many people carrying out specialized functions that it often elude[s] the control of those working on it" (7). Certainly Antena 3, the "family" network whose annual report showed children playing ball on the beach, could not have anticipated that its signature show would focus so heavily on lesbian artificial insemination.

At the time of writing (June 2005), the third season of *Aquí no hay quien viva* is airing from 9.45 to 11.15 on Wednesday nights just before Antena 3's heavily promoted late talk show starring Andreu Buenafuente. This is itself followed by an even later showing of HBO's *Sex and the City* (beginning at 1.30 am). There could be no clearer sign of the persistence of US models (the Spanish girls are almost as graphic in their sex talk as the New Yorkers) even as US programming is shunted to the margins of the Spanish schedule. And, in another distinct cultural difference, *Aquí no hay quien viva* is officially classified as "for all ages" and plays free-to-air in Spanish prime time. Clearly local audiences have no problem with a 12-year-old eavesdropping on very adult dialogue. The intermittent male nudity is no doubt also considered "innocent" and thus in line with current voluntary accords. It was perhaps not such a surprise that the queen of "deep Spain," veteran movie clown Lina Morgan, made a guest appearance on May 20, 2005 as the long lost ex-girlfriend of the caretaker's repellent father.

Aquí no hay quien viva makes no claim to represent reality. But it can be read (like Barcelona's redeveloped port district) as a "magic mirror" that distorts, delights, and provides a focus for urban pride. Certainly it shows that the sitcom, notoriously conservative as a genre, can still give rise to innovations, both temporal and spatial. The lack of laughter track on the Spanish show also implies a very different relationship with the audience from that familiar from US network programming. But if *Aquí no hay quien viva*'s characters, obsessed as they are with money, fashion, and property, reveal that self-worth is now inseparable from consumerist choice, then the show's very title reveals the continuing struggle to survive in a contemporary urban environment. It is a theme that rings true for other European countries: the format was sold to France's M6, which aired a local version under the title *Faîtes comme chez vous (Make Yourself at Home)*.

The decline of the idealized nuclear family is, however, clearly counterbalanced by the show's transparent fondness towards its new elective groupings of friends, lovers, and children. Any critical account of the show thus need not indulge in hostile ideological decoding. *Aquí no hay quien viva*'s finely balanced ambivalences are openly displayed to its widely differentiated audience and clearly engage viewers on a national level. We should be grateful, then, that this assured example of urban witnessing was not banished to a subscription channel and that the Spanish public have been able to indulge communally in its parodic parables of consumerism.

Aquí no hay quien viva (*No-one Can Live Here*, **Antena 3, 2003–)**

Co-creators: Iñaki Ariztimuño, Alberto Caballero
Executive producer: José Luis Moreno
Directors: Alberto Caballero, Laura Caballero
Script editor: Alberto Caballero
Scriptwriters: Alberto Caballero, Laura Caballero, Daniel Deorador, David
   Fernández, David Abajo

Regular cast
Emilio (caretaker): Fernando Tejero
Juan (chairman): José Luis Gil
Paloma (Juan's wife): Loles León
Belén: Malena Alterio
Alicia: Laura Pamplona
Fernando: Adrià Collado
Mauri: Luis Merlo
Lucía: María Adánez
Roberto: Daniel Guzmán

Works cited

"A Survey of Consumer Power." *The Economist* April 2, 2005: 1–16.
Alvarado, Manuel and Ed Buscombe. *Hazell: The Making of a TV Series*. London:
   British Film Institute, 1978.
Bardají, Javier and Santiago Gómez Amigo. *La gestión de la creatividad en
   televisión: El caso de Globo Media*. Pamplona: EUNSA, 2004.
Billingham, Peter. *Sensing the City through Television*. Bristol and Portland, Or.:
   Intellect, 2000.
Bustamante, Enrique. *La televisión económica: financiación, estrategías, y
   mercados*. 2nd edn. Barcelona: Gedisa, 2004.
Colom Esmatges, Ramón. "El cazador de imágenes." *Fotogramas*, April 2001: 262.
Corner, John. *Critical Ideas in Television Studies*. Oxford: Oxford University Press,
   1999.
Díaz, Lorenzo. *Informe sobre la televisión en España 1989–98: la década abomi-
   nable*. Barcelona: Ediciones B, 1999.
Economist, The Pocket World in Figures: 2005 Edition. London: The Economist/
   Profile, 2004.
Ellis, John. *Seeing Things: Television in the Age of Uncertainty*. London: I. B.
   Tauris, 2002.
Jordan, Barry (ed.). *Spanish Culture and Society*. London: Edward Arnold, 2002.
Martín Moreno, Jaime and Amando de Miguel. *La estructura social de las ciudades
   españolas*. Madrid: Centro de Estudios Sociológicos, 1978.
Mills, Brett. "Comedy Vérité: Contemporary Sitcom Form." *Screen*, 45 (2004):
   63–78.

Morreale, Joanne (ed.). *Critiquing the Sitcom: A Reader*. Syracuse: Syracuse University Press, 2003.

O'Donnell, Hugh, "Media Pleasures: Reading the Telenovela." *Contemporary Spanish Cultural Studies*. Barry Jordan and Rikki Morgan-Tamosunas (eds). London: Routledge, 2000, pp. 295–303.

Papathanassopoulos, Stylianos. *European Television in the Digital Age: Issues, Dynamics, and Realities*. Cambridge and Oxford: Polity, 2002.

Pino, Javier del. "Ponga un gay en su tele." *El País: Semanal*, March 24, 2005: 25–31.

Rogers, Richard. *Cities for a Small Planet*. London: Faber and Faber, 1997.

Sánchez, Antonio. "Barcelona's Magic Mirror: Narcissism or the Rediscovery of Public Space and Collective Identity." In *Constructing Identity in Twentieth-Century Spain*. Jo Labanyi (ed.). Oxford: Oxford University Press, 2002, pp. 294–310.

"Special Report: The Entertainment Industry." *The Economist*, January 18, 2003: 11–12, 75–7.

Thompson, Kristin. *Storytelling in Film and TV*. Cambridge, MA: Harvard University Press, 2003.

Trade journals (1989–2005)

Box
Broadcast
Broadcasting and Cable International
Cineinforme
Hollywood Reporter
Moving Pictures
Screen International
Sight and Sound [TV column]
Spectrum
Television
Television Business International
TV World

Electronic sources

Antena 3. "Who We Are." June 6, 2005. <http://www.antena3.com/a3tv_2004/corporativa.htm>.

———. *Informe anual*. 2001–4. pdf. June 6, 2005. Accessed at: <http://www.antena3.com/a3tv_2004/accionistas.htm>.

"Aquí." 6 June 2005. <http://www.miramonmendi.com/aquinohay/aquinohay.htm>.

"Código." "Código de autorregulación sobre contenidos televisivos e infancia." June 6, 2005. <www.ceapa.es/zip/AutoRegulacionTV.pdf>.

Finanzas.com. "Antena 3 y Tele5 enfrentadas a TVE por el dinero televisivo." August 20, 2004; June 6, 2005. <http://finanzas.com/id.7811056/noticias/noticia.htm/>.

Miramón Mendi. June 6, 2005. <http://www.miramonmendi.com/quienessomos.htm>.

"Los responsables." "Los responsables de TVE, Antena 3 y Telecinco sometidos al 'examen' de los lectores." *El Mundo.* November 6, 2004; June 6, 2005. <http://www.elmundo.es/elmundo/2004/11/05/comunicacion/1099660333.html>.

Oliveira Lizarribar, A. "Todo el mundo tiene un vecino que le recuerda a alguno de los personajes de la serie." *Diario de Noticias* March 24, 2004; June 6, 2005. <http://www.noticiasdenavarra.com/ediciones/20040324/television/d24tve0104. php>.

Rodríguez, Juan Carlos. "La psicología navideña de la comunidad más famosa de Espana." *El Mundo,* December 14, 2003. June 6, 2005. <www.el-mundo.es/magazine/2003/220/1071230044.html>.

Vitzthum, Carlta. "Real-Estate Prices Continue their Unabated Rise in Spain." *Wall St Journal* 6 November 6, 2002. November 8, 2002. <http://online.wsj.com/article_email/0,,SB1036525749152507508,00.html>.

5

Telebasura: Trash, Talk, and Reality (*Crónicas marcianas* [*Martian Chronicles*], 1997–2005)

Take 1: When critics attack

In February 2005, La Cubana, perhaps Spain's most popular performance company, brought their new show from Barcelona to Madrid's large, central Teatro Gran Via 66. The logo for *Mamá quiero ser famoso* (a title translated by the group themselves as *Mummy, I wanna be famous*) was of a formally dressed mannequin smiling grimly, his head encased in an old-fashioned TV set. Day-glow colours radiate from the screen. The premise of the multimedia spectacle is that a UK TV company has brought a talent show to Spain. According to the blond-wigged and heavily-accented host, this is the country that has the greatest raw material in Europe, as so many celebrities have been manufactured out of nothing. On entering the theatre the audience, made to play the part of would-be TV stars, is required to sign a mock contract giving away all rights to the fictional company. Any disputes will be settled by the British legal authorities.

Interspersed with audience participation and supported by pre-recorded video footage projected on giant screens, the nine actors of the company run through a dizzying array of skits: the "ordinary family" who are literally weighed down by their brief celebrity (they stagger on stage carrying huge TV sets); the trio of Catalan nuns who have become successful rock music producers and strum ear-splitting electric guitars; a blowsy Andalusian *folklórica*, nicknamed "La churrera de España" ("the fritter seller of Spain," based on gossip favourite Isabel Pantoja, "la viuda de España" ["the widow of Spain"]), who shot to fame after an unscheduled, but affecting, performance of grief over the dead body of Franco; and the little girl forced to sing for the cameras from her hospital bed, as nurses remove bloody swabs from under her sheets. In one running gag, an inoffensive middle-aged accordion duo are repeatedly bumped off the air, only to be broadcast briefly at the end when they are obliged to perform naked. Finally the pretend TV show, whose fluctuating "ratings" are announced minute by minute, is cancelled and replaced by a quick-cut montage of real-life video violence.

There are multiple ironies here. The parasociality of TV is replaced by the genuine sociality of theatre, much intensified by La Cubana's meta-theatrical incorporation of the audience into its parodic variety show. Reality television, itself notoriously inauthentic, is thus self-consciously re-enacted by skilled actors. Where previously La Cubana had taken the distant icons of cinema as the butt of its satire (in *Cegada de amor* [*Blinded by Love*], a parody of Francoist child stars and Almodóvar), here they move the notoriously domestic and tawdry medium of television into the specialized, and indeed costly, space of live theatre. Moreover, as Jordi Milán, the deviser and director of the sophis-ticated spectacle, acknowledges in his programme notes, it is hard to parody something which is already so extreme: reality surpasses fiction (La Cubana). And even the kitschy satirists of La Cubana are led to moralize on this particular topic. The moral of the show is that Spaniards get the TV they deserve.

Much of Milán's material must have felt familiar to Madrid audiences. Since the early 1990s there has been an intense debate around *telebasura* or "trash TV," which focuses on genres such as the reality and talk shows spoofed by La Cubana. The debate peaked perhaps with the March 2004 elections, in which both main parties made bitter attacks on television. By the time *Mamá . . .* came to the capital the Socialist government had already proposed laws aimed at controlling the scheduling and content of public and private channels. *Telebasura*, it would appear, would be legislated out of existence.

The consensus on *telebasura* seems overwhelming, on both Left and Right. And the intensity of the debate seems greater than analogous controversies on "dumbing down" or "moral values" in the UK and US. Yet the definition of *telebasura* has proved elusive. In this chapter I argue that the *telebasura* debate is important because it links politics, ethics, and aesthetics; because it is a focus for anxieties around national identity and society; and because it embraces multiple institutions beyond the electronic media: government, the press, the academy, and audiences. After charting the critiques of the genre from these sources, I go on to address the lesser-known defences of recent televisual trends from Spanish industry practitioners and foreign media academics. It is not the least of the paradoxes of *telebasura* that the same shows attacked by the print media for embodying that ill-defined category are praised by the audiovisual industry for their innovative formats and are enjoyed by audiences that fulfil the criteria for the sought after "quality" demographic (young, educated, and urban). My case study will be the long-running late night talk show *Crónicas marcianas*, which is abused by journalists as trash and festooned by profes-sionals with prizes. *Crónicas* is produced by independent Gestmusic-Endemol, a Barcelona-based Catalan-Dutch entity also notorious for *Gran hermano*, the Spanish version of the reality show franchise *Big Brother*. Both shows are screened by private network Tele5.

Manuel Palacio is the most convincing defender of recent Spanish television and the fullest chronicler of press hostility to the small screen. Yet even he speaks of the "years of lead" (171) in the first half of the 1990s after the belated introduction of commercial television. Defining the "phantom" of *telebasura* pragmatically as those shows which produce "social alarm" in the press and in moralists of all stripes, Palacio reminds readers that as early as 1994, dailies *El Mundo* and *El País* had written of "a year in the rubbish tip" and "television: the enemy within?"; and in 1995 a special Senate committee on television content had reported, proposing the setting up of a Higher Council of Audiovisual Media, a suggestion which would not be acted on until a decade later (174). Palacio notes dryly where the priorities and sympathies of the Senators lay: the bishop of Badajoz, chairman of the Church's media group, was invited to address the committee before the Director-Generals of the television networks had done so.

Skating lightly over half-forgotten shows that exploited *morbo* (morbid curiosity and ghoulish delight) or sex-appeal for briefly increased ratings, Palacio focuses on two more serious factual controversies, which he calls "horror on television" (174): a report by once respected news magazine *Informe semanal* (*Weekly Report*) on a vendetta-style mass murder in rural Badajoz (September 1, 1990); and a live broadcast from talk show *De tú a tú* (*On First Name Terms*) on a similar case in which three young girls were killed in a Valencian village (January 28, 1993). In both shows vulnerable relatives and friends of the victims are provoked to incendiary actions or comments (a father flashes a knife he will use to avenge his daughters' deaths; a brother vows to "catch and kill" his sister's murderer) and are framed by a "mise-en-scène of grief" (the camera shoots a mourning family silhouetted against the setting sun; or moves in, twice, for close ups of a dead child at a wake [176–7]). What is newly at stake here, then, is the complicity of the media with the events they claim to report and the unprecedented blurring of fact and fiction.

There seems little doubt that press use of the term *telebasura* much increased over the following decade. A search of the web archive of *El Mundo* (an independent daily less viscerally hostile to television than the Socialist-supporting *El País*), made on December 15, 2004, reveals that of 25 articles that receive the highest index of relevance (97%), the frequency is one a year from 1998 to 2001, three a year in 2002–3, and no fewer than fifteen in 2004, mostly clustered around the end of the year. The great majority of these last articles are news reports on continuing attempts at government regulation. Thus José María Aznar, then President of the Rightist government, had attacked the broadcasters and producers he held responsible for *telebasura* (May 29, 2003), while "experts" demanded a General Law on Television to require public networks to show "quality programming" and end TV trash (January 6, 2004).

The new Socialist President José Luis Rodríguez Zapatero soon met with "the People's Ombudsman" and "the Children's Ombudsman" ("el Defensor del Pueblo," "el Defensor del Menor") to discuss the banning of *telebasura* during the (as yet undefined) "children's time period" (September 9, 2004). The latter duly declared himself "satisfied" with the meeting, as were groups described as "associations of viewers, consumers, and defenders of children" (October 25, 2004). The same day it was announced that after a grace period networks would be fined for broadcasting *telebasura* between 6 am and 10 pm. Just four days later the government met representatives of public and private channels to agree voluntary regulation on the matter. The verdict was mixed: while viewers' associations had been sceptical and demanded stronger government intervention

116 PAUL JULIAN SMITH

(October 28, 2004), two months later one commentator wrote optimistically "*telebasura* is dead" (December 10, 2004).

Less commonly, *El Mundo* reported TV professionals' attempts to defend themselves. Javier Sardà, presenter of *Crónicas marcianas*, vigorously refuted accusations of *telebasura* made by a listings magazine owned by the same media group that broadcast his show (July 15, 2003). Sardà's boss, the Tele5 Director-General, also claimed there was much "hypocrisy" and "demagoguery" around the *telebasura* "phenomenon" and that most programmes broadcast by the networks had "a high level of quality" (October 20, 2004). Finally representatives of the national networks responded to questions submitted to them by email from concerned readers of *El Mundo* (November 26, 2004). The CEOs of Antena 3 and Tele5 (both Italian nationals), quizzed on *telebasura* (the new head of public television was spared), replied that they were conscious of the legal and ethical limits of broadcasting; did not fear that a country that had relatively recently won its freedom was drifting towards authoritarianism and censorship; and defended the "distinct editorial profile" of each station.

While news reporting was relatively dispassionate, albeit consistently appealing to a term (*telebasura*) which is nowhere defined, opinion pieces showed that subjective dispositions are inseparable from objective positions. Javier Pérez de Albéniz (pen name "El Descifrador" or "The Decoder"), *El Mundo*'s mordant TV commentator, dedicated almost every column in this period to *telebasura*. Thus, in its name he attacks new cultural programming (the PSOE's "puppet" Director-General of TVE has devised a terribly dull book show, scheduled late at night on the minority channel [November 9, 2004]) and new imports of popular formats (the Spanish version of *Queer Eye for the Straight Guy* on Antena 3 reinforces the "social disintegration" typical of trash TV [December 13, 2004]). Pérez de Albéniz returns no less than three times to a musical talent show for would-be child stars, inappropriately scheduled from 10 pm to 1 am and allegedly promoting paedophilia (November 19, 21, 29, 2004).

In Pérez de Albéniz's usage "telebasura" is a term so elastic as to be analytically meaningless, embracing public and private channels, new and old formats, and content and advertising (commercials for violent or gender-stereotyped toys are, we are told, the clearest example of "our daily *telebasura*" [October 26, 2004]). Moreover "The Decoder" is not averse to self-contradiction, warning on one occasion that the anti-trash "crusade," which he has done so much to support, will have pernicious effects: there is a thin line between "control of content" and "manipulation, prudishness, stupidity, and censorship" (November 4, 2004). The motive of this warning is TVE's cancellation of a Saturday afternoon screening of *La buena estrella* ("The Lucky Star" [1997]), an award-winning recent feature film, even though the public broadcaster went ahead, during the same "child-protected" period, with a showing of *La mujer perdida* (*The Immoral Woman* 1966), a superannuated Sara Montiel vehicle backed up by a "report" on a drag queen who specializes in impersonating the famously camp icon.

Pérez de Albéniz's reverent references to French cultural programming (Bernard Pivot's long-running book discussion shows) and sociological theory (Bourdieu on "masculine domination," cited obscurely to damn *Queer Eye*) show that one purpose of his media "decoding" is to protect and promote the distinction of elite print commentary at the expense of popular television. It is a strategy long employed by European journalists, who also choose to focus on low-status TV programmes to the exclusion of "quality" content. In the 1980s Clive James and Serge Daney pioneered elite condescension to television in the national newspapers of the UK and France respectively. Their columns were collected in book form as *The Crystal Bucket* and *Le Salaire du zappeur* (a title punning on "the wages of sin"). In Spain, respected veteran Eduardo Haro Tecglen has long used his "Visto/Oído" (*Seen and Heard*) column in *El País*, ostensibly a broadcasting review, as a vehicle for his unrepentantly old Leftist political commentaries, often with minimal reference and relevance to TV and radio.

It is striking how often in my corpus of articles from *El Mundo* practitioners of other media use TV in general and *telebasura* in particular to stake out a place of distinction for themselves. Typically claims are hyperbolic. The academic director of the Instituto Cervantes blames *telebasura* for the "fact" that "Spain is one of the countries where Castilian is worst spoken" (November 17, 2004); the President of the Press Association (FAPE) wishes to "define the profession clearly and separate it from *telebasura*" (November 1, 2004); a media professor from Madrid's Carlos III University promotes his latest book by voicing "worries" about the effects of television on teenagers (October 30, 2004); a philosopher attacks the supposed effects of *telebasura* on democracy (February 29, 2002); and respected film actor Jordi Mollà bases the plot of his first feature film as director on "fanaticism, guts, and *telebasura*" (February 26, 2003). One journalist, publicizing his new novel, went so far as to say that the victims of war in the former Yugoslavia are as nothing compared with those whose lives are destroyed by reality shows (June 6, 1999).

The most sustained attempt to distinguish between legitimate journalism and illegitimate television is a monograph by Carlos Elías Pérez (2004), a professor of journalism in Madrid's Universidad Carlos III. Elías promises the reader in successive chapters a definition, a brief history, and a "typology" of *telebasura*, before addressing the specific genre of "talk shows" (the name is given in English) and the relation between sensationalism in print and on TV. Following philosopher Gustavo Bueno he distinguishes between "fabricated" and "revealed" *telebasura* (based on the dubious distinction between whether programmes were intended or not by their producers to be trash) (19); revisits notorious news reports; decries the decline of serious journalists such as Sardà into *Crónicas marcianas* (34); and distinguishes between reality shows, docu-shows, talk shows, and celebrity gossip programmes (*crónicas rosa*) (45). For Elías the greatest sin of the talk shows is their undermining of journalistic authority: he professes shock at the way in which "true experts" on a given topic are juxtaposed with "false experts" (unqualified in the area), and even "professional guests" who may well have invented their colourful contributions to the debate (52–7). Elías sketches two cases of the degeneration of politics into trash TV (scandals surrounding local government officials in Marbella and Madrid played out on the small screen) (69–79). To his credit, however, he acknowledges that sensationalism has a lengthy history in Spanish newspapers: *Crónicas marcianas* was anticipated by nineteenth-century scandal sheets such as *El Heraldo de Madrid* (93); and modern journalists receive wholly inadequate professional training (143–70). Straying into the hyperbole and self-importance so characteristic of the *telebasura* debate, however, he claims that a doctor's mistake will affect only one person; a journalist's will affect thousands and could even threaten the stability of the state (170).

Elías thus has no hesitation in linking politics and ethics to trash TV aesthetics (most especially in the dangerously fluid format of the talk show) and in placing television at the heart of anxieties around the changing nature of Spanish identity and society. He takes it for granted that the government, press, and academy should join together to defend vulnerable audiences, whom he compares to children mesmerized by the unsuitable afternoon gossip shows that have taken the place of *Sesame Street*. Spaniards under twenty, he writes, have been subjected to an "intellectual lobotomy", which he blames on the lack of state control of broadcasting (80). However, Elías provides no empirical evidence for this supposed effect of television. And if he attributes huge social and political importance to *telebasura* he is unable to define it. He contradicts the contention of Josep Maria Mainat, Gestmusic CEO and executive producer of *Crónicas marcianas*, that "*telebasura* does not exist," by simply citing an opposing opinion from the then President of the Spanish Government (11); and although he notes Gustavo Bueno's claim that the term *telebasura* is untenable because it is defined only by subjective value judgements (18), he goes on to indulge in just such circular arguments himself. Lacking a theory of ethics, Elías can only find television, the enemy within, wanting when set against the criteria to which he attempts, vainly, to hold his own profession of print media: the informed specialization and disinterested commentary of "true experts."

A theoretical framework is provided by an important collection of essays on media ethics edited in the same year by two moral philosophers, Jesús Conill and Vicent Gozálvez (2004). In their introduction they also make hyperbolic claims (the power of the media may lead to "mental slavery") but propose the antidote of "training" in citizenship for both producers and consumers (9). Adela Cortina advocates "active citizenship in a media society," arguing that the role of the democratic media is to increase citizens' freedom, permit the free expression of opinions, and promote "rational public opinion." This last is founded not on an emotional "multitude" or a self-interested "mass" but on an authentic "public" or "audience" (*público*) (20–2). Almost uniquely in the *telebasura* debate, she also acknowledges that "entertainment" is a legitimate goal of the media: man is as much *homo ludens* as *homo faber* and elite scorn for *la caja tonta* ("the stupid box") is misplaced (23).

In the same volume, Victoria Camps, scourge of *telebasura*, continues the ethical exploration of "public opinion, freedom of expression, and rights to information." Citing John Stewart Mill, she argues that personal freedom must be limited by the harm it causes others and the provisions of the Spanish Constitution, namely the rights to "honour," "privacy" [*intimidad*], and "one's own image" and "the protection of children" (34–5). Camps acknowledges that the balance is a fine one, especially since many individuals have now chosen to sell their private lives in exchange for public fame (37). And she is pessimistic about the possibility of the electronic media expanding democratic participation, citing US studies that suggest the media do not reflect but rather construct public opinion and consent (42, 44). The peculiar characteristics of the audiovisual media, namely "speed" and "spectacle," are serious barriers to what Kant called "the public use of reason" (46, 49).

Camps's broad-brush technological determinism (she mentions no audiovisual product by name) is contradicted to some extent by Vicent Gozálvez's "comparative ethical analysis of the media," which clearly distinguishes between TV, cinema, and internet. Gozálvez also counters some of the most pervasive attacks on television, shared by almost all academic and journalistic commentators: we should not confuse one type of programming (such as the "spectacular") with the whole "universe" of TV; the viewer is neither absolutely "sovereign" nor wholly "manipulated"; and the audiovisual "explosion" can lead to "inductively cultivated dignity," even in the "presentation of life stories" (198). Indeed, argues Gozálvez, the "moral and evaluative perplexity" produced by TV's sheer variety of content may be more "productive" than a "monolithic morality" (199). It is a dissenting view that would be tested to the limit by Camps's participation in the so-called "Committee of Wise Men" (*Comité de sabios*) which was to report on state regulation of television in February 2005.

Take 2: Index appeal

MANIFIESTO CONTRA LA TELEBASURA

1. El término "telebasura" viene dando nombre, desde la pasada década, a una forma de hacer televisión caracterizada por explotar el morbo, el sensacionalismo y el escándalo como palancas de atracción de la audiencia.

La telebasura se define por los asuntos que aborda, por los personajes que exhibe y coloca en primer plano, y, sobre todo, por el enfoque distorsionado al que recurre para tratar dichos asuntos y personajes.

2. Los promotores de la telebasura, en su búsqueda de un "mínimo común denominador" capaz de concitar grandes masas de espectadores ante la pantalla, utilizan cualquier tema de interés humano, cualquier acontecimiento

político o social como mera excusa para desplegar lo que consideran elementos básicos de atracción de la audiencia: sexo, violencia, sensiblería, humor grueso, superstición, en muchos casos de forma sucesiva y recurrente dentro del mismo programa.

Bajo una apariencia hipócrita de preocupación y denuncia, los programas de telebasura se regodean con el sufrimiento; con la muestra mas sórdida de la condición humana; con la exhibición gratuita de sentimientos y comportamientos íntimos. Desencadenan una dinámica en la que el circense "más difícil todavía" anuncia una espiral sin fin para sorprender al espectador.

3. La telebasura, cuenta, también, con una serie de ingredientes básicos que la convierten en un factor de aculturización y desinformación, así como en un obstáculo para el desarrollo de una opinión publica libre y fundamentada:

– El reduccionismo, con explicaciones simplistas de los asuntos mas complejos, fácilmente comprensibles, pero parciales o interesadas. Una variante de este reduccionismo es el gusto por las teorías conspiratorias de no se sabe qué poderes ocultos, que en muchos casos sirven de coartada a determinados personajes y grupos de presión en su labor de intoxicación.

– La demagogia, que suele presentar todas las opiniones como equivalentes por sí mismas, independientemente de los conocimientos sobre los que se sustentan o de sus fundamentos éticos. A ello contribuye la realización de supuestos debates y encuestas, que no son sino simulacros de los verdaderos debates y encuestas, y que lejos de arrojar luz sobre los problemas contribuyen a consolidar la idea del "todo vale."

También la demagogia cuenta con una variante: el despliegue de mensajes esotéricos, milagreros y paranormales, presentados de forma acrítica y en el mismo plano de realidad que los argumentos científicos.

– El desprecio por derechos fundamentales como el honor, la intimidad, el respeto, la veracidad o la presunción de inocencia, cuya conculcación no puede defenderse en ningún caso apelando a la libertad de expresión.

Este desprecio desemboca en la realización de "juicios paralelos"; en el abuso del amarillismo y el escándalo; en la presentación de testimonios supuestamente verdaderos pero que en realidad provienen de "invitados profesionales." Y, por supuesto, en el apoteosis de una televisión de la trivialidad, basada en el protagonismo de los personajes del mundo *rosa y gualda*, cuyas nimiedades y conflictos sentimentales, tratados desde el más descarado amarillismo, son otros de los ingredientes de esta infecta salsa. El problema es todavía más sangrante cuando este tipo de contenidos se difunden a través de las televisiones publicas, cuya obligación moral y legal es suministrar productos, ética y culturalmente, solventes.

4. La telebasura no ha inventado nada: el halago fácil al espectador, el gusto por el sensacionalismo, vienen de muy antiguo. Pero en la actualidad, la enorme influencia social de los medios de comunicación de masas agranda de forma exponencial los efectos negativos de este tipo de mensajes.

– La telebasura se encuentra hoy en un momento ascendente de su ciclo vital. Es como un cáncer, cuya metástasis tiende a invadirlo todo, o quizás como un virus informático, que contamina lo que toca y acaba por impedir el mantenimiento o la aparición en las parrillas de otros modelos de información más respetuosos con la verdad y con el interés social.

5. Ha llegado el momento de que todos los agentes implicados en la actividad televisiva tomen conciencia de su responsabilidad ante la telebasura, que por supuesto varia en importancia según la capacidad de cada uno de condicionar las reglas del mercado.

Responsabilidad, por tanto de los Poderes Públicos, de las cadenas, de los anunciantes. Responsabilidad de los programadores y de los profesionales. Y responsabilidad, también, del ciudadano, que aun sin dejarse engañar por la falacia del "espectador soberano" que por su mero dominio del mando tiene la capacidad de modelar la oferta, debe saber que su decisión de ver un programa no esta exenta de consecuencias, ni para su propia dignidad ni para el propio mercado televisivo.

En la televisión nos enfrentamos con un fenómeno social complejo articulado en grandes compañías de cuya objetividad es lícito discrepar. Detrás de los medios de comunicación existen intereses, poderes y modelos sociales e ideológicos. Por tanto, cuestionar su objetividad y preguntarse el porqué de determinadas insistencias en un tema mientras se ignoran otros, es una forma de empezar a comprender críticamente los mensajes televisivos.

6. Por todo lo anterior, los abajo firmantes queremos manifestar nuestro rechazo y preocupación ante la telebasura y exigimos, como garantía de control social en una sociedad democrática, tanto la elaboración de un código ético de regulación de los contenidos televisivos como la constitución de un Consejo Superior de los Medios Audiovisuales, en los términos en los que fue aprobado por la mayoría de los grupos parlamentarios en la anterior legislatura.

PLATAFORMA POR UNA TELEVISIÓN DE CALIDAD
Asociación de Usuarios de la Comunicación, Unión General de Trabajadores, Comisiones Obreras, Confederación Española de Madres y Padres de Alumnos, Unión de Consumidores de España, Confederación de Asociaciones de Vecinos de España. (Plataforma)

Manifesto against *Telebasura*

1. The term *telebasura* has been used for the past decade to denote a form of television characterized by the exploitation of morbid curiosity, sensationalism, and scandal as means of attracting an audience.

Telebasura is defined by the subjects it treats, by the people it features and focuses on, and, above all, by the distorted perspective it uses to treat these themes and people.

2. The promoters of *telebasura*, in their search for the "lowest common denominator" able to pull in great numbers of viewers, exploit any topic of human interest and any political or social event as an excuse to indulge in what they believe are the basic ways to attract an audience: sex, violence, sentimentality, and coarse humour, often all of them combined in the same programme.

Hypocritically feigning concern and critique, these programmes revel in suffering, showing the most sordid side of human life and the gratuitous display of intimate feelings and behaviour. They set up a spiral of ever increasing excess intended to take viewers unawares.

3. *Telebasura* also appeals to a number of basic ingredients which make it a vehicle for brainwashing and disinformation, as well as an obstacle for the development of a free and well informed public opinion:

– Reductionism, with simplistic explanations of complex matters, making them easily understood but partial and biased. A variant of reductionism is the taste for conspiracy theories concerning shadowy forces, which often serve as an alibi for specific people and pressure groups who are trying to indoctrinate the public.

– Demagoguery, which presents all opinions as equal, without paying attention to what is known about them or their ethical bases. This effect is reinforced by pseudo-debates and enquiries, mere copies of true debates and enquiries, which far from throwing light on problems simply reinforce the idea that "anything goes."

One variant of demagoguery is the broadcasting of esoteric, miraculous, or paranormal views, which are presented acritically on the same level as scientific arguments.

– The contempt for fundamental rights such as honour, privacy, respect, truthfulness, or the presumption of innocence, a contempt which cannot be excused by appealing to freedom of expression.

This contempt leads to "kangaroo courts," the abuse of sensationalism and scandal, the presentation of statements that are supposedly authentic but in fact come from "professional guests" [on talk shows]. And, of course, the highpoint of trivia TV, featuring gossip "personalities," whose every little act and lovers' tiff is treated with shameless sensationalism. These are the added ingredients of this tasteless stew. The problem is all the more acute when this type of show is aired on public channels, whose moral and legal obligation is to show ethically and culturally enlightening programmes.

4. *Telebasura* has not invented anything: facile flattery of the viewer and the taste for sensationalism have a long history. But today the enormous social influence of the mass media increases the negative effect of this type of message exponentially.

– *Telebasura* is now at a growth point in its life cycle. It is like a cancer that spreads and takes over everything, or like a computer virus that contaminates all it touches and prevents other kinds of programme, which show more respect for truth and social concern, from remaining in the schedules or getting on the air.

5. The time has come for all those involved in television to be aware of their responsibility with regard to *telebasura*, which of course varies according to each person's power to affect the regulation of the marketplace.

The responsibility, then, belongs to the authorities, the TV channels, and the advertisers. But also to the schedulers and professionals. And to the citizen, who, without being duped by the fallacy of the "omnipotent viewer" (who can change the programming available to him by using his remote control), must know that his decision to watch a programme is not lacking in consequences, whether for his own dignity, or for the TV marketplace.

In television we are confronted by a complex social phenomenon constituted by large companies whose objectivity is debatable. Behind the media there are special interests, powers, and models, both social and ideological. And so questioning their objectivity and asking why they insist on certain themes at the expense of others is a way of beginning to understand television programmes critically.

6. Because of all the above, we who put our name to this manifesto wish to demonstrate our rejection of and concern about *telebasura*, and demand, as a guarantee of social control in a democratic society, both an ethical code of regulation of television content and the setting up of a Higher Council of Audiovisual Media, as was agreed by the majority of parliamentary groups in the previous government.

Platform for Quality Television
Association of Broadcasting Users, Trade Union Congresses, Spanish Confederation of School Parents, Spanish Consumers Association, Confederation of Spanish Residents Associations.

The "manifesto" reproduced above was posted on the web on December 26, 2001 by a group calling itself "Platform for Quality Television." An influential text, it is even cited by academic commentators such as Elías (17). But perhaps because of its multiple authorship, the manifesto reveals with some clarity the contradictions and prejudices in the critique of *telebasura*. Thus the genre is defined at once and alternately through its purpose (exploitation, the attraction of mass audiences), its subject matter (specific topics and individuals), and its approach to that subject matter (a "distorted" focus). It is attacked for the motives of its producers (they are hypocrites) and its effects on its consumers (they are taken unawares by ever increasing exhibitionism). It is unoriginal (having invented nothing), yet its effects are unprecedented (its social influence is "enormous"). Finally, its nature is at once economic (produced by shadowy media corporations whose interests are dubious) and political (neglected as it is by the Spanish government). More evident than the proliferating categories and repetitions, however, is the extremity, even viscerality, of the language used: TV is not just trash, but a "cancer" that threatens to invade the whole of society. This emotive language is the symptom of a deeply felt anxiety which, I will suggest, owes much to television's troubling "index appeal," its dangerous proximity to hearth and home.

It is instructive to compare the idealized goals of the manifesto with Spanish audiences' real-life viewing preferences. On a typical Thursday night (the evening with the biggest and thus most profitable audience of the week), the top ten programmes show clear evidence of titles and formats accused of *telebasura* (January 20, 2005). *Gran Hermano VIP* (no. 2) is a celebrity version of the reality show in which minor stars are forced to cohabit in a mock household; *Aquí hay tomate* (*Something Fishy Here*, no. 5) is a stridently parodic version of the softer gossip shows *Gente* (*People*, no. 8) and *El diario de Patricia* (*Patricia's Diary*, no. 9). Three million viewers were also tempted by Antonio Banderas in the poor-quality feature film *Original Sin* (no. 6).

However, the number one position is taken by period drama *Cuéntame cómo pasó*, and the remaining three slots by the news bulletins of private network Antena 3 and government controlled TVE1. If Spanish audiences are hungry for star talk and reality shows, then, they are also most attracted to quality domestic drama and information. Moreover, while just over one-quarter of Spanish viewers (26.2%) were indulging in the real-life histrionics of *Gran Hermano VIP*, three-quarters of their fellow citizens were engrossed in other more minority viewing choices. It is thus hardly logical to take the former as representative of the TV public as a whole.

A debate on *telebasura* on website Info-TK also suggests a wider variety of consumer opinions than those given by the associations that drafted the manifesto: correspondents write "Viva la 'telebasura'" (if the bishops are against it, TV must be doing something right); claim they are perfectly able to distinguish between outright entertainment and would-be serious programming (the worst kind of trash); and say that Spaniards are at liberty to watch, or not, whatever they please (although it's a shame smart guys like Sardà can't make better programmes).

Daily *El Mundo*, home to the vitriolic "Decoder" column, has no trouble identifying shows worth seeing on network television every day in its listings, advising readers "Don't miss this." For the week beginning February 11, 2005, it suggests a successful Spanish feature film (Mateo Gil's *Nadie conoce a nadie* [*Nobody Knows Anyone*, 1999]), used as the springboard for a discussion with the director and star in the *Versión española* (*Spanish Version*) strand; documentaries on the ecological threat to the Amazon, on "the evolution of Spanish women since 1978," and on the arrival of a new wave of immigrants: wealthy expatriates from northern Europe; Fred and Ginger starring in a rare musical *Follow the Fleet* (1936); a special debate treating the ill-fated European Constitution; and, finally, there is a screening of a recent French feature film, shot in Barcelona, *L'Auberge espagnole* (UK title *Europudding*, 2002). It is a selection of free-to-air network shows that viewers in other nations might well envy.

If consumers reject the threat of censorship and seem to have more choice of content than critical debate has allowed, TV producers also contest the *telebasura* attacks. Josep Maria Mainat, executive producer of *Crónicas marcianas*, is quoted in *The Economist* on November 11, 2004 as saying that the true trash TV is not his late-night talk show but the political manipulation of news bulletins ("Plumbing").

Meanwhile José Miguel Contreras, an academic and practitioner specializing in audience research and scheduling, empirically disproves the commonplaces of the *telebasura* debate, which are endlessly rehearsed by press and academy alike. Trash does not make money: the most notorious titles were commercial and financial failures. Real profitability comes from durable quality shows (such as *Cuéntame*). Moreover, the programmes are not always the same (Contreras and Palacio, 95). The schedule grid evolves continuously and, indeed, can be transformed almost overnight, as was TVE's with the coming of private channels in 1990 (97). In the decade that followed, supposedly "the years of lead," both production and consumption increased as the "offer-led" shows of a "dictatorial" state monopoly gave way to "demand-led" programming (21). Competition has led to innovation and diversity, with channels catering for at least two televisual Spains (young, educated, and urban vs. older and rural) (187). If rapid changes in format (such as the sudden rise in the reality genre) mark the evolution of viewers' tastes, then changes in viewing habits chart the transformation of everyday life: watching has increased in the late-night and early-morning time-slots. For Contreras scheduling is a tricky art that must combine two competing characteristics sought by audiences: familiarity with creative risk (154).

The now ubiquitous *Big Brother* was itself once a risky innovation in format. And, outside Spain, scholars have vindicated the reality genre with arguments unheard in the *telebasura* debate. As one British TV studies textbook writes:

> An oppositional position has emerged wherein theorists and pundits have been keen to cite these programmes as examples of "democratainment." Within this approach, the emphasis is placed on the participatory nature of reality programming, which, it is claimed, represents a break with traditional forms of factual television. (Casey, Casey, Calvert, French, and Lewis 197).

The rapidly increasing academic literature in the US and UK traces the history of the genre back to *Candid Camera* (1948) (Holmes and Jermyn), explores its relation to social desires and anxieties (Murray and Ouellette), and refocuses attention on TV form (Biressi and Nunn) and the active audience (Hill). All these works have some relation to the "oppositional" or positive appraisal of reality TV mentioned above.

Continental and Latin American scholars have also offered more theoretical explorations of the format. François Jost situates "the television of the everyday" in a place "between reality and fiction." He contrasts two traditional modes: the "authenticating," which makes "true assertions about our world" and whose counterpoint is "error, lies, or falsity" (19–20); and the "fictional," which makes no such claims about the world. But between these two extremes lies a third mode: the "ludic" (21). A genre such as the talk show holds elements of the authenticating and the ludic in unstable combination (22). Unlike the moralizing critics of *telebasura*, who are indifferent to context, Jost argues that images are neither true nor false in themselves. Rather "their 'truth' can be judged only with reference to the genres within which [the images] are inserted" (198). It is through this generic contextualization that Jost attempts to account for troubling paradoxes of content. His example is telling. In 1976 even elite art-house audiences had trouble sitting through a scene in Chantal Akerman's fiction film *Jeanne Dielman*, where the protagonist peeled potatoes for an extended period. And yet, thirty years later, millions are fascinated to watch unknowns carry out similarly banal actions on reality television (199).

This perplexing attraction is what Fernando Andacht labels "index appeal" (29). In his close analysis of the Argentine and Brazilian versions of *Big Brother*, Andacht attempts to navigate between the extremes of critical "rejection" and "renovation" of the boundaries of TV (12) and between "moral condemnation" and "formalist-abstraction" (13). Like Jost, Andacht pays minutely close attention to the content of his shows, focusing on "interactional detail" amongst the participants (16). And like Jost again he argues that the true/false distinction is inadequate: "the basic effect of the index is not truth [but] shock or collision" (29). As is well known, the index is a form of sign which (unlike the icon or symbol) is closely, even intimately, related to its referent. But while Pierce tended to use such examples as "smoke" for "fire," Andacht favours a more bodily example: the warmth of a recently vacated seat denotes a physical presence dangerously (excitingly) close to the observer. For Andacht, then, and for other defenders of reality TV outside Spain, the genre can constitute "a great leap forward in parasocial relations" (92), a leap which may well leave viewers disorientated as the discursive limits of what can be seen or said on television fall away.

Crónicas marcianas: the concept

Crónicas marcianas, the late-night talk show hosted by veteran Javier Sardà four nights a week between September 1997 and July 2005, is generally held to be the most profitable programme on Spanish television. The presenter and independent production company are both said to make some 10 million euros a year ("Sardá, el conductor"). Consistently attracting an up-market audience (young, educated, and urban), it has also won 15 prestigious prizes, both national (TP awards) and international (the Silver Rose of Montreux). Yet it is also the title most cited in the *telebasura* debate.

Returning to the "manifesto," we see that *Crónicas marcianas* would seem to coincide with the criticisms made by the TV viewers' associations. If *Crónicas marcianas*'s purpose is the attraction of mass audiences it has clearly succeeded: some two million Spaniards stay up until 2 am to watch the show. Indeed, sociologist Salvador Cardús credits (or blames) *Crónicas marcianas* for disrupting Spaniards' sleeping habits and lengthening their daily routines (*1000 crónicas marcianas*, 165). The show's subject matter is at best banal, at worst exploitative: guests are typically not the movie stars that grace US late shows but the minor celebrities of reality shows and so-called "freaks" who have some sexual exploit to sell. The producers and, most especially, Sardà are often attacked for hypocrisy: how can a one-time Leftist journalist devote so much air time to silicone-enhanced strippers and cross-dressers? The show is surely unoriginal in concept, parasitic as it is on other notorious examples of trash TV such as *Big Brother*. *Crónicas marcianas* is blamed by some for corrupting Spanish youth (it is indeed watched by schoolchildren) and its political influence is also attacked: critics claim both to perceive the (Rightist) hidden agenda of network Tele5 (part-owned by Silvio Berlusconi) and the radical bias of Sardà (his frequent attacks on the Spanish right-wing and Church, his insistent "promotion" of homosexuality). As *El País* wrote on the occasion of the one-thousandth programme in the series, invoking the extreme language typical of the *telebasura* debate, *Crónicas marcianas* is watched even by those who consider Sardà's influence "toxic" and "diabolical" ("Sardá celebra")

Crónicas marcianas would also seem to infringe the ethical criteria of media academics. It is clearly what Carlos Elías (citing philosopher Gustavo Bueno) would call "fabricated" trash, meticulously planned and executed by its makers. It cheerfully features "professional guests" (recurring visitors to the set) whose salacious stories may well be invented; and it juxtaposes these "false experts" (on pseudo-topics such as "sexual gymnastics") with "true experts" (on matters of legitimate concern such as public health). It could thus be accused of blurring fact and fiction, undermining journalistic authority and endangering social stability. Ethically irresponsible, *Crónicas marcianas* is also politically dubious, fearlessly spoofing public figures. Indeed it is the only Spanish show, to my knowledge, to feature impersonations of King Juan Carlos, a figure who remains untouchable in the media landscape. Surely its sleep-deprived viewers must have received an "intellectual lobotomy" to tolerate such trash? While *Crónicas marcianas* permits free expression of opinions, however bizarre, it hardly promotes rational public debate. Its panelists compete to shout each other down and its vociferous studio audience (which cheers, chants, and boos at the slightest opportunity) is an emotional or self-interested "multitude" or "mass," not an informed democratic "public." On more than one occasion *Crónicas marcianas* has set personal freedom of expression above harm done to others in the way held by Victoria Camps to be typical of television as a whole. After broadcasting a would-be humorous interview with a mentally handicapped youth in October 2002, the show was fined 15,000 euros for breaching the subject's rights under the Spanish Constitution to honour, privacy, and his own image.

Sardà has vigorously defended his creation from the charge of *telebasura*. On one occasion he read on camera explicit small ads for the services of prostitutes printed by a newspaper that had attacked him for purveying trash. Deflecting the charge of hypocrisy onto the print media, he has also attacked TV viewers' associations directly, asking on the show whether they "protect the audience" or "promote ultra-Rightist censorship." More typically the show hosted a spoof visit from a representative of the so-called "Conservative Association of TV Viewers" who argued that images of sex and violence corrupt children and that television does not fulfil its proper mission. This "decent" woman was, however, stark naked. Yet beyond the limited and conflictive confines of the *telebasura* debate, I would argue that *Crónicas marcianas* can best be understood within the context of two factors generally neglected by the general press: industry and audience.

Crónicas marcianas was a vital weapon in Tele5's campaign to re-brand itself as a "quality" network. The channel's annual report of 1998 (the year after the show's debut) claimed to believe that "well managed quality translates into profitability" ("la calidad bien gestionada se traduce en rentabilidad") (Telecinco, 11); and cites *Crónicas marcianas* as an example of the live programming that is a priority for the channel, stressing the flexible content of daily shows that can respond immediately to any "relevant event" (35).

But if *Crónicas marcianas* corresponds to the changing priorities of Tele5's programming at that time, it also testifies to a permanent change in the media landscape: the rise of independent production. Javier Bardají and Santiago Gómez Amigo have recently charted the "management of creativity" in Spanish TV, focusing on a corporate study of Globo Media, independent producer of milestone quality dramas such as *Médico de familia* (*Family Doctor*) and *Periodistas* (*Journalists*). The authors note how during the second half of the 1990s, independent producers became an "indispensable" part of the audiovisual sector and helped to create a true "industry" and "infrastructure" without precedents in Spain (36). Previous pessimism about "invincible US hegemony" and the "atomization" and "financial weakness" of Spanish producers was swept away when the coming of private channels brought both increased competition and a need for new content to fill their programming grids (40).

Specialist sources, directly opposed to general press commentary, thus suggest that greater offer led to increased creativity and quality (42). While in 1993 only three shows in the top ten were made by independents, in the years 1996–2000 all of the top five shows were. Moreover the most productive of these companies is *Crónicas marcianas*'s Gestmusic-Endemol, which has produced more than ten new titles each year since the season of 1996–7, which gave birth to *Crónicas marcianas* (62).

Crónicas marcianas is thus a quintessential example of the new order of Spanish television after the collapse of the public service monopoly, which relied on limited in-house production and US and Latin American imports. It is an order in which (*pace* the latest Director-General of TVE) quality and profitability are not seen as mutually exclusive. Indeed *Crónicas marcianas*'s format, based on CBS's *Late Show with David Letterman*, was unprecedented in Spain. It remains the only show to thrive in the late-night time-slot where, unlike in prime time, viewing has increased year on year. *Crónicas marcianas*'s success is all the more remarkable in that it is broadcast from Barcelona and employs mainly local talent. In an audiovisual industry where Madrid remains dominant, Gestmusic forms part of a "Catalan cluster" of media companies: specialist channels, sport and technical media, and fiction producers ("Sardá, el conductor").

A large-format picture book (*1000 crónicas marcianas*) published to celebrate the one-thousandth episode of the show gives a surprisingly detailed account of the production process of *Crónicas marcianas*. Sardà writes in his introduction that from the first show on September 8, 1997, the aim was to combine "imagination" with "hard work" (9, 10). The initial premise and reason for the name of the series was that the show would look at "our world" from a "different perspective" and observe things "with a certain distance." The concept involved direct communication with the audience. This changed in form from the pencils and paper first handed out in the studio to phone polls, email messages, and, finally, the text messages which now crawl across the bottom of the screen throughout the show, offering instant feedback (21).

The text of the picture book stresses the longevity of the creative collaboration behind the show: the eight-member production team (including Sardà, credited as "director" as well as "presenter," and executive producers Toni Cruz and the brothers Joan Ramon and Josep Maria Mainat) have been together for ten years, and moved together from successful radio shows to TV (61). Even the studio technicians have their moment in the limelight: on the sixth season each show was dedicated to a lighting rigger, make-up person, or hair stylist (61). Moreover the show invented a new profession, that of "live music editor": the whole programme is scored to musical tags and noises reproduced (like the text messages) in real time and thus offering a running commentary on the action (64). Even the set is innovative. As the show developed and the panelists' antics grew more exuberant, the flying-saucer-shaped desk at which all participants sit became larger and even sprouted steps to make (semi-improvised) stripteases or fights more visible and accessible. It is, we are told, a "magic carpet with legs" (68).

The host's role, we are informed, is to be an "invisible man" or "Zelig" (147). Stealthily directing the mayhem, he must not distract from favourite panelists such as the flamboyantly gay Venezuelan Boris Izaguirre (Illustrations 13, 14). Even outside the show Sardà, a "non-practising celebrity" (134), does not give interviews or guest on other programmes. It is thus appropriate that when he published a book of interviews (in another print extension of the lucrative *Crónicas marcianas* brand), all the questions were posed via email by members of the audience. In his responses Sardà treads a fine line between the committed, if idiosyncratic, Leftism of his politics and the ironic distance of his comedy. Asked when he first had a woman, he replies that one does not "have" women as one does houses or cars (Sardà, *Me encanta*, 44) and later claims he couldn't care less if a child of his turned out to be gay (45). He states that Fidel Castro may be enlightened but is nonetheless "a tyrant" (96), names the

13. The host, Javier Sardà

14. The panelist, Boris Izaguirre

"enemies" of the show as conservatives, the Church, and "outdated *progres* [Lefties]" (97) and says that the death penalty is "cold blooded state murder" (101). On the other hand he practises self-deprecation and frivolity: his professional success is in inverse proportion to his sexual potency (47); we can't do without TV, but TV can perfectly well do without us (58); Boris is right: the latest fashion is more important than the most recent Council of Ministers (106).

Sardà is most canny when he discusses his audience and the accusations of *telebasura*. Although he is given complete creative freedom by Tele5 (60), his editorial independence is in the final analysis granted to him by his viewers (62). Moreover, professional prestige is not incompatible with commercial success: his aim is to make a technically perfect live show every night (64). He pours scorn on the public service notion that all TV should form and inform, as well as entertain (which he compares to the belief that the earth is flat) (68) and claims his own show does not deceive but rather is "pure" and "transparent" (129). Revealing the breadth of his cultural references, he notes that the label "trash" (which he gives in English) has long been thought a badge of honour amongst certain US filmmakers, who hold it to be a distinct aesthetic (71); he notes that in Spain the term is applied only to TV, while radio and print are spared (72); and claims that a television show is like a restaurant: the public enters freely and will not return if it finds the menu unappetizing (75).

Beyond the text messages featured on *Crónicas marcianas* itself, the best evidence of audience response is from specialist chat rooms. Info-TK launched a continuing debate on the triumphant occasion of the one-thousandth show (November 21, 2003), when the press (generally out of synch with viewers) grudgingly praised *Crónicas marcianas*. The parasocial power of live TV is clear from the chat room, as are the differing domestic contexts in which *Crónicas marcianas* is consumed: one message poster says the show is "his" and the presenters are "his friends"; another says that everyone at school discusses it the next day; a third writes that after work and dinner he likes to relax, smoking a joint and watching the show with his wife. Many comment from very different viewpoints on the political implications of the show. One blames Sardà for rape and domestic violence in Spain, while another hopes that, thanks to the show, gay marriage and gay adoption will soon be legal. One attacks the show for shifting the blame for the outrage of March 11, 2004 from the terrorists to the Partido Popular, while another thanks the show for "opening the eyes" of young voters to the lies of former President Aznar. It seems clear that in a time of unprecedented national crisis young viewers did turn to *Crónicas marcianas*, an intimate part of their everyday life, to express freely their opinions and anxieties. The fact that public attitudes display moral and evaluative perplexity does not prevent us from reading this electronic debate as evidence for a certain expansion of democratic participation.

Shortly after this time, *Crónicas marcianas* itself experienced something of a crisis. By October 2004 the show had lost 200 thousand viewers and a five-point share (Sanchis); in November executive producer Joan Ramon Mainat died at the age of 53 (the show did not air that night); and January 2005 brought a new and threatening rival in Antena 3's late show starring Catalan comedian Andreu Buenafuente (FormulaTV). Once the undisputed leader in its time-slot, having seen off thirty-seven competitors, *Crónicas marcianas* was now attacked not by moralists for immorality but by the industry for "lack of renewal in its contents" (Sanchis) and by some viewers for an excess of shouting and stripping. As we have seen, this period also marked the high point of the *telebasura* debate and the threatened introduction of government regulation. We can now examine specimen shows from that crucial time for Spanish television.

Crónicas marcianas: specimen episodes

If *Crónicas marcianas* was indeed based on the US talk show format it is longer, later, liver, and louder than the original. Over a three-week period from late January to mid-February 2005 (a time when it suffered unaccustomed competition from rival network Antena 3), the show began at any time between 12.10 and 12.50 am (US equivalents begin at 11.30 pm) and ran for between two and two and a half hours (US equivalents run for one hour), including extended commercial breaks that lasted up to ten minutes. And while Letterman and Leno are "live to tape" (i.e. recorded in front of the studio audience in the afternoon), *Crónicas marcianas* is truly live and thus more open to improvisation. Finally *Crónicas marcianas* is much less decorous than the US shows, frequently escalating into a "dog fight" between noisy participants.

The role of the host is clearly different also. Letterman and Leno come out on stage alone and deliver a comic monologue on topical themes, also alone. Proceeding to a desk that only they are privileged to sit behind, they engage in banter with their sidekicks (leaders of the live bands) and present familiar comic "bits" to camera (the top ten list, the host's mailbag) before the first guest arrives. Sardà, on the other hand, is discovered already seated behind the huge, communal table and immediately introduces his first "collaborator" Boris Izaguirre. Subsequent contributors, whether regulars known as *colaboradores*, recurring visitors known as *tertulianos*, or bemused one-off visitors, are announced at regular intervals and often enter (to loud canned musical tags and accompanied by gyrations from the three scantily-clad hostesses) in groups of up to four or five. As is suggested by the word *tertulia* (a regular discussion group normally held in a café), *Crónicas marcianas* is much more communal than the US shows, which are dominated by their "hosts" (Sardà is described merely as "presenter") and more clearly delineated into segments devoted to individual celebrities, normally focused on promoting their latest film. If the length and lateness of *Crónicas marcianas* testify to the unique rhythm of the Spanish television ecology, then its liveness and loudness testify to its unusual informality and sociability, so alien to the rigidity and individualism of the US models.

After Sardà had ditched successful and long-serving early collaborators (the best known being Galindo, a humorist of restricted growth who was frequently dressed up as a child or doll), the collaborators dignified with a "niche" (*rincón*) on the show's website (Crónicas) number seven in the 2004–5 season: Boris (smart and camp, author of both a coffee-table book on "glamour" and a novel exploring globalization); Juan Carlos Ortega (a young comedian specializing in taped segments with an unusually intellectual bent); Empar Moliner (specialist in bizarre news stories: gay penguins in Germany, prostitutes who advertise as "writers"); Carlos Pumares (a grumpy old man, complaining about mobile phones or "the treatment of the potato"); Rocío Madrid (comely young gossip reporter from Málaga); Carlos Latre (impressionist who takes off celebrities from King Juan Carlos to Almodóvar and the Pope); and Xavier Deltell (vox pop reporter from the streets of Barcelona, now newly accompanied by a naked blond woman).

Where once *Crónicas marcianas* had featured major movie stars and politicians, not one appeared during this time. When an "Oscar-nominated" guest was announced it proved to be not Alejandro Amenábar, celebrated director of award-winning *Mar adentro* (*The Sea Inside*, 2005), but the unknown creator of a short feature. Rather, the show relies on cross-promoting Tele5's TV programming: the main guests in the long first segment are from *Aquí hay tomate* (a scurrilous gossip show, openly hostile to celebrities); *Los Serrano* (an anodyne family sitcom, here illustrated by a montage of saucy clips); and, above all, *Gran Hermano VIP II*, the second edition of a "celebrity" strand of reality pioneer *Big Brother*.

The great majority of the *tertulianos* are also drawn from reality shows. Indeed *Crónicas marcianas* prides itself as a "touchstone" for the conversion of these fragile figures into ongoing stars of the TV ecology. The legibility of the show relies on audience familiarity with the many back-stories of this minor pantheon. A handsome young Cuban, introduced only as: "Dinio: worked as a prostitute" (Illustration 15), is in fact a regular on the show (a "professional guest"), whose hazy account of his alleged sexual experiences is implicitly supported by viewers' knowledge of his appearance on notorious reality show *Hotel Glam* and full-frontal snapshots in scandal magazine *Interviú*. Alessandro Lecquio (billed as "the Count"), a formally dressed Italian who is formidably argumentative even by *Crónicas marcianas*'s standards, will also be familiar for his physical attributes, amply displayed on the beach for eager paparazzi to snap. This network of minor celebrities appears inexhaustible: Dinio introduces his twin brother, who he claims is a soldier, thus segueing into a military-themed striptease on top of the famous table.

Perhaps sensing the growing competition, Sardà begins each show by announcing last night's audience "share" (once more the English word is used) and ratcheting up the sexual content. Regular visitors in this period are a glamorous French sexologist (author of "Diary of a Nymphomaniac") and a middle-aged Spaniard whose unprepossessing appearance suggests he may indeed be a "genuine expert" with professional credentials in sexual dysfunction. During January–February viewers are treated to frequent lesbian (and gay

15. The guest, Dinio ("worked as a prostitute")

male) kisses, erotic massage, and "light" displays by professional sex workers. Sushi is eaten off taut stomachs and ice cubes are traced around erect nipples. The "freaks", who have spawned their own feature-length DVD spin-off, are conspicuously absent, with the exception of a long-time collaborator, the elderly and ugly Carmen de Mairena, who gamely stands in as the booby prize in a recurring audience-participation segment: young men are obliged to kiss her grotesquely swollen lips as a proof of love for their girlfriends.

If true celebrities are replaced by reality "stars" and current affairs take the back seat to sex, then apparently unscripted, even unfocused, discussion replaces traditional comedy. Only Juan Carlos Ortega's innovative taped segments, sometimes surprisingly erudite in inspiration, come close to this definition. One "bit" staged an interview with Vermeer's milkmaid (a phone handset is held up to the canvas), supposedly suggested by Hölderlin's longing to speak to the young girl depicted in the classic painting. Elsewhere Ortega satirizes intrusive TV reporting. A tremulous elderly couple, convincingly authentic, are interviewed in their tiny urban flat, which, in their longing for their native village, they have converted into a smallholding: one picks carrots or tends pigs as the other watches TV or does the ironing. The same couple (we now know they are actors) are shown on another night with a unique way of saving money: they produce electricity by frenetically pedalling on an exercise bike.

Such humour clearly relies on the competence of the *Crónicas marcianas* audience, who are able to distinguish between the three strands that have made up the show since it began: news, gossip, and comedy. But a frame of legibility is also built into the show, in order to prompt ignorant or inattentive late-night viewers. *Crónicas marcianas* frequently cites itself, most blatantly in the intermittent opening segment known as "mix," which montages spectacular and often topical moments from recent shows (e.g. Latre re-creates Fidel Castro's fall; Boris, in wedding gown, marries a handsome horse in honour of the coming of same-sex marriage in Spain). On the set, plasma screens placed behind the guests flash up pictures of the reality stars, helpfully captioned, as they are referred to in discussion, or endlessly repeat relevant video clips: Fidel falls down the steps, over and over. The real-time sound accompaniment also prompts audience response. Amongst other things, *Crónicas marcianas* is thus an education in how to watch TV: panelists endlessly dissect the interactional details of the Big Brother household, frequently focusing on the motives and status of words and actions. Are the housemates sincere or disingenuous, serious or playful? *Crónicas marcianas* thus encourages both parasocial engagement with reality TV (panelists experience it every night just as we do) and sceptical, even cynical, dissocation from it (they noisily argue over its interpretation and speculate that each new interaction is a set-up [*montaje*]).

Sardà has frequently stated that he prefers a "humorous" discussion of *Big Brother* to a would-be serious discussion that fails to do justice to its subject matter. And he makes the difficult distinction between the "content" of the show (which he claims does not matter) and the "climate" or "atmosphere" (which is indispensable). I have suggested that one aspect of this atmosphere is the sociability of *Crónicas marcianas*, guided but not dictated by its "invisible man." The second is the viewer's complicity with the sometimes distant, ironic Sardà, who for the most part remains safely outside the "circus" he has created. Indeed he boasts that on one show he was obliged to leave the set for a few minutes and discussion continued imperturbably without him.

Ironic sociability and complicity are also played out on the set, however, in the central relation between sober Sardà (always dressed in black suit and white shirt) and Boris (more likely to be impersonating a Venezuelan Miss World). Sardà has often spoken of his affection for Boris, typically joking that they could be a couple, if only Boris wasn't taller than him. And if *Crónicas marcianas*'s sociability is horizontal, without clear hierarchy, still (taking their lead from the "presenter") guests defer to Boris, as arbiter of elegance. The book published for the one-thousandth edition clarifies his ambivalent and self-consciously Wildean pose: Boris promotes "frivolity," the only thing that differentiates the merely "intelligent" from the "divinely superior" (46); he tries to "educate" ignorant Spanish tastes, still stuck in the slums (*modos chaboleros*) (49); and he is no gay activist, but contributes nonetheless to the "acceptance" (*normalización*) of homosexuality (58). In his open gayness and proud Latin Americanism Boris is thus a unique public figure in Spain. In one typical joke, Sardà brought together the two elements: when Boris claimed to be descended from a Native American tribe, the host assured him that that was clearly the

source of his *pluma* (both "feather" and "campery"). While some gay viewers
may be disturbed by Boris's "undignified" behaviour (and we have seen that the
right to "dignity" is protected by the Spanish Constitution and thought to be
endangered by *telebasura*), the complicity and familiarity displayed night after
night by Sardà's Catalan straight man and Boris's knowing South American
queen is surely a model of inductively cultivated intimacy. It might even be seen
as an example of the electronic extension of democracy to groups long excluded
from formal politics.

Let us now examine a single show during the specimen period, which aired
on the night of Monday, February 7, 2005. After a teaser preview that shows
presenter, collaborators, and hostesses joking and dancing behind the scenes,
we break for eight minutes of commercials for new movies, life assurance,
honey, internet providers, tissues, mints, mobile phones, watches, and Suzuki
automobiles (the proud "sponsor" of the show). After the brief credits with their
"red planet" logo, we cut to the set where Sardà sits ready at the table, claiming
that the audience's cheers are excessive: maybe they are celebrating the Spanish
handball team's victory that day (more cheers). Boris comes on the set, soberly
dressed in jeans and navy V-neck sweater (0:01), followed by pretty Rocío
(0:02), and "Kika Matamoros" (0:03), a loud, bald man in drag. The latter is an
invention of impersonator Carlos Latre: the supposed sister of recent *Big
Brother* contestant Kiko Matamoros, a frequent guest of *Crónicas marcianas*.
Two minutes later three more guests appear (mere *tertulianos* rather than the
previous *colaboradores*), including the Italian "count" Alessandro (0:05).

Now the panel is complete for this segment, angry discussion of *Big Brother*
ensues for half an hour. This is punctuated by three short clips from today's
episode of the reality show (screened on Tele5 but not made by the same independent producer as *Crónicas marcianas*) and by another eight-minute
commercial break. Discussion turns around one gay housemate who is supposedly attractive to three female contestants and is thus (according to Boris) the
true sex-object in the show.

Sardà then abruptly dismisses some panelists (Boris and the Count remain)
and welcomes five new guests, including well known TV priest Father Apeles
and ex-Catalan separatist member of parliament Pilar Rahola (0:39). Abruptly
changing tone, the presenter shows a clip from an afternoon talk show in which
a gay man living with his legally recognized partner has been refused the sacra-
ment by a local priest (0:42). The eloquent Father Apeles argues that the Church
cannot give communion to a "public sinner," while Pilar Rahola hoarsely
decries the Church's "ultra-Rightism" and "homophobia."

No conclusion is reached before we switch to another topic, an extreme form
of wrestling whose name is given as *vale tudo* (sic; 0:47). A Syrian-born Spaniard who promotes the sport is introduced, before we see a one-minute montage
of exceptionally violent moments of it taken from Tele5's scandalous news
magazine *TNT*. Back in the studio, Rahola attacks the sport as "barbaric" (0:49)
while Apeles pronounces in favour of it. As panelists continue to argue, the
Arab guest, apparently unfamiliar with the format in spite of his unaccented

Castilian, repeatedly complains that he "hasn't finished speaking" before he is interrupted. He justifies the game as "freedom of expression" (0:56). More footage from *TNT* claims to link the bouts to the "ultra-Right" (01:01). Boris now intervenes, attracted by the lycra shorts worn by the wrestlers (01:03). Isn't this ultra-violent sport just a little bit gay? Do the participants get an erection when they fight? The promoter, anxious to change the subject, claims that he is organizing a special bout "for charity" (01:07). Suddenly we cut to a spoof *vale tudo* fight between housewives (portly men in drag hammering each other with their handbags).

Sardà next announces that Almodóvar has resigned today from the Spanish Cinema Academy, in protest at its unfair prize giving (01:09). (On a subsequent night Latre will impersonate him tearing up his driving licence as a protest against Spanish road traffic.) There follows a party game in which Sardà asks panellists whether old movie stars are alive or dead (01:11). A further segment begins with tape of a weeping gossip journalist on Tele5's *A tu lado* (*By Your Side*, 01:19). Rahola calls her a "clown" (01:34). Making unusually explicit the conventions of TV, she praises the "humour" and "irony" of late-night *Crónicas marcianas*, so different from the lachrymose self-importance of day-time talk shows (01:25). Behind her the tears of the clown are endlessly repeated on the plasma screens.

With another abrupt change in tone, Sardà leaves the desk and walks into the audience (01:29). Eighteen young people have recently been killed in Castellón by fumes from a gas heater. The host asks detailed questions of a representative of the Catalan association of gas fitters. There are safety demonstrations with three heaters in the studio. Sardà unobtrusively corrects the native Catalan speaker's faulty Castilian at one point. We cut back to the table before a final commercial break (01:38), returning only for a further parlour game of identifying theme tunes of old TV series (01:53). Sardà, briefly impersonating the commander of *Hill Street Blues* (the quality US drama par excellence), gives a final address to his doughty "team," warning them to "be careful out there" (01:59). The news bulletin that follows takes up topics discussed in *Crónicas marcianas*: the funeral of the gas victims of Castellón and the return of the victorious handball team.

From this outline it is clear that *Crónicas marcianas* tends to blur distinctions that remain relatively clear in the original US format: between host and guests, between one segment and another, between news, gossip, and humour. And if Sardà remains relatively distant, it is clear that his power to choose *tertulianos* is vital. Often they hide contradictions which prove fruitful in debate. For example, Father Apeles is both a highly conservative Catholic anxious to promote his cause and a preening creature of the media whose appearances on shows such as *Crónicas marcianas* have been disowned by his superiors. Pilar Rahola is at once a radical separatist politician and a fierce critic of Islamic terrorist violence, unlikely to be sympathetic to a Syrian kickboxing promoter. While the dangerously fluid format of the talk show makes for bewildering changes in topic and tone, it seems unlikely that the audience is incapable of reading those shifts. Indeed *Crónicas marcianas*'s self-reflexivity demands a sophisticated familiarity with the programme's form and content.

While frequently the show lapses into dullness (echoing the rhythm of everyday life), it takes fire at those unpredictable moments when it enters that third mode between the "authenticating" and the "fictional" which François Jost calls the "ludic." Boris's sly taunts to the boxing promoter are thus neither true nor false, but rather, playful assertions of camp in the most macho of contexts. The Syrian's squirming, indignant response feels genuinely dangerous, threatening as it does to transgress the rules of a game that are based on the same "freedom of expression" that he himself invokes.

This is clearly the kind of "shock" or "collision" which Fernando Andacht finds characteristic of reality TV. Watching live, in real time, we are intimately connected to referents that may well arouse, amuse, or anger us. This is the elusive "index appeal" which, as Sardà knows so well, can transcend banal content. Indeed one critic of *Crónicas marcianas* unknowingly reiterates Andacht's bodily definition of the index in a homophobic slur the show itself would surely denounce: *El Mundo* wrote that no "right-thinking" (*íntegro*) person would sit in the seat recently left warm by Boris Izaguirre (*1000 crónicas marcianas*, 165).

From content to climate

Spaniards are not great readers. In May 2003 only 39% read a daily newspaper and more than a quarter of those chose the sporting press. Football paper *Marca* far outsells *El País* and *El Mundo* (AIMC). Meanwhile, in the same month, 90.7% watched television every day. The phantom of *telebasura* can be traced back to the "black legend" of press attacks on TV which emerged in the 1970s in the context of late anti-Francoist resistance. It is a blanket attack on a hugely popular medium, an attack that is clearly not shared by the great majority of the Spanish population.

Many educated Spaniards are anxious at what they see as the new vulgarity of their television. But it is clear that the "crusade against *telebasura*" makes good copy for the restricted readerships of the daily press. Ironically, the educated demographic who read newspapers are also disproportionately fond of shows such as *Crónicas marcianas*. It is a further irony that the anti-American newspapers do not see fit to champion the home-grown TV shows that have trounced US competition on the small screen. The contrast with cinema is instructive. The conspicuous success of domestic gross-out comedies does not encourage Spanish film critics to dismiss the medium as a whole; nor does it stop them patriotically supporting Oscar-winning features such as Amenábar's *Mar adentro*. Television is considered too domestic, too intrinsically trivial, to play a part in representing the nation in international cultural competition.

The Manifesto against *telebasura* attacked "simulacra" of debates in which "anything goes." But even *El País* acknowledged on one occasion that *Crónicas marcianas*'s "parodies of debates" (which it branded "frivolous, demagogic, and superficial") served the "difficult art of entertaining" (*1000 crónicas marcianas* 162). I have argued that in such a fluid medium and genre it is hard to separate politics, ethics, and aesthetics. Political intervention is, moreover, continuous. When the "Committee of Wise Men" finally published their report, Juan Pérez de Albéniz (*El Mundo*'s "Descifrador") noted that the word "control" appeared 166 times (February 23, 2005). While *Crónicas marcianas*'s appeal to "freedom of expression" is hardly sufficient in itself (simply negating as it does the possibility of harm to vulnerable citizens), Sardà's hostility to censorship is avowedly shared by some of the anti-trash campaigners, incensed by government meddling in news media. And the line between participatory "democratainment" and rabble-rousing demagoguery is hard to draw. *Crónicas marcianas*'s politics is exceptionally ambivalent, embracing as it does mavericks from both the cultural Right and Left, such as Father Apeles and Pilar Rahola.

But it seems that the pieties of old-Leftism are no longer acceptable to young audiences: when Sardà interviewed José Sacristán, a veteran actor with a long history of political activism, he spoofed "constructive conversation" by dressing as a building worker and posing on a girder in front of a New York backdrop from the 1930s (*1000 crónicas marcianas*, 155). But if working-class politics is hard to carry off, this need not mean that *Crónicas marcianas* is apolitical. Sardà's unforced Catalanism (he vigorously defends his accent) is unusual on Spanish national TV, as is his consistent support for gays. *Crónicas marcianas*'s ordinary guests may seem as bizarre as the contestants parodied by La Cubana and as sadly fixated on becoming famous, but they are rarely ridiculed by the host. Rather they are left to describe themselves. *Crónicas marcianas* may not provide a training in citizenship, now the public service virtues of "formation and information" have been so undermined; but it surely provides an education in sensibility: in irony and tolerance. Indeed, while we saw that Victoria Camps attacked the "speed" and "spectacle" of the unethical electronic media as inimical to the "public use of reason," close analysis of *Crónicas marcianas* reveals that it does not fit this bill. The show is typically slow in pace and unshowy in aesthetics, relying on group discussion for segments up to one hour long.

I would suggest that, as with reality programming proper, it is precisely this sense of proximity to everyday life, of close (too close) bodily contact, that is the secret of the show. And it is this closeness that signals its break with traditional factual programming (which relies on "genuine experts") and its adhesion to the new mode of participation. This intimacy or inductive presentation of life stories, however bizarre, results in an evaluative perplexity which challenges monolithic morality. Certainly the Church takes very seriously *Crónicas marcianas*'s parodies of the Pope, encouraging Catholic viewers to complain to the network (*1000 Crónicas marcianas*, 170).

Crónicas marcianas might be described as a surrealist soap opera. It is a phrase which catches the elusive ambivalence of the show on many levels. Thus host Javier Sardà must combine familiarity and novelty (always seeming the same, always being different) and the reality "stars" and "freaks" must seem at once recognizable and strange to the audience. Even the set combines the mundane and the extraterrestrial: the domestic set-up (all the guests crowded around the table) is complemented by the Martian backdrop, so different from the US urban decors of Letterman and Leno. This distinctively "ludic" element (poised between true and false) is confirmed by one controversial aspect of the production process: while Sardà claims the whole show is scripted (and four writers receive a credit), contributors claim that they prefer to improvise. If, as François Jost suggests, the ludic image can be judged only within the context of the genre into which it is inserted, then the extreme fluidity of *Crónicas marcianas*'s genre renders interpretation especially perilous.

Evaluating "climate" and not "content" is a tricky job best not left to legislators or moralists. But it is one that suggests that aesthetics (set design, sound-mixing, interactional detail) are as important for the meaning of a show as are politics and ethics. Certainly the formal differences between US versions of the late talk show and *Crónicas marcianas* suggest a specifically Spanish form of sociality based on the group discussion of the *tertulia* or *sobremesa*. As an electronic version of this longstanding tradition, *Crónicas marcianas* carries a trace or, more properly, an index of social practice into the television ecology. This is in addition to the fact, admitted even by some academic commentators, that a citizen is a *homo ludens* and entertainment can be a legitimate civic good.

Crónicas marcianas's executive producer once claimed the show would be studied in universities. Sardà modestly dissented, suggesting it would soon be forgotten (Sardà, *Me encanta*, 79). The current website offers an uncanny after-life to over twelve hundred nights of live performance in innumerable clips and still photos that are deprived of dates. Web surfers thus enter an uncanny time-less time which simulates perhaps the hazy perception of live viewers, drunk, drugged, or somnolent as they may well be. *Crónicas marcianas* may not be a great leap forward in parasociality, although its sheer abundance and longevity are unprecedented. Its host, now showing signs of age, may be trapped: one skit saw his head encased in a cardboard TV set like the manikin on La Cubana's poster. But at its best *Crónicas marcianas* retained in 2005 its ability to shock and surprise the viewer.

At the end of Ray Bradbury's science fiction novel from which the show took its name, an Earth-born colonist of Mars takes his children to look at Martians:

> They reached the canal. It was long and straight and cool and wet and reflec-tive in the night.
> "I always wanted to see a Martian," said Michael. "Where are they, Dad? You promised."
> "There they are," said Dad, . . . and pointed straight down.
> The Martians were there. Timothy began to shiver.
> The Martians were there – in the canal – reflected in the water. Timothy and Michael and Robert and Mom and Dad.

The Martians stared back at them for a long, long, silent time from the rippling water . . . (235)

There could be no better image of reality television, with its combination of the familiar and bizarre, than Bradbury's uncanny canal. The new media landscape threatens many Spaniards who feel themselves, like Martian colonists, to be strangers in a strange land that may, in part, be of their own making. But those not mesmerized by the phantom or black legend of *telebasura* clearly take pleasure in recognizing themselves in newly exotic and innovative TV genres.

Crónicas marcianas (*Martian Chronicles*), Tele5 1997–2005

Presenter and director: Javier Sardà
Executive producers: Toni Cruz, Josep Maria Mainat, Joan Ramon Raimat
Scriptwriters: Jordi Roca, Miquel José, Xavier Vidal, Joan Tresserras
Panelists (2004–5): Boris Izaguirre, Juan Carlos Ortega, Empar Moliner, Carlos Pumares, Rocío Madrid, Carlos Latre, Xavier Deltell

Works cited

1000 crónicas marcianas. Madrid: Gestmusic, 2003.
Andacht, Fernando. *El reality show: una perspectiva analítica de la televisión*. Buenos Aires: Norma, 2003.
Bardají, Javier and Santiago Gómez Amigo. *La gestión de la creatividad en televisión: El caso de Globo Media*. Pamplona: EUNSA, 2004.
Biressi, Anita and Heather Nunn (eds). *Reality TV: Realism and Revelation*. London: Wallflower, 2004.
Bradbury, Ray. *The Martian Chronicles*. London: Flamingo, 1995.
Camps, Victoria. "Opinión pública, libertad de expresión, y derecho a la información." In Conill and Gozálvez pp. 33–50.
Casey, Bernadette, Neil Casey, Ben Calvert, Liam French, and Justin Lewis. *Television Studies: The Key Concepts*. London: Routledge, 2002.
Conill, Jesús and Vicent Gozálvez (eds). *Ética de los medios: una apuesta por la ciudadanía audiovisual*. Barcelona: Gedisa, 2004.
Contreras, José-Miguel and Manuel Palacio. *La programación de televisión*. Madrid: Síntesis, 2001.
Cortina, Adela. "Ciudadanía activa en una sociedad mediática." In Conill and Gozálvez, pp. 11–32.
Cubana, La. *Mamá quiero ser famoso*. Theatre programme. Madrid: Gran Vía 66, 2005.
Daney, Serge. *Le Salaire du zappeur*. Paris: POL, 1988.
Elías Pérez, Carlos. *Telebasura y periodismo*. Madrid: Libertarias, 2004.
Gozálvez, Vicent. "Análisis ético-comparativo de los medios." In Conill and Gozálvez, pp. 187–232.

Hill, Annette. *Reality TV: Audiences and Popular Factual Television*. London: Routledge, 2005.
Holmes, Susan and Deborah Jermyn (eds). *Understanding Reality Television*. London: Routledge, 2004.
James, Clive. *The Crystal Bucket*. London: Picador, 1981.
Jost, François. *La Télévision du quotidien: entre réalité et fiction*. Brussels: INA/De Boeck University, 2001.
Murray, Susan and Laurie Ouellette (eds). *Reality TV: Remaking Television Culture*. New York: New York University Press, 2004.
Palacio, Manuel. *Historia de la televisión en España*. Barcelona: Gedisa, 2001.
Sardà, Xavier. *Me encanta que me hagas esta pregunta*. Madrid: Santillana, 2004.
Telecinco. *Informe anual 1998*. Madrid: Telecinco, 1999.

Electronic sources
AIMC [Asociación de Investigación de Medios de Comunicación]. "EGM: año móvil octubre 2002–mayo 2003." September 25, 2003. <http://www.aimc.es/02 egm/resumegm203.pdf>.
Crónicas. Crónicas marcianas: web oficial del programa de telecinco. February 23, 2005. <http://www.cronicasmarcianas.telecinco.es/>.
Descifrador, El. "Descontrol." *El Mundo*, February 23, 2005. February 23, 2005. <http://www.elmundo.es/elmundo/2005/02/23/descodificador/1109116634. html>.
FormulaTV. "*Crónicas marcianas* logra sus mejores resultados de la temporada." *FormulaTV*, January 16, 2005. February 23, 2005. <http://www.formulatv.com/ 1,20050116,755,1.html>.
Info-TK. "*Crónicas marcianas* tiene buena prensa." 21 November 21, 2003. February 23, 2005. <http://infotk.blogs.com/infotk/2003/11/crnicas_marcian. html>.
Mundo, El. Archive search: "telebasura". December 15, 2004. <www.elmundo.es>.
Plataforma por una televisión de calidad. "Manifiesto contra la telebasura." March 4, 2005. <http://www.arrakis.es/~pedra/tvbasura.htm>.
"Plumbing the Depths: A Forlorn Effort to Get Rid of Rubbish on Spanish TV." *The Economist*, November 11, 2004. January 24, 2005. <http://www.econo-mist.com/displaystory.cfm?story_id=3387797>.
Sanchis, Luz. "*Crónicas marcianas* pierde en un año 267.000 telespectadores." *Periodista Digital*, October 16, 2004. February 23, 2005. <http:// periodistadigital.com/boletin/object.php?o+33211>.
"Sardá celebra mil noches en el planeta Marte." *El País*, November 17, 2003. February 4, 2005. <http://www.elpais.es/articulo/elpepirtv/20031117elpepirtv_1/ Tes/Sard%E1%20celebra%20mil%20noches%20en%20el%20planeta%20Mar te>.
"Sardà, el conductor de *Crónicas Marcianas*, gana 10 millones de euros al año con el programa." *Noticiasdot.com*, July 18, 2003. February 4, 2005. <http:// www.noticiasdot.com/publicaciones/2003/0703/2207/noticias220703/noticias22 0703-14.htm>.

6

Almodóvar on Television: Industry, Thematics, Theory

Industry

Almodóvar's first fifteen feature films are framed by references to television. In *Pepi, Luci, Bom* (1980) Carmen Maura's unlikely heiress Pepi sets herself up as an advertising producer. Her first project is a spot for knickers with a twist: they will absorb gas and urine or, when necessary, double as a dildo. In the final titles which bring *La mala educación* (*Bad Education*, 2004) to a provisional and unsatisfactory close, we read that the mercenary and murderous actor played by Gael García, known variously as Ignacio, Juan, and Angel through the course of the complex plot, will spend ten years as a movie star before "now work[ing] exclusively in TV series." While *Pepi* gleefully incorporates parodies of pop or mass culture such as television into its defiantly heterogeneous filmic text, *Education* seems to posit television as a radical other to cinema, a fate for an actor (and perhaps a director) that is almost worse than death.

Television is the dark continent of Almodóvar's oeuvre. While references are constant in his films (Mark Allinson claims that in the first thirteen features there is only one in which characters fail to watch television [54]), there is almost no criticism that addresses this vital topic (Allinson himself is the only one to write at length on the medium). The neglect is no surprise. Spanish critics of film and indeed TV despise television, a position which Almodóvar would seem to share in *Education*; foreign critics lack familiarity with a notoriously domestic medium. What I argue in this last chapter, however, is that television, however repressed or disavowed, is indeed central to Almodóvar's work over the course of twenty-five years. Indeed his later "blue period," which I have argued elsewhere resurrects the artistic distinction of "art cinema," can be profitably re-read in the light of TV studies. After all, Almodóvar himself has acknowledged the ubiquity of television. In interview on the US release of *Kika*, his most savage critique of the medium, he is reported as saying:

> It is an omnipresent eye in everyone's life. In every country, any place, there is a television. I don't think there is a day in the year in which we don't see an image in that square frame. So if there is an open window, then I thought that someone with a camera could be watching. (Willoquet-Maricondi 102–3)

Television is thus equated not only with the space-time matrix of everyday life but with vision and surveillance (seeing and being seen) in the city: the window quite simply equals the small screen.

The first approach to television in Almodóvar is industrial. While Almodóvar's independent production company El Deseo, helmed by his faithful brother Agustín, has permitted him a wide degree of artistic freedom, it is striking how often El Deseo works in collaboration with TV companies. Even before the setting up of El Deseo with *La ley del deseo* (*The Law of Desire*, 1987), *Matador* (1986) had been co-produced by Iberoamericana and the then monopoly broadcaster Televisión Española (it is characteristic that state support for the goriest of Almodóvar's films provoked no controversy). *Carne trémula* (*Live Flesh*, 1977) was made in collaboration with French film producers Ciby 2000 and TV channel France 3; *Todo sobre mi madre* (*All About My Mother*, 1999) with Pathé's Renn, France 2, and premium cable channel Canal +. *Hable con ella* (*Talk to Her*, 2002) had minority financial interests from the Spanish free-to-air private network Antena 3 and digital platform Vía Digital. Finally *Bad Education* was part funded once more by Televisión Española, by now locked in bitter competition with the private webs, and the Spanish subsidiary of the premium channel Canal +, which had long relied on local feature films to attract subscriptions.

What is striking, then, is the Almodóvars' increasing recourse to TV production funding during the recent blue period, in which Pedro set his sights on the elite distinction of art or auteur cinema. Interestingly, at the same time, Almodóvar also took to collaborating with actors mainly familiar to Spanish audiences from television, albeit casting against their accepted type: inoffensive romantic lead Toni Cantó played the cruel transsexual father in *All About My Mother*; tubby, buffoonish Javier Cámara played both the troubled nurse in *Talk to Her* and the camp sidekick in *Bad Education*. Both actors had featured in early seasons of Tele5's urban sitcom *7 Vidas* (*Seven* or *Nine Lives*, 1999–). In fact El Deseo had long turned to TV for both funding and distribution. To take a few examples at random: Almodóvar's own career was arguably launched by his musical performances on the legendary TV show of the *movida*, *La edad de oro* (*The Golden Age*) in the early 1980s; in 1990 (soon after the setting up of his independent production company and the huge commercial success of *Women on the Verge*) he sold his entire back catalogue to TVE for the then unprecedented sum of 200 million pesetas (Smith, *Desire*, 101). Explicit gay melodrama *The Law of Desire* was first networked at prime time in April 1991, once more without controversy (Smith, *Desire*, 89). Given the current wholesale exclusion of foreign-language cinema from British network schedules, it is a shock to remember that *Mujeres al borde de un ataque de nervios* (*Women on the Verge of a Nervous Breakdown*, 1988) played on BBC2 on Christmas Eve 1992 (Smith, *Desire*, 102). In spring 2004, *Talk to Her* was in rotation on HBO Latino, the Spanish-language channel of the respected and innovative premium US cabler. Almodóvar, perhaps the only foreign-language filmmaker to achieve theatrical distribution for all of his movies in all major territories, thus also nurtured his audience and increased his cultural profile through screenings on mass television at home and select minority channels abroad. It is perhaps unsurprising that El Deseo, who have expanded their feature production outside

Spain and into English, claim themselves to have at least two TV series in development.

Two collaborations by Almodóvar himself with Spanish television are especially significant. *Trailer para amantes de lo prohibido* (*Trailer for Lovers of the Forbidden*, 1984) is a promotional short made to tie in with the release of *¿Qué he hecho yo para merecer esto?* (*What Have I Done to Deserve This*, 1984). Shot on low-definition video, it boasts features typical of Almodóvar's mid-period film work, but exaggerated and coarsened. The cursory plot is of a desperate housewife who abandons her home for a young lover, a decision that inevitably leads to murder. More interesting is the form: the story is told entirely through stylized sequences of lip synching to old songs. The mise-en-scène (settings and wardrobe) is apparently improvised and gaudy, while the cast is relatively unknown (with the exception of long-time collaborator Bibi Anderson). Like the little-seen and extravagantly titled super-8s that came before *Pepi, Luci, Bom*, *Trailer* seems something of an embarrassment to the Almodóvars, perhaps because its low production values came at a time when Pedro was first beginning his long march to high art. Considered of only academic interest, *Trailer* was screened with a preview of *Bad Education* to a select group of specialist scholars at the conference held at the Universidad Castilla-La Mancha to celebrate Pedro's donation of his archive in 2003. Most interesting in *Trailer* (whose very title proclaims allegiance to film even in a work made for TV) is the integration of documentary footage of the première of *What Have I Done* into the fictional plot. Already Almodóvar's cinematic history is inseparable from television.

Much later, in 2000, comes the programme broadcast by state minority channel TVE2 celebrating the twentieth anniversary of the theatrical release of *Pepi, Luci, Bom*. As Nuria Triana notes (142), this curious show marks the definitive "canonization" of Almodóvar: *Pepi* is the first film to be shown in a series known somewhat paradoxically as "Clásicos modernos" and in a strand called, with gentle irony, *Versión española* ("Spanish version" is a label normally applied by cinemas to dubbed Hollywood films). In a format familiar on Spanish TV, but little known in the UK or US, studio discussion bookends the screening of the feature. While the show was promoted because of the first appearance together for many years of the director and one-time diva Carmen Maura, cinematic history is also embodied by its attractive and articulate presenter: Caetana Guillén Cuervo had just appeared as the main character's best friend in *All About My Mother* and is the daughter and sister respectively of the two actors who played father-and-son detectives in *The Law of Desire*. As ever, TV is a family business. While Pedro was clothed in a basic black top and jeans and Carmen in a relatively modest wrap-around dress, one unusual feature of the studio set-up heightened the potential conflict of the confrontation: the three speakers were confined to an arena-like circle around which the camera crew were shown at work. A crane even gave alarmingly vertiginous high angles looking down on the contestants.

Somewhat tense studio discussion was cross-cut with short pieces to camera by the presenter which introduced brief messages from survivors of *Pepi* and the *movida*, some sadly decayed, wishing all involved a "happy birthday", and documentary footage of momentous historical events of the period: the passing of Franco, the legalization of the Communist Party, and the death of Tierno Galván, popular and progressive Mayor of Madrid. Interestingly this public narrative (electronically treated to resemble gaudy *movida* graphics) was juxtaposed with the personal history of Pedro and Carmen's dramatic relationship, presented with on-screen titles: "a very special union," "falling out," "re-encounter," "to be continued." Famous film careers were thus likened to episodes in a humble TV series.

In conversation Maura stressed how much she had learned about filmmaking from the extended and improvised shoot of *Pepi* (although she was already an established actress), while Pedro claimed Carmen was a perfect "instrument" for his direction (although he had received no training for this, his first feature). Maura's wary looks and guarded comments contrasted with Almodóvar's unperturbed fluency. Triana is surely right to stress how this prime time broadcast marked a definitive change in what is understood by "Spanish national cinema": the shift from an exclusive definition of "quality" or "social realist" film to an inclusive "discourse of diversity" which permitted a wider range of "generic and aesthetic choices" (142). However, what we find here, in the emblematically named strand *Versión española*, are two modes of perception which, as we shall see, are typical of the televisual medium: a pedagogy or education in personal and national history; and a witnessing or working through of issues, whether subjective or objective, which can have no definitive conclusion.

Thematics

The last three decades have seen the post-Franco reform of state broadcaster TVE, the coming of regional and commercial channels, the *telebasura* controversy, and the recent explosion of locally produced quality fiction. If we leave the industrial aspect and look at the content of the films themselves, we see that over the course of that same period Almodóvar has given us a hidden history of TV (or, rather, of the electronic image) in Spain.

A brief survey would look something like the following: with *Pepi* we have not just the commercial for pants-you-can-pee-in mentioned earlier but also the policeman's rape of neighbour Charo as a black-and-white talk show plays unheeded in the background. *What Have I Done . . .?* (1984) gives us a commercial for hot coffee you'll never forget (the consumer's face is scarred for life), and the idiosyncratic performance of traditional song "La bien pagá" by Almodóvar and musical crony McNamara. *Matador* (1986) begins with a clip tape of slasher footage enjoyed in fevered isolation by a serial killer, and an early attack on partisan news reporting (a strident journalist denounces the "breathtaking cynicism" of the lawyer defending a client accused of murder). In

The Law of Desire (1987) the main character Pablo, a gay film director, is interviewed by a more indulgent arts reporter. In *Women on the Verge* (1988) Pedro's own mother plays an unlikely newsreader. The director in *¡Átame!* (*Tie Me Up! Tie Me Down!*, 1990) is addicted to the porn videos of his star, played by Victoria Abril. The latter also plays a newsreader who confesses to a murder live on air in *Tacones lejanos* (*High Heels*, 1991). *Kika* (1993) is structured entirely around the new genre of reality TV. *La flor de mi secreto* (*The Flower of My Secret*, 1995) begins with closed circuit TV intended to train transplant surgeons and features a song by Chavela Vargas heard by main character Leo on a TV playing in a bar. *Live Flesh* (1997) and *All About My Mother* (1999) show glimpses of classic movies broadcast to very different households (Buñuel's *The Criminal Life of Archimbaldo Cruz* in a junkie apartment and Mankiewicz's *All About Eve* in a loving household headed by a single mother). The serious-themed *Talk to Her* features a single farcical scene in which a prurient talk-show host literally holds down her interviewee on set. Finally *Bad Education*, as we have seen, condemns its anti-hero, ambitious for a film career, to a post-cinematic living death in television fiction (Illustrations 16, 17, 18).

While the sheer persistence of Almodóvar's engagement with television is striking, confirming as it does the ubiquity of the medium, other preliminary observations can be made. First, his films cite a wide range of TV genres: commercials, variety, news, and reality shows (but significantly, perhaps, not drama). Secondly, they cover several related but distinct electronic media: broadcast television, home-edited videotape played on a private VCR, professionally recorded videotape broadcast live and recorded, and closed-circuit TV used in the workplace. Finally, the features reveal a number of modes of reception or consumption: intense solitary voyeurism, sociable family viewing in the home, distracted communal attention in public places, and the hermetic loop of the closed-circuit camera and monitor, at once private and public (in *All About My Mother* the main character's son, a non-professional, sits in on one video training session).

It is evident, then, that Almodóvar "makes room for TV," in all its variety and heterogeneity, even in his last films, which clearly constitute love songs to cinema as a medium. If we look more closely at three specimen features from the early and late periods ("rose" and "blue"), pivoting as ever on the problem picture that is *Kika*, we see changes in the relationship between the TV elements and the films which frame them. For example, it is striking how often Almodóvar cuts straight into a TV sequence without giving the audience any formal cue in the editing (the equivalent of an establishing shot) to orientate us. Thus with *Pepi*, the commercial, which was actually shot before the film itself and thus constitutes a unique fragment of pre-cinema in Almodóvar's oeuvre, simply begins to play in full frame. While the product is wilfully bizarre, the formal conventions of traditional advertising are observed: the omniscient voice-over, the direct address to camera, mood music, and final tagline punning on the brand name ("Whatever you do, wear knickers/*Ponte* knickers"). After the commercial finishes Almodóvar cuts to a screening room. As the lights

16. *Carne trémula* ("Live Flesh"): Elena (Francesca Neri)

17. *Hable con ella* ("Talk to Her"): Lydia (Rosario Flores)

18. *La mala educación* ("Bad Education"): Ignacio/Juan/Angel
(Gael García Bernal)

come up the main characters give desultory opinions on what now stands revealed as Pepi's debut spot. The cheerful scatology of the advertisement and its fragmentary nature ally it with the rest of the film, composed as it is of barely connected episodes (musical performances, vérité reportage, hand-drawn inter-titles, etc.).

By the time of *What Have I Done?* TV material is more integrated. Once more Almodóvar cuts directly into the bizarre musical number in which he and Fabio, dressed as nineteenth-century lovers, lip-synch to a campy traditional song. But this time we are given a brief wide shot of the studio which includes the cameras trained on the set, and would thus be inaccessible to the audience watching at home. We then cut to that domestic audience, in this case the enthusiastic grandmother and her grandchild, nauseous after drug-taking. Almodóvar then cuts to a third location: the bedroom in which Carmen Maura's Gloria pleads with her husband for money as he makes perfunctory love to her. While the lyrics of the song clearly comment on the main action (the modern housewife is compared to the ill-paid prostitute of the past), what interests me more here is the depiction of a fantasized, deconstructed "family viewing" precipitated by a grotesquely implausible variety show, a genre which, as we saw in chapter 4, survived longer in Spain than in other territories. While TV professionals sometimes talk of the "two televisual Spains" (elderly and rural versus modern and urban [Contreras and Palacio, 187]), Almodóvar posits TV viewing as a kind of ironic communion between social extremes, analogous to the other comic activities performed together by this odd couple: school homework, the forging of signatures, and the gathering of sticks from the dismal suburban park.

High Heels reveals increasing interest in the apparatus and, indeed, industry of recently deregulated Spanish television. A member of Almodóvar's newly up-market professional milieu, Victoria Abril's Chanel-suited Rebeca is a newsreader married to the mysteriously murdered CEO of a fictional private web. The sequence of her televised confession is pivotal in the film. In this case, and for the first time, Almodóvar focuses on the variety of audiences brought together by live national broadcasting. Rebeca's improvised performance is re-doubled on screen by the alarmed sign-language interpreter and framed by cutaways to her professional colleagues (the news-conscious director, who instructs his production team not to pull the plug on the unfolding media event) and her private acquaintances (her celebrity mother and the judge who doubles as a transvestite chanteuse). The public display of intimacy (Rebeca shows family snapshots to the camera) is easily read as typical of that (con)fusion of performance and essence held to be characteristic of postmodernism. To anticipate my own argument on televisual modes of perception, however, I would suggest it points rather to a witnessing of the media event, which implicates spectators emotionally even as they remain impotent observers: Rebeca's mother, strong-willed Becky, stares dumfounded at the screen, powerless to participate.

With *Kika*, Almodóvar's least successful film for the critics, televisual dynamics have wholly invaded cinematic space. As I have written elsewhere, in this early scattershot critique of reality shows (made some ten years before the genre was widely programmed in most markets), Almodóvar explores what Paul Virilio called "the vision machine": the confusion of presentation and representation; the passage from vision to visualization; the waning of reality under the onslaught of technology (Smith, *"Kika"*: 38). More precisely *Kika* tracks the transition from one medium to another: celluloid, with its sense of dialectical duration, gives way to video, with its new stress on the paradoxical incident or accident (39). However, the film's attitude towards this social and technological change is fatally flawed. While it is at the very least ironic to see Almodóvar, once the champion of popular culture, editorialize against new forms of mass entertainment, his own cinematic vision comes to be shadowed by the electronic medium he critiques. Arguably the most dynamic scenes of the film are when Victoria Abril's cyborg reporter tracks down "the worst of the day" for her exploitation programme of that name. And in his defence of the notoriously extended rape scene, Almodóvar appeals to precisely that confusion of presentation and representation characteristic of the vision machine: he argues, unconvincingly, that the real violation of Kika is not her physical rape but the broadcasting of it on television. Moreover, a blurry haze of low-definition video pixels bleeds over into the movie, contaminating the typically and incongruously glossy big-screen production values of Almodóvar's mid-period.

But even here the vision of television is not wholly negative: *Kika* also re-creates the unlikely book discussion show "We Must Read More," hosted by Almodóvar's aged mother (for whom the film itself is named). Greeting the foreign author played by dubbed American actor Peter Coyote, she offers him a "little sausage" (*choricico*), the regional diminutive increasing the sense of TV's local particularity and domesticity. And if we turn to early sequences in three recent films of the more artistically ambitious "blue" period, we see that television remains central to Almodóvar's depiction of Spanish forms of sociality. *Flower* begins, typically, without editorial warning, with scenes of organ transplant donation, which are only later revealed to be closed-circuit training videos. Almodóvar then cuts to his heroine Leo, asleep in the stylish, cluttered apartment where she is attempting to resurrect her career as a serious author. Here the video performance on "brain death," which precedes the representation of the "real" world, is by no means inauthentic but rather stands as a privileged metaphor for a creative life and a romantic love that are also on life support (Leo's husband, like the romantic fiction she writes but despises, has betrayed her). In *Live Flesh*, junkie Elena's viewing of Buñuel's Mexican melodrama fully exemplifies the "distracted attention" that TV is often held to embody (heedless of the movie, she is desperate for a fix). But once more the material shown on television embodies a vital precedent for the cinematic action to come: a fatal bullet rings out on screen and in the flat; a look of love will change lives on TV and in the film. Finally, in *All About My Mother*, Almodóvar establishes the deep bond between mother and teenage son by having them watch TV together. While the dubbed transmission (i.e. "versión española") of *All About Eve* highlights the themes of female community, rivalry, and theatricality which will be developed throughout the film, the circumstances of *Eve*'s consumption are perhaps more important: Manuela and Esteban sit together during an extended two-shot, sharing the frame as they share the sofa, casually (intimately) discussing the movie and their own lives. Television, no less than the theatre which is a medium more prominently featured and discussed in the film, serves as a precious opportunity for working through issues that are at once public and private, social and personal.

Theory

TV studies, writes John Caughie (9), are haunted by the memory of film. In the final section of this last chapter I would like to offer a modest proposal which inverts the hierarchy: that Almodóvar's recent films are best understood using analytical concepts derived from TV studies. After all, if television is as ubiquitous as Almodóvar himself acknowledges, in interview as in the body of his work, it is hardly surprising that the small screen should leave some aesthetic and theoretical residue in the large.

It is a proposal that seems counterintuitive. After all, a film like *Talk to Her*, for which Almodóvar won the Oscar for best original screenplay, is as frank a hymn to cinema as one could imagine. It not only re-creates a 15-minute black-and-white silent movie in the style of Murnau, it also sets a pivotal scene in a real-life Madrid art house, the Cine Doré, which screens the repertory programmes of the Filmoteca Española. Almodóvar's camera lovingly tilts up the recently restored façade. Elsewhere I have written that the "blue period" films stage a transparent and successful bid for the resurrection of that endangered species the "art movie" (Smith, *Contemporary*, 144–68). Boasting expert camerawork, pseudo-classical scores, and luxury casts, *Flower*, *Flesh*, *Mother*, and *Talk* also treat themes designed to attract cultural distinction. They are literate and literary films in which characters are often shown writing and reading; they are sexually dissident films intended to appeal to sophisticated cosmopolitan audiences; and they are highly urban films, which address for the first time social and political issues, albeit framed by and subordinated to personal and emotional imperatives.

Yet three aspects of Almodóvar's filmmaking coincide more closely with televisual modes of perception and production than those of the feature film. The first is regularity. Unlike the few surviving auteurs of a previous generation, Almodóvar has kept up a regular rhythm of production: fifteen features in twenty-four years. One comparison would be with a director often cited as the consummate Spanish art director, Víctor Erice, who has completed just three acclaimed feature films in thirty years. In spite of their highly professionalized publicity campaigns, Almodóvar's films cannot be seen as the unique "events" typical of current art-movie practice but read rather as part of a regular, rhythmic flow, more characteristic of TV drama.

The second aspect is familiarity. To domestic and, increasingly, foreign audiences Almodóvar's creative universe (his motifs, styles, actors, even his music and production design) is immediately identifiable and lodged in popular, communal memory as TV is supposed to be. In Spain, unlike in the UK, there is no popular television narrative which has lasted as long as Almodóvar's consistently successful cinematic serial. Indeed it is precisely this excessive familiarity which has denied him in Spain, at least until very recently, the cultural prestige so readily given to other less prolific auteurs, especially those working in the critically privileged social realist genre.

Finally, there is openness. Where movie plotting is conventionally unified and closed (dictated by the three-act structure, the character arc, the satisfying conclusion), Almodóvar's scripts are defiantly plural and inconclusive. Within each film, plot strands spiral off from the main narrative (indeed it is often impossible to identify a main narrative), straining against the restraints of a feature-length ninety minutes. Conclusions are cursory: in *Flower*, Leo, having lost a husband, toasts a new, sexless partner who is hardly a substitute; in *Flesh*, a new birth in Madrid both brings us back to the opening sequence of the film and suggests a whole new beginning; in *Mother*, Manuela returns once more to Barcelona where the other characters are shown to be living stories that are, in the familiar formula, to be continued; finally, *Talk* ends with the briefest of final sections as inter-titles announce a new relationship (Marco and Alicia) which has yet to commence.

Moreover, plot elements link up with or loop back from one film to another in a way which is also reminiscent of the looser associative forms of television drama: the closed-circuit transplant scene of *Flower* is replayed and expanded in *Mother*; *Mother*'s main actresses recur as uncredited extras at the party scene in *Talk*; *Talk*'s brief and enigmatic shot of a young man swimming in a pool is expanded into a central scene of *Education*. While such thematic continuities were often seen as distinguishing signs of cinematic auteurism, the formal discontinuities of Almodóvar's idiosyncratic scripts (often attacked by perfectionist Spanish critics) come close to the restless, boundless innovations of television drama.

Almodóvar's recent films also allow us to witness and work through social issues as they are implicated in daily life, a distinguishing feature of that everyday medium, television. *Flower* places NATO and PSOE decadence in the context of Leo's disastrous love life; *Flesh* contrasts urban spatial practice (the street) under democracy and dictatorship; *Mother* addresses issues from AIDS to Alzheimers rarely shown in Spanish cinema, but the stock-in-trade of recent TV drama in Spain. Almodóvar's cinema has become "pedadogic" without being didactic or preachy, educating audiences on social and ethical responsibility and making them think about their world with open-ended ambivalence. For example, the rape in *Talk*, unlike that in *Kika*, is conspicuously attacked within the film itself. Marco says Benigno is crazy even to speak of his relationship with the comatose Alicia as a marriage. Benigno is finally imprisoned and dies a suicide, in an almost unique example of criminal justice in Almodóvar. Yet we are also led to sympathize with Benigno's emotional history, stunted and deformed as it is. It is not just in *Bad Education* that Almodóvar seeks to educate his audience.

But before turning to a reading of this fifteenth feature, I would like to make explicit the TV scholarship on which I have been drawing here and to which I have appealed throughout this book. In *Seeing Things: Television in the Age of Uncertainty*, his history of television focusing on the UK and US, John Ellis stresses the "profound uncertainty" of television at the millennium (1). His new modality of perception "witness" is, we remember, defined as "a particular form of representation that brings with it a sense of powerless knowledge and complicity with what we see" and his two distinct eras of television in consumer society are mass-market and public service "scarcity" (2) and diverse and differentiated "availability." Television no longer offers a mass audience definitive programming, but rather works through or worries over issues and emotions interminably. The everyday quality of TV is thus positively valued for its social utility (4), and the medium is not to be dismissed out of hand.

We also saw that Ellis's version of the shift from public service "scarcity" to consumerist "availability" was borne out in Spain by Manuel Palacio's *Historia de la televisión en España*, stressing as it does the social importance of the medium, its communal history, and role in socialization (11). In spite of the particular problems he notes in studying television in Spain (the lack of archival resources and the near universal condemnation of the medium), Palacio identifies "pedagogy" as a key term historically and theoretically. Likewise the Spanish audiovisual industry and audience have long coincided in believing that television is educational, in the broadest sense of the word, and should be criticized if it fails to achieve that basic function.

Now it may merely be a happy accident that Almodóvar should have named his fifteenth feature as he did. But *Bad Education* does explore aspects of electronic visuality examined by Ellis and Palacio above. This is not to deny that it is gloriously cinematic, with its mobile cinematography, subtle, probing score (by the sole composer for the "blue period," Alberto Iglesias), and expert cast. Yet *Bad Education* was immediately drawn into an intense televisual controversy which overshadowed its release in Spain: shortly after the terrorist atrocity at Atocha, Almodóvar at first suggested and then denied at press conferences that the People's Party was conspiring before the 2004 elections to do away with democracy. The continuing drama of Almodóvar's relation to the press here veered perilously into the territory of *telenovela*. And, in spite of such novel elements as the casting of Latin America's hottest young star, Gael García Bernal (rigorously schooled in a European accent), and the period setting, *Education* remained reassuringly familiar to Spanish audiences with the recurring motif of the drag queen, the central figure of the film director, and the brief uncredited appearance of Leonor Watling, the comatose Alicia in the previous *Talk*, as a wardrobe worker. Our distracted attention thus "bleeds over" from one film to another, suggesting a continuing flow of themes and figures beyond the limits of a single feature. The device of the final titles used to end the film is also wilfully provisional, projecting the action far beyond the last scene that we are shown and sketching out reversals worthy of a day-time soap: the blackmailer is himself blackmailed and murders his obsessive tormentor. One distinguished Spanish critic simply listed the many plot points *Education* reruns from 1987's *The Law of Desire*, suggesting this was just another episode in a continuing drama that spanned decades (Heredero).

In his notes to the DVD which was released as a special promotion with the newspaper *El País*, Almodóvar claims his film is a commentary neither on the *movida* of the 1980s nor on the Catholic paedophile-priest scandals of the present time. Yet, as at once Almodóvar's most historical and most contemporary feature, *Education* witnesses or works through what is transparently a major social issue, even if the one million pesetas which the junkie Ignacio seeks to extort from the former priest pales in comparison with the billions of dollars paid in legally mandated reparations for similar cases in the US. (The scandal is at an earlier stage in Spain.) The education Almodóvar presents or represents to us works on a number of levels, often ambivalent or mutually contradictory. The hypocritical teaching of the Francoist church is condemned even as its ritual is depicted with a fetishistic reverence worthy of Zurbarán. The youthful training in camp enjoyed by the innocent youths on their trips to see movie stars like Sara Montiel is replayed by the ambitious and cynical Juan-Ignacio, who literally takes lessons from the Montiel impersonator he insults as a "queer." Finally the driven director Enrique learns the truth about Juan-Ignacio-Angel, but can never penetrate his mind as he does his body. Arguably the director, who, we are told in the very last title, "still makes cinema with passion," is the one character who fails to develop, never learning a lesson about love in the workaday world but frozen in his self-inflicted cinematic seclusion.

As in *Talk*, Almodóvar seems more willing than he once was to denounce ethical crimes such as rape. In "The Visit" (the film within the film), drag queen Zahara tells the first priest: "you don't 'love' a child of ten years: you rape and abuse him." And, threatening blackmail, Zahara invokes the changing times which, with the coming of democracy, have undermined past certainties: "This society values my freedom more than your hypocrisy." But even here there is ambivalence. After all, was it inevitable that Spain would pass so quickly from the censorship of dictatorship to the lurid sensationalism of democratic mass media? And Zahara's relatively sympathetic words are echoed by the demonic real-life transsexual Ignacio in the second half of the movie. Blackmailing the second priest, he notes complacently that "sexual abuse is frowned upon." Even the impenetrably dark Juan is given a certain moral alibi. In his final confrontation with Enrique, the confidently gay man-about-Madrid, he says: "You can't imagine what it was like to live in a village with a brother like mine." The film thus worries away at issues such as homophobia and paedophilia without coming to any definite conclusion. Both priests persist in calling their obsessive passions "love." As Sr Beranguer, abandoned after helping Juan to murder his brother, weeps in the rain we can only look on, implicated, impotent, and perhaps complicit.

We saw in chapter 5 that there are two narratives of Spanish television during the period Almodóvar made his recent art movies. In the first, much repeated by *El País*, Ellis's era of media "availability" has led to a flood of *telebasura*: trash TV, which threatens individuals and society alike with its commercially motivated stupidity and venality. In the second, much less known narrative, media scholars and practitioners such as Palacio and his collaborator José Miguel Contreras, the offer of Spanish television has been transformed for the better by independent producers of the quality fiction which has banished from the small screen previous imports from the US and Latin America and outdated local shows. The watchword here is not trash but "innovation" in both technology and content. TV workplace drama of the last five years has actively sought "quality" audiences (young, wealthy, and urban) and tackled risky social issues such as euthanasia, even before they were tardily targeted by earnest moviemakers: Tele5's *Periodistas* aired the issue of mercy killing not only long before the release of Alejandro Amenábar's prize-winning feature film *Mar adentro* (*The Sea Inside*, 2004) but even before the final curtain had come down on the real-life drama on which the movie was based. As we saw in chapter 4, new-style sitcoms, modelled on quality US shows such as *Frasier*, have spurned the traditionalist stars and formats of yore in search of the same quality demographic, featuring amongst their colourful casts sexual dissidents who are the equal of Almodóvar's cinematic cousins. Ironically, then, even as Almodóvar has distanced himself publicly from Spanish television (he claimed that *Kika* was inspired by celebrity sex trials on US TV [Willoquet-Maricondi, 103]), the audiences for quality drama in the two media have converged. It is thus no accident that Almodovar has borrowed actors from such TV shows, or plans to produce them with his own company, or that his own films are screened on prestigious minority channels abroad.

The glossy ads for mobile phones and luxury cars that punctuated the *Versión española* screening of the grungy *Pepi, Luci, Bom* inadvertently revealed how Spain has changed for some at least during Almodóvar's lengthy career. An age of media abundance has also brought an unprecedented abundance of consumer goods to many Spaniards. El Deseo is a remarkable example of Spain's ability to keep up its profile in a highly competitive global media marketplace. Almodóvar's collected works are the nearest thing to a shared national narrative in a country where television, ever beset by controversy, has not historically provided such continuity. And they offer us, to a highly developed extent, the best properties of cinema: the chance to dream and to desire. But I have argued that, like television, Almodóvar's recent cinema also prompts us to think about the world and our place in it. It is not to diminish Almodóvar's achievement to suggest that his films, framed and permeated as they are by televisual references, have something in common with a medium that he and other right-minded Spaniards would prefer to ignore, if only its ubiquity did not make it inescapable.

156 PAUL JULIAN SMITH

Works cited

Allinson, Mark. *A Spanish Labyrinth: The Films of Pedro Almodóvar*. London: I. B. Tauris, 2001.

Almodóvar, Pedro. Production notes reproduced in DVD of *La mala educación* sold with *El País*, in its collection "Todo Almodóvar," 2004.

Caughie, John. *Television Drama*. Oxford: Oxford University Press, 2000.

Ellis, John. *Seeing Things: Television in the Age of Uncertainty*. London: I. B. Tauris, 2002.

Heredero, Carlos F. "La vida, la ficción" [review of *La mala educación*]. *El Mundo: Suplemento El Cultural*, March 18, 2004: 47–8.

Palacio, Manuel. *Historia de la televisión en España*. Barcelona: Gedisa, 2001.

Palacio, Manuel, and José Miguel Contreras. *La programación de televisión*. Madrid: Síntesis, 2001.

Smith, Paul Julian. *Desire Unlimited: The Cinema of Pedro Almodóvar*. 2nd edn. London: Verso, 2000.

———. "*Kika*: Vision Machine." In *Vision Machines: Cinema, Literature, and Sexuality in Spain and Cuba, 1983–93*. London: Verso, 1996, pp. 37–58.

———. "Resurrecting the Art Movie: Almodóvar's Blue Period." In *Contemporary Spanish Culture: TV, Fashion, Art, and Film*. Cambridge: Polity, 2003, pp. 144–68.

Triana, Nuria. *Spanish National Cinema*. London: Routledge, 2003.

Willoquet-Maricondi, Paula (ed.). *Pedro Almodóvar: Interviews*. Jackson: University Press of Mississippi, 2004.

Conclusion: A Day in the Life of Spanish Television

Whatever their political positions, all Spaniards agree that today, Thursday, June 20, 2005, is "historic." Before dissolving for the summer, the Spanish parliament, led by the Socialists, votes in favour of extending marriage rights to same-sex couples on the same terms as heterosexuals. The government also announces that the commission of enquiry into the terrorist attacks of the previous year, which left nearly two hundred dead, will stand down. Neither decision is uncontroversial, with the opposition People's Party accusing the Socialists of exploiting both events for partisan purposes. While the hastily convened "Forum for the Family" (surely not unconnected to the conservative TV viewers' associations) has mounted large demonstrations against gay unions, President Zapatero claims that the new law enhances the dignity and freedom of all citizens and queer groups stage a massive, festive Pride carnival on the following Saturday.

Keeping the nation's calendar, Spanish TV also prepares itself for the long summer holidays. The schedules are awash with gossip and variety shows. On Saturday night TVE airs a traditional "gala" featuring the sentimental songs beloved by Spanish grandmothers. Meanwhile Tele5's talk show *Salsa rosa* (*Pink Sauce*, classified as suitable for "over 18s") extends for an interminable four hours from 10 pm Saturday to 2 am Sunday. In one lengthy studio segment the intrusive panelists grill a minor celebrity (hapless or clueless?) who has agreed to submit to their questions: how can she claim her marriage was happy when she starting dating other men so soon after her husband's death? The audience's text messages, for and against the merry widow, flash over the bottom of the screen. On Tele5 the big coup is the summer return of reality talent franchise *Operación triunfo* (*American Idol* in the US, *Pop Idol* in the UK) for its fourth season. Dropped by public broadcaster TVE, which refused to pay the high fees charged by Gestmusic-Endemol (the independent producers of *Crónicas marcianas*), it has now resurfaced on the private channel with a popular new host: openly gay Jesús Vázquez, who the press claim will soon marry his male partner. *Crónicas marcianas* itself, continuing its policy in recent seasons, hitches its cart to reality programming, with current episodes relying heavily on the newly revitalized *Operación Triunfo*. After over 1250 episodes, *Crónicas* is now scheduled to come off the air on July 21. Weddings are in the news here too: Boris Izaguirre interrogates his fellow panelist Rocío Madrid on whether she had sex with her new husband just before their recent ceremony.

TV, even at its most trivial, thus runs parallel to politics. And showing that public service is by no means impossible in the current climate, TVE1's weekend news update *Informe semanal* (*Weekly Report*, airing at 9.35 pm on Saturday) has a sympathetic segment on same-sex marriage. As well as covering current events from a fresh angle (focusing on parents who support their gay children), the journalists also investigate the historical background to the story, airing rare interviews with elderly gay men and lesbians from Barcelona, including veteran activists from the 1970s. While such coverage evidently supports the policies of the ruling Socialist Party, whose leader Zapatero is so publicly committed to the extension of marriage rights, it continues a tradition of TV pedagogy which, as we have seen, stretches back at least as far as the transition to democracy some thirty years earlier. Clearly 2004–5 is another historic period, as the coming of the most Leftist government since the Republic has brought rapid and unexpected social and political change. There is much material for television to witness and work through for bewildered Spanish citizens.

As the season ends (in politics as in television), the texts studied in this book remain vital. *Cuéntame cómo pasó*, which had ended its sixth season as early as February, is still the most popular drama in the country, although it has strayed far from its domestic beginnings. One expensive plotline had characters visiting the Soviet Union as part of a trade delegation. In an exploration of a historical phenomenon only now being widely reclaimed, the father (played by Imanol Arias) bonds with a Spanish exile who was sent to Moscow as a child in the Civil War. A special episode to celebrate the one-hundredth episode, "Días de blanco y negro" ("Days in Black and White"), relies on footage from NO-DO newsreel to illustrate the older actors' memories and anecdotes of the long lost 1970s.

Although willing to pay for such prestige independent productions as *Cuéntame*, TVE's continuing financial crisis makes the cost of genres such as the classic serial prohibitive when set against the likely audience benefits. No such shows are visible in the schedule. But TVE still announces documentary series with aspirations to national heritage, both spatial and temporal. New for the summer is *España, entre el cielo y la tierra* (*Spain between Heaven and Earth*), twenty-six episodes of aerial photography spanning the nation from north to south (we begin with Cervantine windmills for the four-hundredth anniversary of *Don Quijote*). The state broadcaster also trails the development of a historical documentary on the Civil War called *Memoria recobrada* (*Memory Recovered*; *Emisiones.TV,* 10).

Meanwhile, *Cine de barrio*, still fronted by the gaffe-prone Carmen Sevilla, continues its own idiosyncratic investigation of Francoist history. On Saturday, July 2 it shows Rafael Gil's *Currito de la Cruz* (1965), a bullfighting drama starring the respected Francisco Rabal. Between period picture and cozy chat, *Cine de barrio* swallows up a leisurely three hours in TVE's late afternoon and early evening (Spanish *sobremesa*) schedule. Antena 3's *Aquí no hay quien viva* remains more frenetic in both style and rhythm of production. Closing a mammoth third season of thirty-two episodes (the previous seasons reached only fourteen), the programme with the highest rating and share in Spain says goodbye for the summer with an episode in which the residents are seduced by the spurious promise of a free beach holiday (June 29; 5,718,000 rating, 35.5% share). Taking advantage of the show's popularity, María Adánez, who plays the pretty, posh girl Lucía, features in ubiquitous print ads for seaside resorts. The tagline mimics her show's title: "Así sí hay quien viva" ("Yes, people can live like this"). Television's intimate association with the everyday could hardly be more explicit than here.

Finally, Almodóvar also chooses this moment of mixed history and holiday to announce that he is about to start shooting his sixteenth feature. *Volver* (*Going Back*), his first film to star Carmen Maura in almost twenty years, marks a return to ruralism, with an all-female cast of characters returning to La Mancha, the depopulated regional home which Pedro himself abandoned long ago for the big city. The ghost of TV's *Crónicas de un pueblo* thus haunts Spain's most celebrated cineaste. Viewers may remember that it was on television's *Versión española* that Pedro and Carmen were first reunited. Meanwhile El Deseo's first ever TV series is scheduled to be broadcast in Spring 2006. Inevitably, it is called *Mujeres* (*Women*).

Current movie releases in theatres also reveal the long shadows of both Almodóvar and television. Ramón Salazar's *20 centímetros* (*8 Inches*) features a transsexual "mother" anxious to lose her manhood and boasts wilfully tacky dance numbers that could pass muster on *Cine de barrio*. Chus Gutiérrez's *El Calentito* is the period story of a girl group from the *movida*, which incorporates footage of Pedro in drag from his early *Laberinto de pasiones* (*Labyrinth of Passions*, 1982) and cast members from *Aquí no hay quien viva* masquerading as Francoist reactionaries. In an extension of the sitcom's lucrative brand into print, 2005 also sees the publication of a book supposedly written by the residents of the apartment building and named after the inescapable (and inexplicable) catch phrase of the show's ill-treated caretaker: *Un poquito de por favor* (*A Little Bit of Please*; Antena 3 TV).

Aquí no hay quien viva is also bitterly criticized by the Forum for the Family for a plotline held over from the previous season in which the gay characters seek to become parents ("Las conservadoras"). The parallel between broadcasting and politics continues in the prestigious summer schools held by Madrid's Complutense University at El Escorial (the monumental monastery built by Philip II, which features so frequently in Francoist newsreel). Parallel sessions treat "Television: industry or means of communication?" and "Homosexual cultures in Spain." In the first, Carmen Caffarell, Director-General of TVE, lectures on the thorny question of "quality" content. Many other producers cited in this book are interviewed in the third-anniversary number of trade journal *Emisiones.TV,* given out to delegates at El Escorial. Maurizio Carlotti reflects on two years as Antena 3's Director-General, during which he successfully turned around the private channel, as he had Tele5 in the previous decade (12–14). An Italian citizen, he defends himself against what he calls "provincialist" insults made against him by the critics of private television (13).

Josep Maria Mainat, independent producer of *Crónicas marcianas*, attacks the government's media policies as a waste of time, reserving particular ridicule for the "committee of wise men" whose recommendations have failed to tackle the "black hole" of TVE's finances (28–30). How could they expect an Academician who boasts of not having a TV set in his house to solve the riddle of public broadcasting? Mainat contrasts the bloated TVE with the slimmed down BBC, with its current policy of aggressive job and cost cutting (29). A brief interview with Eduardo Ladrón de Guevara (52), still scriptwriter and coordinator for *Cuéntame* four years after the show made its debut, reveals once more the collective nature of TV authorship. After he designs the "narrative arc" for the season and a team of writers draft the scripts, the actors contribute at the "table read", where their comments and opinions serve to "enrich" the teleplays.

As we have seen before, then, producers, in the broadest sense, are inextricable from institutions. The national government continues to complain about programming standards (threatening that if TV does not take itself in hand then they will); network executives and independent producers complain of political meddling and bias towards TVE. Only writers seem happy, with Ladrón claiming that, once treated "like shit," their creative contribution is now properly valued by a newly competitive TV system.

Meanwhile the figures for April 2005 carried by *Emisiones.TV* (20) confirm a historic reversal: TVE1 is no longer the most popular channel, its 19.4% share beaten by both Tele5 (22.7%) and Antena 3 (20.2%). The first year of a Socialist government which has bitterly attacked Spanish television has coincided with a significant fall in the ratings, both relative and absolute, for the embattled public broadcaster. One recommendation of the "Committee of Wise Men" appointed by the government will surely exacerbate this financial crisis: in Autumn 2005 subscription channel Canal + (part of the Socialist-supporting Prisa conglomerate) will become a new free-to-air national channel ("Cuatro"), thus competing with TVE for ratings and revenue. The ranking of most popular shows for April, moreover, confirms the dominance of long-running domestic fiction aired on the private networks. *Aquí no hay quien viva* appears no less than four times in the top five. The only US programme listed is the forensic drama spin-off *CSI Las Vegas* at a lowly nineteenth position.

In *El ojo digital*, his valuable compilation of journalistic pieces on TV audiences in Spain, Ricardo Vaca Berdayes also notes the "fidelity" of the public to long-running quality series and their discrimination between different episodes of those series. The Russian excursion of *Cuéntame*, which was exceptionally dramatic, brought in the highest audiences in the show's history (201). This success shows that it is still possible (and highly profitable) to attract a general audience that mirrors in its diversity the different ages and interests of the fictional Alcántara family. With proper investment, both financial and creative, such audiences can be sustained over a period of years. But if studies such as Vaca Berdayes's give the lie to the commonplaces of the *telebasura* controversy (namely that only trash makes money and that the shows are always the same), then the management of creativity is fraught with problems. Carlotti, CEO of

Antena 3, predicts that the government's reluctance to dialogue with the still small Spanish audiovisual industry could endanger the current boom in content production (*Emisiones TV*, 13).

In spite of this constantly changing institutional framework, we have seen that there is nonetheless a certain aesthetic continuity which stretches across the genres of serious drama, classic serial, sitcom, and talk show. Two factors seem specific to Spain, at least when compared with the US and UK. The first is time. In spite of rapid modernization and one of the most flexible economies in the EU, Spain retains a distinctive timetable which is reflected and reinforced by its television programming. TV viewing is not just later than elsewhere (with audiences continuing to grow in a late-night slot that lasts past 2 am); it is also longer, with formats stretched to at least twice those typical of Britain and America. This suggests a certain tolerance for tardy, lengthy, and irregular timeslots that does not exist elsewhere. If, as Alonso Zaldívar and Castells have argued (68–9), Spain escaped that rationalization of time that was brutally enforced by the industrial revolution, it has retained a distinctively pre-modern temporality into a postmodern era.

The second factor is collectivity. Spain is not without TV stars, although some of the best known (such as *Cuéntame*'s Imanol Arias) began their careers in feature films. However, the shows I have studied here, amongst the most highly valued both objectively and subjectively in the history of Spanish television, are all ensemble pieces. And frequently individual stars are replaced by the constellation of minor celebrities known in the dismissive Spanish diminutive as *famosillos*. From *Cuéntame* to *Aquí no hay quien viva*, through the two *Crónicas* (*de un pueblo* and *marcianas*), the dramatic focus is on interaction within a community rather than on action by an individual. While Anglo-American dramas also often focus on a well populated workplace, there are few equivalents of the Spanish ensemble shows in the genres of sitcom and talk show. It seems likely that, as in the case of the time factor, this collectivity is deeply engrained in Spanish culture. It also confirms that television, not cinema, is the true inheritor of the teeming nineteenth-century novel of Galdós and Alas. Certainly collectivity is a distinctive element that suggests a particular preference for community (in an extended family, village, or apartment building) and for group sociability (in the studio simulacrum of the *tertulia*, or group discussion, traditionally held in a bar).

Taking the two distinctive factors of temporality and collectivity together we find strong evidence for Castells' thesis that globalization leads not to cultural homogenization but to the newly intensified power of regional identities (*The Information Age*). Even when production processes are imported directly from Hollywood, familiar formats take on strange new forms in the distinctive Spanish televisual ecology. David Letterman would find that *Crónicas marcianas* (originally based on his late show) is, in its final season, a very different kind of broadcasting. There is no doubt that Spanish programming has grown increasingly domestic and locally specific over the last decade. My stress on the positive aspects of televisual parasociality and festivity thus suggests a new and more sympathetic way of reading a phenomenon frequently noted and hated by commentators on Spanish TV: the celebrity gossip shows that are so much more prevalent in Spain than elsewhere.

The national is, of course, problematic in a state made up of self-governing regions some of which are actively seeking independence. And I have not treated in this book the popular programming in minority languages already studied by Hugh O'Donnell. But I have attempted to address the six problems for TV studies raised by John Caughie, which I cited in the first chapter. We have thus seen that the specificity of television is clear in a Spanish context, even when its themes (ruralism, urbanism, sexuality) coincide with feature films. Spanish television is also intensely verbal, with participants clearly taking great pleasure in speech for its own sake. Secondly, we have seen that Spanish television has a distinct history. While it would be impossible to address the whole range of programming over years, I have selected vital shows from four decades, attempting to rescue them from the amnesia to which broadcasting was especially prone before the advent of DVD. Thirdly, we have treated Spanish television as text, paying particular attention to repetition and familiarity as they intersect with innovation and creativity. Fourthly, we have addressed the national as a continuing (albeit weakened and qualified) sense of public service, heritage, and pedagogy. Fifthly, we have attempted to place Spanish TV in the context of the everyday life which it both reflects and refracts. Here TV can be uniquely sensitive to changing social conditions: the diverse households of *Aquí no hay quien viva*, formerly taken for granted, suddenly seem more controversial in series three when same-sex marriage becomes a political football.

Finally, Spanish television raises the question of value with unusual, even uncomfortable, insistence. Few national broadcasting systems can have been subject to such continuous and bitter hostility. The mere mention of the medium to educated Spaniards will elicit a torrent of abuse. Yet those same Spaniards will, on closer questioning, admit to watching and even enjoying selected shows. Unconsciously echoing the tagline of the US premium cable channel, they seem to believe that the programmes they favour are, like those on HBO, "not TV." This book was first prompted by the sheer pleasure I have felt in discovering, watching, and analysing the best Spanish programming and by the belief that it is of significant aesthetic value and social interest. It will have served its purpose if it encourages closer and more sympathetic viewing of television in Spain.

Works cited

Alonso Zaldívar, Carlos and Manuel Castells. *España, fin de siglo*. Madrid: Alianza, 1992.

Antena 3 TV. *Un poquito de por favor: manual para sobrevivir en una comunidad de vecinos*. [Book ostensibly written by characters of *Aquí no hay quien viva*.] Madrid: Antena 3/Temas de Hoy, 2005.

Castells, Manuel. *The Information Age, Volume 2: The Power of Identity*. Oxford: Blackwell, 1999.

Caughie, John. *Television Drama*. Oxford: Oxford University Press, 2000.

Emisiones.TV, 25 (May–June 2005).

O'Donnell, Hugh. *Good Times, Bad Times: Soap Operas and Society in Western Europe*. London: Leicester University Press, 1999.

———. "Media Pleasures: Reading the Telenovela." In Barry Jordan and Rikki Morgan-Tamosunas (eds). *Contemporary Spanish Cultural Studies*. London: Routledge, 2000, pp. 295–303.

Vaca Berdayes, Ricardo. *El ojo digital: Audiencias 1*. Madrid: Ex Libris, 2004.

Electronic source

"Las conservadoras creen que fueron una burla: Varias asociaciones polemizan sobre las alusiones a la manifestación del sábado en 'Aquí no hay quien viva.'" July 12, 2005. <http://elmundo.es/elmundo/2005/06/16/comunicacion/1118923 005.html>

APPENDICES

Timeline: chronology of television in Spain

1956 Televisión Española (TVE), the monopoly state channel, begins broadcasting.
1966 TVE2, the minority cultural channel, begins broadcasting.
1975 Death of Franco.
1977 Election of Rightist UCD Government.
1980 Statute of Radio and Television, reforming RTVE for the democratic era.
1982 Election of PSOE (Socialist) Government.
1984 Third Channel Law, regulating public regional channels, which begin broadcasting throughout Spain over next six years, following the lead of Basque-language ETB-1 and Catalan-language TV3.
1988 Private TV Law, granting licences to commercial channels.
1989 Setting up of FORTA, the consortium of public regional channels, as a counterweight to Madrid-based channels.
1990 Private national channels Antena 3 and Tele5 (free-to-air) and Canal + (subscription) begin broadcasting.
1995 Cable Law, grants franchises for cable and satellite broadcasting.
1996 Election of PP (Rightist) Government.
1997 Canal Satélite Digital (Prisa) and Vía Digital (Telefónica) begin transmission as competing platforms.
2003 Canal Satélite Digital and Vía Digital merge.
2004 Election of PSOE (Socialist) Government.
2005 Report by "Committee of Wise Men," calling for further reform of TVE.
—— Private national channel Cuatro (formerly Canal +) begins broadcasting free-to-air.

Glossary of names

Amenábar, Alejandro. The best known young filmmaker in Spain, with four prize-winning features.
Apeles, Father. Conservative Catholic spokesman, frequent guest on TV talk shows.
Arias, Imanol. Former movie star and heart-throb of the 1980s and 1990s for directors including Almodóvar; TV star in drama *Querido maestro* (*Dear Teacher*, 1996–8), the mini-series on Spanish Nobel Prize winner *Severo Ochoa* (2001), and *Cuéntame cómo pasó* (*Tell Me How It Happened*, 2001–).

Arias Salgado, Fernando. A conservative Director-General of TVE during the Transition to democracy.

Ariztimuño, Iñaki. Young co-creator of hit sitcom *Aquí no hay quien viva* (*No-one Can Live Here*, 2003–)

Aznar, José María. President of the government led by the Partido Popular (1996–2004).

Belén, Ana. Successful singer and prolific actress in film and TV (*Fortunata y Jacinta*, 1980), once known for her radical politics; with her son, performs the theme tune of *Cuéntame cómo pasó* (*Tell Me How It Happened*, 2001–).

Berlanga, Luis García. Veteran filmmaker, famed for his black comedies satirizing Spanish archetypes; occasionally directs for TV (e.g. *Blasco Ibáñez* [1997]).

Berlusconi, Silvio. Italian President and media mogul; part owner of Spanish channel Tele5.

Bernardeau, Miguel-Ángel. Producer of *Cuéntame cómo pasó* (*Tell Me How It Happened*, 2001–).

Blasco Ibáñez, Vicente. Valencian novelist whose works have sometimes been adapted for TV (e.g. *La barraca* [1979]).

Buenafuente, Andreu. Catalan comedian, host of a late-night talk show.

Bustamante, Enrique. Media scholar and member of the "Committee of Wise Men."

Caballero, Alberto. Young co-creator and director of hit sitcom *Aquí no hay quien viva* (*No-one Can Live Here*, 2003–).

Caffarell, Carmen. Director-General of TVE, appointed by the PSOE government elected in 2004.

Camps, Victoria. Philosopher, critic of *telebasura*, and member of the "Committee of Wise Men."

Camus, Mario. Film and TV director, best known for literary adaptations for both media in the 1980s (*Fortunata y Jacinta*, 1980).

Carlotti, Maurizio. Chief executive officer of Tele5 and, subsequently, Antena 3.

Carrero Blanco, Luis. Right-hand man of dictator Francisco Franco; assassinated 1973.

Chico, Florinda. Popular star of film comedies and occasionally TV, especially in the later Franco period.

Contreras, José Miguel. TV commentator and professional, founder of GECA.

Duato, Ana. Female star of film and TV, known as Imanol Arias's wife in *Severo Ochoa* (2001) and *Cuéntame cómo pasó* (*Tell Me How It Happened*, 2001–).

Erice, Víctor. Quintessential art-movie director of Spanish cinema, maker of just three prize-winning features in thirty years.

Fernán Gómez, Fernando. Veteran actor of some two hundred Spanish films; occasional guest star on TVE: *Fortunata y Jacinta* (1980), *Cuéntame cómo pasó* (*Tell Me How It Happened*, 2001–).

Gómez, Carmelo. Respected film actor; male lead in TVE's adaptation of *La Regenta* (1995).

Gutiérrez Aragón, Manuel. Director of feature films and TVE's mini-series *El Quijote* (1991).

Haro Tecglen, Eduardo. Leftist journalist and media commentator in *El País*.

Izaguirre, Boris. Flamboyantly gay Venezuelan panellist in talk shows on Tele5 and Cuatro.

José Antonio [Primo de Rivera]. Founder of the Falange (Spanish Fascist Party); executed 1936.

Ladrón de Guevara, Eduardo. Former anti-Francoist militant and TV creator and scriptwriter of the democratic era, including *Querido maestro* (*Dear Teacher*, 1996–8) and *Cuéntame cómo pasó* (*Tell Me How It Happened*, 2001–).

Landa, Alfredo. Favourite comedian of late Francoist cinema; occasional star of TV sitcoms.

Leblanc, Tony. Veteran film and TV star.

León, Loles. Extravagant supporting actress in Almodóvar films and first two seasons of sitcom *Aquí no hay quien viva* (*No-one Can Live Here*, 2003–).

Machado, Antonio. Poet and teacher of the Republic; an icon of liberal tolerance.

Mainat, Josep Maria and Joan Ramon. Catalan brothers, producers of successful talk and reality shows with Gestmusic-Endemol.

Martínez Soria, Paco. Coarse comedian of late Francoist films, now rerun on Spanish TV; archetypal *paleto*.

Méndez-Leite, Fernando. Director for cinema and TV (*La Regenta*, 1995).

Mercero, Antonio. Veteran TV creator and director, best known for TVE's *Crónicas de un pueblo* (*Chronicles of a Village*, 1971–4) and *Verano azul* (*Blue Summer*, 1981–2), and Antena 3's *Farmacia de guardia* (*All Night Chemist*, 1991–5).

Miró, Pilar. Film director, head of film production under the first PSOE government, and previously director for TVE (e.g. *Curro Jiménez*, 1976).

Moix, Terenci. Novelist and classic movie enthusiast; sometime TV presenter.

Montiel, Sara. The greatest star of Spanish musical comedies; occasional guest on TV talk shows. A sequence from *Esa mujer* (*That Woman*, 1969) was used by Almodovar in *La mala educación* (*Bad Education*, 2004).

Moreno, José Luis. Executive producer of variety shows and sitcoms.

Morgan, Lina. Much loved comedienne in Francoist film and, subsequently, TV sitcom.

Muñoz Molina, Antonio. Distinguished novelist and occasional media commentator.

Panchos, Los. Long-lasting Mexican vocal group, famous in Spain for their romantic ballads.

Pantoja, Isabel. Singer and staple of the TV gossip shows; widow of a famous bullfighter.

Parada, José Manuel. Creator and first presenter of TVE's *Cine de barrio* (*Neighbourhood Cinema*, 1995–).

Parrondo, Gil. Prize-winning production designer in Hollywood and for Spanish TV (*La Regenta*, 1995).

Pérez de Albéniz, Javier ["El Descifrador"]. *El Mundo*'s acerbic TV commentator.

Rahola, Pilar. Former Catalan member of parliament and frequent talk-show guest.

Raphael. Extravagant singer and movie star of the 1960s, now an intermittent guest on TV.

Rodríguez de la Fuente, Félix. Respected pioneer of nature shows on TVE.

Rodríguez Zapatero, José Luis. President of the PSOE-led government elected in 2004.

Ruiz del Río, Emilio. Special effects designer in film and TV (*Fortunata y Jacinta*, 1980).

Sacristán, José. Movie star of the Transition to democracy, known for his Leftist politics; occasional TV appearances.

Sánchez Gijón, Aitana. Star of movies and TV drama (*La Regenta*, 1995).

Sardà, Javier [Xavier]. Former radio journalist and presenter of Tele5's *Crónicas marcianas* (*Martian Chronicles*, 1997–2005).

Sevilla, Carmen. Musical comedy star of Francoism and, latterly, TV presenter.

Umbral, Francisco. Long-time columnist for *El País* and subsequently *El Mundo*; habitual critic of TVE.

Vázquez, Jesús. Popular, openly gay host of TV reality and game shows.

Vázquez Montalbán, Manuel. Celebrated crime novelist, gastronome, and influential critic of TVE.

Glossary of institutions and Spanish terms

13, rue del Percebe. Long-running comic about an apartment building, drawn by Francisco Ibáñez; graphic precedent for sitcom *Aquí no hay quien viva* (*No-one Can Live Here*, 2003–).

Antena 3. Private national free-to-air channel; began broadcasting in 1990, aiming for a "family" audience.

Canal +. Private national subscription channel; began broadcasting in 1990, specializing in films and sport.

Canal 9. Local Valencian channel; began broadcasting in 1990.

casposo [literally "dandruffy"]. Dismissive adjective used for old-fashioned, low-quality programming.

cateto. Pejorative term for country-dweller ("bumpkin").

Cineinforme. Long-established trade journal for cinema and TV in Spain.

Comité de sabios ["Committee of Wise Men"]. Group set up by PSOE government in 2004 to make proposals for the reform of television.

costumbrista. Concerned with local customs and manners; often applied to comedy.

Cuatro. Private national free-to-air channel; began broadcasting in 2005.

Cubana, La. Popular experimental theatre company, much influenced by cinema and television.

Deseo, El. Film production company set up by Pedro Almodóvar and headed by his brother Agustín; ventured for the first time into TV production in 2006.

destape. The increasing vogue for nudity in Spanish cinema of the Transition.

Españolada. Dismissive term for a Spanish production.

Falange. Spanish Fascist Party.

famosillo. A minor celebrity, habitué of talk or reality shows.

folklórica. Dismissive or affectionate term for female stars of musical comedy or traditional song.

FORTA. The consortium of public regional channels, set up in 1989.

Forum for the Family [*Foro de la Familia*]. Conservative pressure group, active in campaigning against same-sex marriage, abortion, and education reform.

Fuero de los Españoles. Law setting out the rights and responsibilities of Spaniards during the Francoist dictatorship; stressed the Church and family as fundamental institutions.

GECA. Research and consultancy group for Spanish audiovisual media.

Gedisa. Barcelona-based publisher, specializing in film and TV studies.

Gestmusic-Endemol. Independent Barcelona-based production company, specializing in reality and game shows.

Marca. Football journal, the best selling newspaper in Spain.

Miramón Mendi. Independent producer of variety and sitcoms.

movida. Cultural renaissance of the post-Franco period.

Mundo, El. Daily newspaper of the centre-right.

NO-DO ("Noticiarios y documentales cinematográficos"). Francoist newsreel.

País, El. Daily newspaper of the centre-left.

paleto. Pejorative term for country-dweller ("bumpkin").

Partido Popular or PP ["People's Party"]. Right-wing party, in power 1996–2004.

Plataforma por una televisión de calidad ["Platform for Quality Television"]. Umbrella group attacking "trash TV."

PSOE. Socialist Party, in power 1982–96, 2004–.

Prisa. Media conglomerate, identified with the Socialist Party, including newspaper *El País*, radio station Cadena SER, and TV channels Canal + and, subsequently, Cuatro.

RTVE. The state broadcaster of TV and Radio.

rosa ["pink"]. Adjective describing shows devoted to celebrity gossip.

SGAE. The official body representing Spanish authors and publishers; carries out annual surveys of cultural consumption.

SOFRES. Standard source for audience research.

Statute of Radio and Television (1980). Legislation introduced in the Transition to democracy, intended to reform the state broadcasting system.

Tele5. Private national free-to-air channel; began broadcasting in 1990 and at first notorious for poor-quality programming; later pioneered home-produced drama.

Telebasura ["trash TV"]. Much derided, but ill defined, poor-quality programming, especially of the 1990s and 2000s.

Teleclubs. Early collective form of TV viewing, sponsored by the Francoist dictatorship.

telenovela. Long-running serial, normally produced in Latin America and a staple of afternoon programming in Spain.

tertulia. Regular group conversation, traditionally held in a bar, now re-created in talk shows by *tertulianos* (panellists).

TP. TV listings magazine and website; host of a well known TV award.

Transition. The period between the Francoist dictatorship and the consolidation of democracy, generally held to begin with the death of Franco in 1975 and end with the election of the first Socialist government in 1982.

TV3. Catalan-language public free-to-air channel, began broadcasting in 1984.

TVE. The state TV broadcaster, with two national channels ("la Primera" and "la 2").

Valle de los caídos ("Valley of the Fallen"). Grandiose memorial to the Nationalist dead in the Civil War, often featured in Francoist newsreels.

Vanguardia, La. Conservative Barcelona-based Spanish-language newspaper.

Zarzuela. Spanish operetta, formerly televised by TVE2.

INDEX

NB Page numbers in bold type refer to illustrations and their captions.

Lightning Source UK Ltd.
Milton Keynes UK
UKHW021528231119
353999UK00003B/154/P

9 781855 661363